A journalist with the BE ... Australia in 1987 to wor... one of his most controve... led to the publication in ~~~~ ~. ~.~ ~... bestseller, *The Rise and Fall of Alan Bond*.

Since then, he has dominated the bestseller lists, with *The Rise and Rise of Kerry Packer* named the Number 1 biography of the decade, and *The Rise and Fall of Alan Bond* Number 3.

His work as an investigative journalist has won numerous awards; *The Rise and Rise of Kerry Packer* was shortlisted for the 1994 Banjo Award for Non-Fiction, and *Going for Broke* for the 2000 Colin Broderick Award.

Paul Barry writes for the *Sydney Morning Herald* and lives in Sydney.

For all honest Australians

GOING FOR
BROKE

PAUL BARRY

BANTAM BOOKS
SYDNEY • AUCKLAND • TORONTO • NEW YORK • LONDON

Going for Broke

A BANTAM BOOK

First published in Australia and New Zealand in 2000
by Bantam
Paperback edition first published in 2001 by Bantam

National Library of Australia
Cataloguing-in-Publication Entry

Barry, Paul, 1952– .
 Going for broke.

 Includes index.
 ISBN 1 86325 198 7 (pbk.).

1. Bond, Alan, 1938– . 2. Businessmen – Australia –
Biography. 3. Bankruptcy – Australia. 4. Fraud
investigation – Australia. 5. White collar crime
investigation – Australia. 6. Corporations –
Corrupt practices – Australia. I. Title.

364.1680994

Transworld Publishers,
a division of Random House Australia Pty Ltd
20 Alfred Street, Milsons Point, NSW 2061

Random House New Zealand Limited
18 Poland Road, Glenfield, Auckland

Transworld Publishers,
61–63 Uxbridge Road, Ealing, London W5 5SA
a division of The Random House Group Ltd

Random House Inc
1540 Broadway, New York, New York 10036

Typeset by Midland Typesetters, Maryborough, Victoria
Printed and bound by Griffin Press, Netley, South Australia

10 9 8 7 6 5 4 3 2

Contents

Acknowledgements

There are several people without whose help this book would never have been written. Foremost among them is Jo Puccini, who worked tirelessly and cheerfully to trace the players in this story. If anyone could raise the dead and make them talk, it would be her. Natalie Young, who worked briefly on this project back in 1995, when I first started looking at the idea, was also excellent. Her contacts, her knowledge of the law and her filing system were invaluable.

More recently, Mark Drummond from the *Australian Financial Review* has kept me up to date with developments in Perth and has helped me generously and unselfishly, even when I have been writing for a rival newspaper. So too has Jamie Fawcett, another long-time Bond watcher.

A host of people have told me their Bond stories or provided me with valuable evidence, but I suspect that they would prefer to remain anonymous, so I will let them do so. They know who they are, and without their frankness and courage, this book would not exist. So thank you.

It would, I think, be safe to thank the following, who also helped make this the book it is: Liam Bartlett, Lionel Berck, Paul Bowen, David Chaikin, The Hon. Michael Duffy, Lloyd Higham, David Kerr, Wayne Lamb, Anne Lampe, Pam Lesmond, Peter Lundy, David Michael, John McGlue, Bruce Phillips, Joe Poprzeczny, Anna Quilter, Colleen Ryan, Martin Saxon, Lee Tate, Ros Thomas, Garry Trevor, John Urch, Fiona Wingett, Mark Zanker and Julian Zakaras. Also, everyone in the registry at the Supreme Court of South Australia and in the libraries of the Art Gallery of New South Wales and the National Gallery of Australia.

I also want to thank all those at *Four Corners* who worked on the various Bond programs all those years ago but, in particular, Adelaide Beavis, Ian Carroll, Alec Cullen, Penny Lysaght, Rosemary Meares, David Pearson and Gary Russell, who all helped make *Rich Man, Poor Man* which introduced Jurg Bollag to the Australian public in 1993. Also Ann Connor and Jonathan Sequeira, who organised stills from the video. I owe a bigger debt to producer Stuart Goodman, who, in a moment of inspiration, sliced his name off his business card and gave it to me for Alan Bond to stamp on. It provided a moment of television that Alan Bond and I will certainly never forget. And all thanks to Stuart's Swiss army knife.

Finally, I want to thank all the people at Random House who made this book a reality. Shona Martyn had the faith to commission it in 1998, and since then, Annabel Blay, Jody Lee, Maggie Hamilton, Fiona Henderson, Karen Reid and Katie Stackhouse have encouraged me, supported me and nudged me towards the finish line. Richard Potter's and Anne Flahvin's legal advice and Michael Sexton's comments will, I hope, keep me out of trouble.

Finally, I want to say a special thank you to my two talented editors, Amanda O'Connell and Vanessa Mickan. It was a great pleasure working with you. Your comments made this a far better book. You were great.

Prologue

A rape, a rape,
You have ravished justice.

John Webster, 1612

3 May 1994

It's three years since Bond's business empire finally collapsed
with debts of around $5 billion. And Alan has brought
sandwiches for lunch.

They're in a green plastic bag he clutches in the dock. The
press are impressed. Poor old Bondy.

He's sitting like a zombie, staring into space, popping
the occasional pill, as if he's nigh on brain dead. We're in the
Federal Court in Sydney, and his interrogator is asking about
bank accounts in Switzerland, companies in Panama and an
accountant's office in Jersey. He seems surprised that the
questions are for him.

On occasion, he pauses for a minute, then asks for the
question to be repeated. He's trying hard, but he keeps on
losing the plot. The trouble is he can't recall. There were so

many companies, it was so long ago, and he's not been well.

He shuffles out of court, a small figure in a crumpled rain-coat, bent and pale. A shadow of his former self.

Round a couple of corners, he's out of sight of the pursuing press. He steals a look, straightens up and tosses the bag away.

Later, he's at the Sheraton Wentworth, making the phones run hot. He's calling Switzerland, Singapore and the USA. Dealing, dealing. Doing business.

The next day, I decide to test his memory. Surely no man can forget whether he has millions of dollars overseas. Surely this is an act?

I catch him walking up the street to the Federal Court and hand him a business card. 'I'm Paul Barry from *Four Corners*. Remember me?' He stamps on it, dances on it, grinds it into the pavement, and tells me to keep away. 'Keep right away.'

'So you do remember me,' I say, 'you do remember me.'

Back in the court, the questions continue. Bank accounts in London in the name of A. Bond, transfers to Switzerland in 1989, a few million dollars here, a few more million there. No. It doesn't ring a bell to Bondy. He can't recall a thing.

15 April 1995

One year later, and it's just like old times. Australia's greatest salesman is back with his 10,000 kilowatt smile. His skin is glossy, and he's rude with health. He's plump, shiny and pros-perous in white tie and tails. He's puffed up with pride like a black-and-white bullfrog.

If he ever had brain damage, he's forgotten it now.

Outside Sydney's Museum of Contemporary Art, crowds of reporters, photographers and camera crews push and jostle to get close to Alan Bond's new bride. He is marrying a beautiful woman sixteen years younger than him. He has escaped from bankruptcy with the bulk of his fortune intact.

He has a second marriage, a second chance, a second coming. Good ol' Bondy is back in business. He's a winner again.

One has to say, he looks better in this role than when he's being hounded by those reptiles of the press. Adulation suits him so much more. He has always been puzzled by criticism, pained by the barbs of those who don't believe. It's been one of his greatest assets, the unshakeable conviction that he's done nothing wrong.

It can be hard not to admire someone so utterly devoid of guilt and shame, so completely unstoppable in the face of adversity, so consummately good at getting away with it. And as he likes to tell everyone, at least *he* stayed to face the music.

But there is another view of what Bond has achieved by his remarkable escape from the wreckage of his empire. And it is this. He has made a monkey out of the law and brought the legal system into disrepute. He has shown in the most public way possible that if your pockets are deep enough and your lawyers good enough, you can tie the system in knots forever, or at least until the most tenacious and bloody-minded pursuers give up. Nerve, stamina, self-belief, and access to a stash of cash, are all it takes. As long as you go for broke.

This is the story of how the bankruptcy laws of Australia failed to get hold of Alan Bond's fortune. And how they will always fail to catch people like Skase and Bond.

It's also a story about a man whose incredible resilience is, sadly, far greater than his respect for the truth.

1

Oh Lucky Man

If ... the bankrupt be convicted, he shall be set
upon the pillory in some public place for the space
of two hours, and have one of his ears cut off.

Bankruptcy Act 1623

Alan Bond is lucky he didn't go bust 150 years ago,
because creditors in those days had the right to lock
debtors in jail and throw away the key. The rules then were
simple. If you borrowed money, you had to pay it back. Full
stop.

There were no compromises, no settlements, no lengthy
court battles, and no living high on the hog while debts
remained unpaid. And the mere fact that court proceedings
had started was enough for a creditor to have the debtor
arrested by the sheriff, so that he did not abscond.

London's notorious Newgate prison was full of such
wretched people who often rotted inside for years over debts
as small as a few shillings. Sometimes they died there, because
if they couldn't pay what they owed, they stayed behind bars
until their creditors decided to release them ... if they ever did.

Once jailed, there was also no guarantee that these poor

debtors wouldn't starve to death, as an English judge once reminded an unfortunate subject in passing judgement:

> Neither the plaintiff nor the sheriff is bound to give him meat or drink ... If he has no goods, he shall live off the charity of others, and if others give him nothing, let him die in the name of God ... for his presumption and ill-behaviour brought him to that imprisonment.[1]

It was all a world away from our current lax attitude to credit. In those days, people who ran up debts that they couldn't pay were regarded quite simply as criminals.

Conditions in the jails were horrendous, with no attempt to segregate by sex or by gravity of the crime. And since many prisons were owned privately and run for profit, they typically demanded payment from their inmates for the most basic comfort. At Newgate, for example, there was an entrance fee of three shillings, a weekly rent of two shillings and sixpence, and a further weekly payment of one shilling and sixpence to share a straw mattress with another prisoner. In the debtors' section, where by definition no one had money to purchase such things, you fought for floor space and scraps of food with murderers, rapists, footpads and anyone else who happened to be there. The inmates at Newgate called the debtors' section Tangier, because it was reminiscent of the suffering inflicted on British sailors by Arab pirates off the Barbary Coast.

But the punishment for people who could be shown to be concealing assets from their creditors was even more severe, as England's 1623 Bankruptcy Act made clear:

> If upon such indictment the bankrupt be convicted,

he shall be set upon the pillory in some public place for the space of two hours, and have one of his ears cut off.

And after 1705, if you failed to hand over all your assets to the King's Commissioners so they could be shared among your creditors, you could find yourself being sent to the gallows, which is almost certainly where Alan Bond would have ended up.

Bankrupt ... Not Broke

Your property now vests in me as your Trustee in Bankruptcy and is available for division amongst your creditors.

Letter to Alan Bond on the day of his bankruptcy, 14 April 1992

Between 1983 and 1991 Bond and his family spent their way through more than a million dollars every seven weeks. Or roughly what the average Australian earns in a working lifetime. Yet when he was eventually made bankrupt in April 1992 there was virtually nothing to show for it.

The assets that Alan declared in his statement of affairs amounted to an $8,000 Hyundai car, a partly completed ocean racer, three paintings by a minor Australian artist called Strawb O'Brien, around $2,600 in cash and shares, and two loans of questionable worth—one of which was to a trust company that had bought a house for his girlfriend, Tracey Tyler.

So how on earth had it come to this?

Well, the Bond family still had money, of course, and had it by the bucketload. Along with cars, houses, horses, boats, jewellery, paintings, farmland, property and bank accounts with lashings of cash. But Alan had made damn sure that his creditors wouldn't be able to get their hands on any of it.

Even his personal super fund, with its $2.7 million in investments, had a special clause designed to keep the money safe in the event of his bankruptcy. And the other Bond family assets were locked away in family trusts that couldn't be cracked.

When it comes to keeping your creditors at bay, there's no substitute for practice. And few people had had more of that than Alan Bond. He had spent the first twenty years of his business life as a land developer in Perth being chased round town by people wanting payment, and had frequently escaped bankruptcy by the skin of his teeth. Then, in 1974, the Australian property market had gone into free fall as interest rates had rocketed, and he had found himself comprehensively broke.

He had kept his head above water on that occasion because his biggest creditor Citibank had been squeamish about sinking him while he was challenging for the America's Cup, and because he had fought harder than any other entrepreneur to stay afloat. But he had also engineered his business empire to ensure that his private company would be repaid in full before the banks saw any money, so there had been no great incentive for the banks to put him under.

Bond was already an expert back then in how to keep his own money safe while other people lost theirs. But this close shave in the early seventies had made him put his personal assets even further out of reach. And this was why, in the 1990s, he was so well protected. Back in July 1975, months after the property crash had nearly put him out of business, the Alan Bond Family Trust No 1 had been formed to keep his money safe. Its 'prime beneficiaries' were supposedly the Bond children, but Alan and Eileen clearly derived substantial benefit too, because the first asset transferred to it was the

Bonds' vast—and vastly expensive—home on the banks of the Swan River, where the Bonds lived, courtesy of the trust, without paying rent.[1]

The house, which was a magnificent example of a Perth palace, had been built in the midst of the 1974–75 crisis for around $1.5 million, at Bond's shareholders' expense. Laid out on four levels, and standing on six blocks of land, it rose from the Swan River like a huge white fortress. There was a cinema, a squash court, seven bedrooms, ten bathrooms and a ten-car garage. There was marble on the floors, gold on the taps, and Jacuzzis everywhere. In the garden was a resort-sized swimming pool that Bond had added in the late 1980s, which was built round a large sunken bar. The palm trees around it had been flown in from Queensland, with labourers to dig the holes, which had pushed the cost above $1.5 million. By 1992, the pool and the house were worth five times that, or around $7.5 million.

And the house wasn't even the half of it. By the time of his bankruptcy, the Bond Family Trust No 1 also owned 16,500 hectares of prime farmland at Dandaragan, two hours north of Perth, along with 40,000 sheep and a large herd of beef cattle that went with it. There were also some historic farm buildings and modern feedlots that brought the total value to $11 million or more.

And there was much much more that the family could call its own. There were three Perth restaurants, including the famous Mediterranean, which Alan had bought for his son Craig for $2 million in December 1988; there were four bowling alleys worth around $6 million; and a block of land on Adelaide Terrace in central Perth with great potential for development. There was more land on the river at Dalkeith worth close to $1 million; a huge apartment in West Perth with river views, worth around $850,000; and a string of units in Claremont, owned jointly by his daughter Susanne and wife Eileen, which were worth another $1 million. Then there was Craig's magnificent waterside home in Brisbane, worth $3 million, and his other son John's house in swanky Peppermint Grove, worth around $2 million, which John's wife Gemma owned, and a couple of suburban shopping centres worth $6 million or more, which John had bought. And then there were the cars, the boats, the paintings, the sculptures, some $640,000 worth of furniture belonging to Eileen, and finally the jewellery, which was worth $20 million or more.

In January 1990, Bond gave an interview to a British journalist called Teresa Poole from Britain's *Independent* newspaper. Looking fit, healthy, unruffled, and certainly not contrite, despite the billions of dollars that his creditors were seeking, he assured her that he would never be destitute. And provided he kept on good terms with his family, this was undoubtedly the case.[2]

His fun-loving wife Eileen had hardly earned a dollar in her life. Susanne, his elder daughter, likewise. Younger son Craig had typically lost money when trying to make it, and only John had made anything approaching a million for himself. Yet here they all were with their fingers in a pie worth around $80 million gross and perhaps $70 million net, after borrowings had been netted off.[3]

Almost all this wealth had been derived from Bond Corporation, which at the time of Bond's bankruptcy owed some $4,500 million. Most of it had come via Alan Bond's private company Dallhold, which owed some $520 million. And typically it had flowed through the personal bank accounts of Alan Bond, who owed some $600 million. But thanks to Alan's lawyers, the vast bulk of this fortune would not be available to creditors because it was held in the name of family members or their trusts.

In 1981, a phalanx of trusts had been set up for the Bond family, with John, Craig, Susanne, Jody and Eileen each acquiring a trading trust, an investment trust, and a trustee company to run them, making a total of ten new trusts in all. Various others were added later to bring the grand total for the Bond family to seventeen. And even though it was Alan's millions that had been poured into these various entities, the millions were now out of reach of the people who had lost their savings by backing Bond.

To the ordinary person, this may seem like an outrage, especially since Alan had no intention of living like a pauper. But it was hardly news to those who knew anything about the ways of entrepreneurs and high finance.

The famous Costigan Inquiry into the Painters and Dockers Union in 1984 uncovered a whole bunch of bankrupts who kept their assets in trusts or parked them with friends who could later return them. Despite being officially broke, they lived in big houses, drove fast cars, and cruised the coast in flashy yachts, in the knowledge that neither their creditors nor the taxman could ever confiscate the loot.

In an attempt to deal with the problem, the Hawke Labor Government passed tough new legislation in 1988 that gave trustees in bankruptcy far greater power to inquire into who the real owners of the assets were. But while this doubtless made it harder for people to park assets with their mates, it made far less difference where trusts were concerned, because it did not attack the fundamentals of trust law, which dated back to eleventh-century Norman England.

The entirely legitimate purpose of trusts, way back then, was to hold money on behalf of someone who was incompetent to handle it, either because they were too young, too reckless, too stupid, or simply insane. It was to stop money being wasted.

But in modern times, and in the last thirty years in particular, trusts have been adopted by clever lawyers and accountants as the number one way of protecting assets from the taxman and creditors. In fact, the discretionary trust in particular is now de rigueur for cheats, crooks, crims and bankrupt businessmen, because it allows them to hang on to their ill-gotten gains, while denying, quite legally, that they own them.

The legal fiction of such an arrangement is that assets are handed over to an independent trustee who has absolute discretion to pass them on to anyone he or she thinks fit. But in practice, of course, the wealth is not given away to charity. And woe betide the trustee who runs off with it. Typically, there is a 'letter of wishes' that gives the trustee a very short list of people to consider when handing out money, and often there is someone they are required to consult beforehand. But once again, the legal fiction is that the trustee is entirely at liberty to ignore advice.[4]

There is little question that such trusts can make a mockery of the bankruptcy laws, by making it easy for bankrupts and their families to park assets legally out of reach of creditors. But few politicians or public servants would be game to abolish them, since this would involve overturning 800 years of English property law. And many Australian politicians have benefited from the shelter they provide.[5]

So in the meantime, lawmakers have struggled to find other ways to tackle the problem, either by catching the money as it goes into the trusts, or grabbing it on the way out. And their efforts had an impact on the way in which Bond went bankrupt, or at least on the determination with which he resisted it.

As Bond revealed in his statement of affairs in April 1992, he had indulged in an absolute orgy of gift-giving in the previous six years. Jewellery, paintings, land, restaurants, cars, apartments and cash had rained out of the Bond firmament like manna into the desert. Multi-million-dollar debts had been forgiven with ne'er a cross word. When it was all totted up, Alan had given away $32 million to his family and friends, including $13 million worth of jewellery to his wife Eileen.[6]

Christmas 1988 had been the climax. At a time when the financial wizards at Lonrho, a UK company that Bond was trying to take over, were suggesting that the Bond Group was insolvent, Alan embarked on a massive spending spree, buying a $350,000 bracelet for his daughter Susanne, lavishing $4.3 million on diamonds for Eileen, and throwing in a brand new Bentley Turbo for her Christmas stocking. The following week, he forked out another $300,000 in cash, and couldn't even remember whom he had paid it to.

The bankruptcy laws, as they stood in the early 1990s, allowed creditors to claw back gifts like these, but only if the debtor had made them in the two years before bankruptcy. In Bond's case, this meant anything he'd given away after 14 April 1990. But by an extraordinary stroke of luck, his great glut of giving had come to an abrupt halt exactly one month before that.

It seemed like a remarkable coincidence that Alan had given away his fortune just in time. And so unlucky for his creditors. But it was really no such thing, because Bond had fought like mad to delay his bankruptcy, so that these gifts would not be clawed back, and had succeeded in keeping the bailiffs at bay for more than a year.

The process of sending him broke began officially in March 1991, and would normally have been complete by June or July, but Bond's lawyers managed to spin out the process so that it was not until 26 September 1991 that the first bankruptcy notice was issued. And this only marked the start of the fun and games.

Over in Perth, a process server called Kevin Munns was given the job of finding Bond and handing him the papers. He called Bond's solicitors and offered to serve them by appointment, so it could all be done quietly and without fuss, but he was told he would have to catch Bond himself.

Munns had no idea, of course, that Alan had good reason to avoid him. Or should one say five million good reasons. For the Bond family would hang on to another $5 million if Alan could stave off bankruptcy for another six months.

3

Never Say Die

It's not over till the fat lady sings
Alan Bond's motto

Kevin Munns knew that his best chance of catching Alan would be in the early morning, either at the office, or before he left home. But by the time he got to the Bond mansion in Dalkeith at around 7.30am, a TV crew from Channel 7 had already beaten him to it.

He sat in his car for a few minutes, hoping not to be noticed, then decided he wouldn't get anywhere by doing that, and went to bang on the back gate. Before long, a gardener appeared and told him to push off, slamming the gate in his face, so he then asked the news crew if he could sneak into the house with them when they went inside for the interview. The reporter, Howard Gratton, was keen to film him serving the bankruptcy notice on Bond, which is why he was there in the first place, but was not prepared to smuggle him into the house by subterfuge. So that failed too.

Had Munns been allowed to push the bankruptcy notice

through the letter box and leave, it would have been over then and there, because Bond was definitely in the house and would be sure to get it. But court rules say the papers have to be handed to the debtor in person, so Munns either had to talk his way through the front door or wait until Bond came out. And Alan was quite clearly going to do everything he could to avoid him.

In fact, Bond had given another firm of process servers the slip in Sydney the day before. They had staked out three five-star hotels where they thought he might be staying, and had then tried a series of different restaurants where he had booked in for dinner. But after a frustrating twenty-four hours they had discovered he was flying back west. The original bank-ruptcy notice, stamped by the court, had then been entrusted to a special courier service, to be hand-delivered to Munns's home in South Perth shortly before midnight.

Now, back at the Dalkeith house, the Channel 7 crew had told Bond that a process server was waiting outside, and had passed the news to Munns that Alan wasn't going to let him in. So, with an hour already wasted, he decided to have another go at the gardener. This time there were two large dogs to contend with, who were equally adamant that they weren't going to let him onto the property. But just as they were all arguing the toss, a white Range Rover emerged from the nearby driveway, with the unmistakable figure of Alan Bond at the wheel, whereupon Munns jumped into his Toyota Landcruiser and set off in pursuit.

For twenty minutes the two four-wheel drives careered around the back streets of Perth at breakneck speed, playing Mad Max games with each other. Bond's version to the *West Australian* next day was that he had no idea that anyone was trying to serve a bankruptcy notice on him, and that an unidentified maniac had tried to force him off the road.

> I was quite concerned because I didn't know who it was; whether it was somebody with a gun, a thug or who it might be. He had a red sort of a Toyota truck with great big bumper bars. He tail-gated me up the street and then he came alongside and tried to drive me into the actual kerb ... it could have caused a very nasty accident ...[1]

Bond could hardly have not known that it was Munns who was chasing him, because Gratton had told him minutes earlier that a process server was lying in wait outside his house, but he clearly had no intention of stopping or of letting himself be served with the papers. And if Munns is to be believed, Bond was risking life and limb to stop that happening.

> He was driving rather erratically. I went up to pass him, to beckon him to pull over. As I pulled up next to him he swerved his car very heavily to the right, forcing me onto the grass verge. My car slid sideways. I again pulled up behind him, went to pass him with ample room and again he swerved violently to the right. I thought then I'd better stay close to him but stay behind him. On three occasions he slammed his brakes on, causing his car to skid, and I've even got photographs of the skid marks. I can only assume he wanted me to ram him in the back which would then put me in trouble with the law.[2]

Munns has spent most of his working life chasing people who

don't want to be caught, and being greeted with anger and abuse. But he regards this clash with Bond as one of the most difficult of his thirty-year career. As anyone who knows Bond can tell you, he can be enormously charming and persuasive when things are going his way, but he has a fearsome temper when things go wrong.

Munns says today that he still believes Bond deserves a medal for winning the America's Cup and for transforming the port of Fremantle, but otherwise he has no time for the man at all. And it's largely because of what happened next.

Having led the process server on a high-speed chase through the suburbs, Bond drove to the unmanned police station at Nedlands to file a complaint. Munns, who was still following him, stopped his car outside and got out to identify himself, at which point a violent argument started by the side of the road. Bond's version in the *West Australian* was that he told Munns:

> 'Look, you'd better come inside because I'm going to charge you for dangerous driving.'
> With that, he rolled up two pieces of paper and threw it at me and said, 'There's your writ', with some other adjectives to go with it.

Munns's story is that he *handed* the bankruptcy notice to Alan Bond, who screwed it up and threw it in the gutter. He then told Bond he had been properly served, and started to walk back to his car. In his version, Bond then chased him and shoved him in the back:

> I turned around and he shirt-collared me. A number of people, hearing him yelling and

screaming obscenities at me, gathered around the vehicles. And then the television crews turned up again ...

I put my hands out to protect myself, because he was quite violent at the time. He was shaking me as hard as he could with one hand up on my collar and one on my shoulder. I don't remember the words at all but they were quite loud, aggressive, obscene.[3]

The Channel 7 crew caught only the end of this altercation, but their news report that evening showed Munns with his shirt collar bent up and his tie yanked halfway round his neck, so it was clear that he had been attacked. An eyewitness to the confrontation confirmed on camera that an angry Alan Bond had been the aggressor. Yet the old salesman told Channel 7's viewers, just as he told the papers, that he had been an entirely innocent party, had not been trying to avoid service, and had merely been chased by an unidentified thug.

The same TV news report showed clips of an interview with Bond that had been recorded in Alan's garden beforehand, in which Alan claimed that his telephone was 'almost choked with well-wishers'. It was encouraging, said Bond with that sincere smirk that he does so well, that 'in these difficult times for all Australians', people understood the difficulty he was in.[4]

At this point, it's important to explain why Bond was being made bankrupt in the first place, because he has implied time and again that it should never have happened. But the cause was simple, and Bond had only himself to blame. In January 1990 he had given personal guarantees for US$194 million as security for a huge new loan that three banks were about to make to his master private company Dallhold.

For the banks, it had been an extraordinary moment to be lending Bond new money, because his empire was teetering on the brink of collapse. Receivers were in control of Bond Brewing, another lot had briefly been sent into Dallhold, Bond Corporation was sinking fast, and just about every other banker in the world was trying to get his money out. But the Hongkong Bank, Tricontinental and Bank of New Zealand all stood to lose a fortune if Bond went down at that moment, because they had already lent hundreds of millions of dollars, which was secured against shares in Bond Corporation that were now worth next to nothing.

Their only chance of getting this money back was to get their hands on the one asset in Bond's empire that was actually producing cash, the Greenvale nickel mine in North Queensland. And this is what the new loan was designed to achieve. By putting in US$300 million of new funding, they were able to both get their old loans out and take security over an asset that could be sold for a decent price if the Bond empire finally collapsed. Plus they were able to extract personal guarantees from Alan Bond himself.

But the new loan hadn't saved Bond or his empire. And the banks had received neither a cent in interest nor a penny of principal on their US$300 million. So, in March 1991, as Bond's businesses had begun to disintegrate, they had decided to seize the nickel mine and call in the personal guarantees, and to this end they had served notices of demand on Bond and his various companies, in Brisbane, Perth, New York and Sydney, to pay the money or be put under.

Bond and his lawyers soon made it clear that they would make it a long and difficult battle. And by arguing every point of law and exploiting every technicality, they managed to slow the process down so much that it was four months before the case even came to court. Then, on the day before the hearing was due to start, they announced that they would argue that the notices of demand had been served incorrectly.

Now there was no question that Bond and his companies had actually received the notices, because Bond's lawyers had caused them to be served no less than three times over a space of four months. But Australian courts are so obsessed with the letter of the law that they're perfectly capable of sending everyone back to square one just because a name is spelt wrongly on a court document or, as in this case, because a writ had been delivered successfully to Dallhold's new offices, instead of to the old (and unoccupied) address that had been specified back in 1990.

But fortunately for the banks, the case was being heard in the New South Wales Supreme Court by a judge who was famous for his intolerance of such legal nonsense. And while Justice Andrew Rogers couldn't stop the point from being argued, he was not likely to be at all sympathetic. Indeed, when it came to his judgement two months later, he attacked Bond's lawyers' tactics as 'a gross violation of the rules' that was in 'flagrant contravention of the purposes and practices of this court'. And in case there was any doubt as to his views, he added that he was delighted the tactic had failed because 'legally successful but otherwise meritless technical arguments do nothing to engender public confidence in the rule of law'.

The substance of Bond's case, in Rogers's view, wasn't a whole lot better. According to Alan, the banks had demanded his personal guarantees from him but had promised not to call them for at least two years, so that he would have enough time to sell the Greenvale mine for a decent price. Bond swore black and blue that the head of the Hongkong Bank, Willie Purves, had promised this himself in his office in Hong Kong. Yet there was nothing in any of the agreements about this, and the bankers and lawyers all denied it absolutely. What's more, as Rogers said, it was inconceivable that the banks would have been so stupid as to bind themselves hand and foot when the Bond Group was on the verge of collapse.

Bond tried hard to sell his story to the court, but Justice Rogers wasn't buying:

> The printed words of the transcript cannot give an approximation of the charm and salesmanship of Mr Bond in the witness box. Unfortunately, having seen the principal players in the witness box, in my view, the only person to whom he sold the notion that he was free for two years was himself ... The circumstances cry out in disbelief at such an arrangement.[5]

So, on 23 September 1991, Rogers gave judgement to the banks, Bond was given four weeks to pay US$194.6 million that he didn't have, and Kevin Munns was despatched to give him the good news that bankruptcy beckoned. But as Bond was soon boasting to the papers: 'It's not over till the fat lady sings'. And by the time Australians were reading about the bizarre outbreak of road rage in Perth, his lawyers were lodging an appeal.

At this stage, Bond may well have felt that he could still avoid bankruptcy altogether, for there is no doubt that he genuinely believed that the banks had dudded him. But all he succeeded in doing was keeping the bailiffs at bay for another three months, because in mid-December, Justice Michael Kirby turned down Bond's appeal. And a week after that, Bond was denied permission to take his case to the High Court and argue all over again.

So, two days before Christmas 1991, a new bankrupcty notice was issued (remedying deficiencies in the old one) and Basil Faulkner went down to the Dalkeith mansion to see if he could do any better than Kevin Munns.

As Faulkner sat outside in his ancient Falcon station wagon, there was a fair bit of activity in the Bond household. A couple of parties were planned over Christmas, so there were marquees to put up, and chairs, tables, food and drink to be delivered. A little matter of US$194 million wasn't going to stop the Bonds from having fun. And as a consequence, there was a steady stream of delivery vans, plying to and fro, with occasional forays by the family Mercedes or the big white Range Rover.

Occasionally, Faulkner gave chase to the Bond family cars in the hope that Alan might be driving, or lying out of sight in the passenger seat. Several times, Eileen told him firmly that Alan wasn't there. But although he hadn't set eyes on him, Faulkner was convinced that Bond was still hiding in the house, so for five days over Christmas he parked himself in the road outside with his thermos and sandwiches. He was not invited in for turkey.

Then, just after Christmas he got a tip-off that Bond had booked a flight and gone to Bali. Which meant, of course, that at some stage, he would almost certainly come flying back. And at 6.30am, on the day before New Year's Eve, he did just that, walking straight into the arms of a young lawyer who had come out to Sydney's Mascot Airport to welcome him.

It must be said that a good Hollywood scriptwriter would make more of such an opportunity than Alan and the lawyer managed to do, but it was a historic conversation nonetheless, given that Bond had been caught at last. According to the court affidavit, the exchange went like this:

> 'I'm Hamish Young, a solicitor with Mallesons.'
> 'Yes.'
> 'I'm here to serve you with this bankruptcy notice.'
> 'Thank you.'

At this point, most people would have gone quietly. But within three weeks, Alan's lawyers were marching into yet another court, Sydney's Federal Court this time, to have the bankruptcy notice set aside. There was no way now that they could do any more than delay the arrival of the bailiffs. But there was still $1 million to be saved if Alan could stave off bankruptcy till the end of February. So more dollars and yet more ridiculous arguments were now wheeled out in an attempt to persuade the courts that the latest bankruptcy notice was invalid.

This time, Bond's argument was that the banks had used the wrong exchange rate to convert his US$194.6 million debt into Australian dollars. The lawyers who acted for the banks had been pretty careful in doing this, and had followed the law to the letter, by phoning three different banks to ask them what their rate would have been at 11.00am on 19 December, and then swearing a statutory declaration to the court. But they had forgotten to specify the size of the transaction, so Bond hadn't got the best deal available. And as a result, he was being asked to pay A$252,243,451 instead of $251,738,805.

Now this extra half a million dollars would have been a serious matter if there had been the slightest possibility that Bond was going to pay any of it. But given that he didn't have a brass razoo, the amount was entirely academic. Yet it tied up some of the best brains in the Australian legal system for another three months before Justice Morling was able to dismiss it. Then there was yet another week while Bond appealed Morling's decision to the full bench of the Federal Court, where he lost once again. And only then was yet another bankruptcy notice issued.

But even now, the game wasn't over. For they still had to get the notice served, and as the *Sydney Morning Herald* soon reported, Bond was in London lying low.[6] He had been living it up in America with his girlfriend Di Bliss, watching the America's Cup and shouting meals for friends in expensive restaurants, but had since been spotted by a journalist called Eric Ellis, sitting in the front room of 14 Selwood Place in Chelsea, which had long been one of the Bond family's homes in the UK. He had refused to answer the door, and had then issued an angry press release, decrying his treatment by the banks and denying that anyone had told him they were trying to serve a bankruptcy notice on him.

For Bond, going back to Australia at this point was not the most attractive proposition. He was due to face trial in May 1992 on criminal charges over the Rothwells rescue that could put him in jail for a long stretch, and the Australian Securities Commission had said publicly that other charges were imminent. Now, as he saw it, he was also going to be humiliated by bankruptcy. Meanwhile, he was being sued for $23 million in the Western Australian Supreme Court, and was facing divorce proceedings in the Family Court in late April after thirty-seven years of marriage to Eileen, who had finally grown tired of his girlfriends.

At this stage, he still had a passport and was free to travel. But however tempted he may have been to do a runner and follow Christopher Skase into exile, he resolved to fly back to Perth and face the consequences. There was a minor consideration of $100,000 bail that he would lose if he didn't.

This, however, would be the last chance he would have to flee, because on 14 April 1992, Bond was finally made bankrupt and his passports confiscated. (The court had eventually permitted the banks to serve notices on his lawyers instead.)

Bond was not in Sydney's Federal Court to see it happen or to meet his new master, Robert Ramsay, who would be his trustee in bankruptcy. Ramsay would have the job of running Alan's bankrupt estate and dividing his assets, but as the banks had already discovered, there was virtually nothing to share out. Crucially, Bond had held off bankruptcy for so long that almost all of the $32 million he had given to family and friends since 1986 was now safe from attack.

4

Divorce

You toss off rumours of other women for a long
time, but eventually you have to stop and think
about it. But Alan was no different to many men ...
There's a lot of girls willing to put their names to
someone with power and money.

Eileen Bond 1994 in Public Lives, Private Passions[1]

The decision to get divorced after thirty-seven years of
marriage had been Eileen's entirely. It was not, as others
suggested, a ploy to safeguard Alan's fortune or ensure that
she was not taken down by his demise, because all that had
already been taken care of.

She confessed that she had been unhappy for some time and
felt that Alan no longer listened to her. They had not been
communicating, had grown too far apart and had got used to
living separate lives.

For a long time she had hoped that things would come right,
but gradually she had realised that they wouldn't. Finally, over
a period of about eighteen months, she had decided to get on with
her life alone. Later, she would explain with a tinge of regret:

I thought, 'Well maybe it's time to do what my
friends say I should do.' Having started the ball
rolling it's hard to stop.[2]

25

On several accounts, she loved him as much as ever, and they were certainly still friends. But they had seen little of each other in recent months, or even years. And what was really remarkable about the marriage was that it had held together so long.

Alan, for a start, had always had girlfriends, whom he had rarely bothered to hide from his wife, and had recently been going to singles parties for the under-forty-fives that a friend had organised in Perth. But he had also conducted a very public love affair with Diana Bliss since the early 1980s and the two of them had recently reunited after a three-year break. This, no doubt, had helped convince Eileen that the marriage was over.

Alan had first met Diana Bliss in 1976 when he had spotted her behind the bar at a posh Sydney hotel and asked her to join his group of friends, only to be slapped down with the rejoinder that she wasn't 'that sort of girl'. Three years later they had met again in Perth, where Di and a girlfriend were lunching at a trendy eatery called O'Connors. Once again, Alan had been with a party of people and had come over to introduce himself, as he did with countless other women over the years. And, as Di told *New Weekly*, they were immediately off and running:

> 'Hello, I'm Alan Bond' he said, looking directly into her eyes.
>
> 'And that was it . . .' Di smiles as she recalls the scene.
>
> 'I remember I was quite formal and of course I called him "Mr Bond". He said "Please call me Alan." He was slightly daunting, but he was very charming and relaxed. He had this air of confidence.'[3]

He was sixteen years older than she was, had four children, and was still very much married to Eileen, but he had never let such things cramp his style. She was in her early-twenties and looked like a teenager. A picture of the two of them from around this time shows her in a high-collared lace shirt with hair down to her shoulders, looking like the clergyman's daughter that she was, and apparently young enough to be one of Alan's own children. By this stage she was an air hostess with TAA (since merged with Qantas), and before long, she was doing the same job on one of Bond's corporate jets.

During the 1980s, they travelled the world together as he flew from one deal to the next, with Alan rarely bothering to be discreet about the arrangement and parading her openly in London at public functions. In 1982, according to Bond, they were invited to St James's Palace together, with a select bunch of twenty other guests, for Christmas carols with the Queen. And soon afterwards they were asked to dine with Princess Michael and Princess Margaret.

Their photo album pictured them on boats, on beaches, at dinner, or just relaxing in a host of different locations with a host of different hair and clothing styles, so it was obvious that they had seen a lot of each other down the years. Diana told interviewers that they were just good friends, but those who knew them knew better. In March 1986 they had bought a terrace house together in one of the best streets in Sydney's fashionable Paddington, which was named The Nest.

Eileen certainly knew about the affair, but somehow learnt to live with it, as wives of tycoons often do, turning a deaf ear to gossip and a blind eye to photographs of Alan and his pretty young companions. She could see no point in doing anything else, but she also had a family to look after and was a loud, fun-loving, vibrant person who was good at enjoying herself.

In her own words she 'never got sick of parties', so she sur-rendered herself to a world of Dom Perignon and lunches that lasted till well into the afternoon. She also whisked friends off on shopping trips to Sydney or Singapore, taking another Bond corporate jet, minus Diana, or up to Cockatoo Island Resort, which was owned by Dallhold. Rather than refer to Diana by name, she talked about her dismissively as 'Alan's sandwiches on the plane'.

But Perth was a small town and it was inevitable that they would run into each other from time to time. On one famous occasion they both turned up for lunch at the Mediterranean restaurant, where Perth's fast-money merchants used to gather in the 1980s to boast about their deals and drink French cham-pagne. A furious Eileen spotted Diana across the room and ordered the restaurant manager, Vito Ceccini, to 'throw the bitch out'. Ceccini refused, then watched, aghast, as Alan arrived and was greeted by his girlfriend with a kiss.

As the story goes, and it has no doubt been embellished over the years, Eileen then vented her anger on a friend of hers who was lunching with Diana, which resulted in Miss Bliss deciding to leave.

In late 1988, however, Alan and Diana split up. She had moved to London to chase her dream of being a theatre pro-ducer, and the strain of living on opposite sides of the world, or her decision to put career first, became too much for the relationship to bear.

For the next three years, Alan filled the vacant slot with another dazzling blonde called Tracey Tyler and travelled the world with her instead. She had also been an air hostess, but was now able to add London, New York, Colorado, Hawaii, South Africa, Japan and the South of France to the list of places she had visited. Tracey, too, received the mandatory house, car and jewellery. For Christmas in 1988 he gave her a mink coat. The following year it was an Omega gold watch. For her birthday in 1990 he gave her a new white Mercedes.

Friends noted that the two women looked remarkably similar, which was perhaps why Alan had chosen her. According to Diana Bliss, who told the story to friends in London with a twinkle in her eye, Alan showed her a photograph of his new flame over lunch in 1989 after their love affair had ended. 'Isn't she lovely?' Alan supposedly asked her. 'Just like you, only younger.'

But in 1991 this affair also came to an end and Diana re-emerged as the Bond girl. The first public sign, however, did not come until two months after Alan's divorce and bankruptcy, when Diana told *Woman's Day*:

> Alan is a dear friend and I feel that this is the time
> I should prove that I am a friend to him. Anyone
> can be a friend when times are good. It's when
> times are tough that real friends come through.[4]

It was the first time that Diana had publicly admitted that she was anything more than a good friend of Alan's mother Kathleen, which had been the hurried explanation that a flustered Bond had given his own *60 Minutes* program back in 1989. And while many knew that they had been lovers for ages, it was significant that she was at last confirming it. 'Bondy's blonde tells all' was the come-on to readers, and in a very tasteful manner she was at last admitting it:

> I suppose it would be easy to stay silent or pretend
> that Alan and myself had barely met. But I feel

defiant and want to say loud and clear that I will
not let him down this time.[5]

In the 1970s and 1980s, Alan and Eileen had talked of divorce
several times, and had even come close to reaching a settlement.
But Alan had apparently decided he couldn't afford the split.
Geoff Summerhayes, an architect friend, had discussed the
problem with the Bonds over breakfast and told Alan that he
and his ex-wife had divided their wealth down the middle, to
which Alan had scoffed: 'Yes, but that was two pounds of fuck
all'.

With Alan now on the skids, however, money was no longer
an issue, since he had nothing more to give away. And in the
meantime, his commitment to the marriage had just about
dried up.

Diana, by all accounts, is a lovely woman, and it was
entirely in character that she would come back to him when
others were walking away. Small, quiet, demure and determined, she was not one for extravagance or display, and in
many ways she was the opposite of Eileen. While she dined
out and liked parties, she would not stand up on the table to
lead a chorus or shower other guests with champagne as Big
Red might well have done. Nor would she have burst out of
a huge cake as Eileen once did to sing Happy Birthday to the
impresario Robert Stigwood.

Diana was a good-hearted, strong, honest woman whom
some people thought naïve, but most described as the best
thing that had ever happened to Alan. In her wide circle of
friends and acquaintants it would have been almost impossible to find anyone with a word of criticism. She was 'lovely',
'delightful', 'remarkable', 'positive', and almost universally
respected by her fellow professionals in the theatre.

She, for her part, was obviously in love with Alan, though most found it hard to see why. Perhaps the clue lay in her love of theatre, for the great characters of drama and fiction are not accountants or bankers or scrupulous citizens, they are people who are not bound by rules, who have boundless energy and galvanise others into action. And this was what Alan Bond was like. Whatever crimes he might have committed down the years, or lies he might have told, and whatever he lacked in self-awareness and empathy, he had the ability to enliven and motivate, or to aggravate and infuriate, in equal measure. And this was surely what Diana found so attractive. In her own words, he was the most positive, the most energetic person she had ever met. And plenty of others shared this view.

Those who bought the Bond package saw him as a wonderful entertainer and an amazing salesman who could talk anybody into anything. This, after all, was what had enabled him to borrow $14 billion from the banks of the world. Yet the same people sometimes suggested that he was not particularly smart and that he was not really interested in anyone but himself. As one friend uncharitably described him, he was a dysfunctional person who came from a dysfunctional family and was driven to impress a disapproving father. All agreed, however, that he was a junkie, a man who lived for the thrill of the deal.

David Michael, who was Alan's personal assistant in the 1980s, still marvels at his old boss's ability to enliven everyone who worked for him, Michael included. But in other ways he was far less impressed:

> In virtually every aspect he was, and still is, a very
> ordinary man. He has no great brain-power, and

no analytical skills whatsoever, but he is one of the most cunning operators around. His driving force is 'sticking it up his rivals', and at the same time, showing the world that he has done so. It is no more complicated than that.[6]

Bond was a great dealmaker, whose supreme talent was to borrow vast amounts of money from the banks and risk it on projects that others thought reckless. He bought oil wells, gold mines, breweries, TV stations, a telephone company and properties all over the world, but he could only play the game while markets were rising, for he was a buyer and a seller rather than a manager of businesses, and he needed to keep assets moving or revalue them and borrow more money if the ship was to stay afloat. Once prices started falling this was not possible.

He was, however, quite capable of manufacturing profits artificially for Bond Corporation by selling things to his mates. In David Michael's words:

As he was cunning, so he was prepared to bend the rules until they roughly corresponded with what he wanted them to mean. So it was that year after year, spectacular deals were done, or seen to be done, at about the end of the financial year. Great profits were made and ever larger dividends paid out.[7]

It escaped attention for many years that his private company Dallhold needed these dividends to stay solvent and that a lot of the deals contained clauses enabling them to be unwound after the end of the financial year. But in March 1989, the

ABC's *Four Corners* program exposed two huge deals that had produced $150 million of bogus 'profit' in the 1988 accounts, and this both rocked his bankers' confidence and caused his auditors to book huge losses in the 1989 accounts.

The crash was inevitable. By the end of the 1980s, asset prices were falling, Bond Corporation and Dallhold were desperately short of cash, and the banks were already baying for money. By late 1990, Alan had been forced to resign and Bond Corporation was in the hands of the receivers. The collapse of Dallhold and Alan's bankruptcy followed hard behind.

Bond's America's Cup victory in 1983 had given him access to money beyond his wildest dreams and caused bankers to beat a path to his door, but it had also brought extravagance and excess on a massive scale. By the end, Bond Corporation was running a fleet of four long-range jets that cost nigh on $20 million a year, and maintaining two huge ocean-going yachts, *Southern Cross II* and *III*. The larger of these cost US$10,000 a day to keep, even if she was just sitting idle at her mooring in Antibes in the South of France.

Dallhold, meanwhile, handed out cash by the fistful to Bond and his family, and maintained several hugely expensive properties around the world, including the entire English village of Glympton that Alan had bought in 1986.

And that was not the end of the largesse. A business mate of Alan's had received a $6 million finder's fee for introducing a land deal in Victoria, while Dallhold had picked up $10 million on a gold deal and $30 million for 'finding' the Emu Brewery site in Perth for Bond Corporation. The group's three top executives—Peter Beckwith, Peter Mitchell and Tony Oates—had also done well, with secret $1 million profits on a Bond Corp land deal and the notorious Golden Handcuffs of 1988, which promised them $25 million if they stayed with the company that they were driving into bankruptcy.

It was thus that Alan and his mates had managed to do what most people had considered impossible. They had owned a brewery in Australia and still gone broke.

5

Friends

A friend in need is
a friend indeed

It was hard when you looked at Bob Ramsay, Alan's trustee in bankruptcy, to avoid the conclusion that his battle with Bond might be the mismatch of the century.

Here was a quiet, conservative, cautious accountant up against a salesman whose ability to paint dreams had enabled him to borrow more than any other man in Australian history.

Here was a decent, honest, moral man who believed in truth, fairness and moderation, on the trail of a story spinner who had grave trouble telling fact from fiction.

And here was a man who played his golf on a public course, pitched against a spender of heroic proportions, who could give away $300,000 and not remember whom he'd paid it to.

Alan Bond was truly a champion in everything he had done. He had won the America's Cup against all odds, built one of Australia's biggest companies from scratch, run up the country's biggest corporate loss, followed it with the biggest ever corporate collapse, and then capped it with one of the world's biggest bankruptcies.[1]

And now this charming, serial self-deluder was about to do battle with an ordinary human being like Bob Ramsay. And to do so, paradoxically, with far more money than his poor creditors would ever be prepared to provide. It did not seem like a fair fight.

Ramsay could have been forgiven for being overawed by his opponent, but it was his lack of spark that gave cause for concern, for he looked like Walter Matthau at his most morose. He was tall, yet you hardly noticed it. And his grey pin-striped suit, matched with grey-striped shirt and purple tie, was doubtless expensive, but looked like it had cost less than Alan spent on dinner.

Insolvency practitioners normally have a certain dash about them, as if they've rubbed off some of the gloss from the entre-preneurs they've buried, but poor Bob looked as sombre as an undertaker.

Ramsay had not exactly been everybody's tip for the job, for Bond was the biggest and highest profile bankrupt Australia had ever seen, and Ramsay was hardly the biggest name in the insolvency business. But in fact he had experience of the big time, for he had wound up Ian Johns's estate in the late 1980s (after Johns had lost a fortune for Tricontinental) and had followed that with Reuben Lew's company, Estate Mortgage Financial Services. And on both of these he was judged to have done well by the banks who hired him.

There was also a suggestion that he might just relish this contest, for inside Robert Ramsay there was a hint of a flash cat yearning to scratch its way out. He wore a diamond-and-gold ring on his right hand and a chunky gold signet ring on his left, with the initials RR emblazoned upon it. He was also an expert on insolvency, had tough new laws behind him, was stubborn and determined, and had an excellent team of people. And he was not going to stand for any nonsense.

Only minutes after the court had made Bond bankrupt, a letter from Ramsay was winging its way to Bond's Sydney solicitors to inform him of his obligations, and Bob was jumping on a plane to Perth to talk to Bond face to face. The letter told Alan he had fourteen days to prepare a statement of affairs listing all his assets and liabilities, plus names and addresses of all his creditors. He was warned that failure to do so could land him in prison for contempt.

He was also advised that his worldly goods would have to be surrendered for division among his creditors. All he would be allowed to keep were 'necessary wearing apparel, necessary household property, ordinary tools of trade, and a motor vehicle' worth no more than $2,500.

Finally, he was told that he would be forbidden from obtaining credit of more than $500 without telling the lender he was bankrupt, and would be prevented from travelling overseas unless he had his trustee in bankruptcy's permission.

But if Bond ever bothered to read this letter, he did not seem to be convinced that these onerous restrictions should apply to him. Only a matter of hours after he had been made bankrupt, he met Bob Ramsay in Perth and told him that he wanted to leave Australia the next day to spend three weeks in Europe. He was angry that he had been forced to come back to Australia and interrupt an important business trip. And he now demanded to be allowed to catch a plane to Saudi Arabia, where several sultans and princes were expecting his visit.

Ramsay was clearly aghast at the way in which Bond travelled round the world first class, 'in the manner that you and I might catch a tram'. And three years later he was still marvelling that 'the standing of the people Bond dealt with all over the world, the high-level wheeling and dealing, was incredible'.[2] But he was not going to be bullied into letting Bond skip the country like that other notorious 1980s entrepreneur had done ten months earlier.

Christopher Skase had fled justice in 1991 only hours after being made bankrupt for $164 million, having persuaded a tame trustee to give him his passport back. And Ramsay was determined not to make the same mistake, so he told Bond there was no prospect of him getting permission to travel, at least until his statement of affairs had been completed, and promptly confiscated Alan's Australian passport so that he couldn't take off on his own.

Bond, however, also had a British passport which he was reluctant to hand over, and he at first refused to reveal where it was, except to say that it was in London awaiting a Saudi Arabian visa. It took more than a week before he agreed to surrender it, and by that time he was loudly demanding the return of his Australian passport so that he could jump on a plane to Europe. In fact, by the end of the month, he had made no fewer than five attempts to persuade Ramsay to let him go, and had even applied to the Federal Court to have the trustee's decision overturned. Ramsay told the court that he was not only concerned that his charge might not come back, but was also determined that Bond should take his legal duties seriously, which meant helping to decipher his appallingly complex financial affairs.[3]

Boxes and boxes of documents had by now been shipped across from Perth by Bond and his family companies, and back at Bird Cameron's office in Melbourne, where Ramsay was based, there was already a huge room of files devoted to the investigation. There, nine accountants were trying to make sense of the vast mass of paperwork and drawing up a list of 100 detailed questions about bank accounts, properties, jewellery, cars and even a storage lockup that Alan had rented in January 1991.

At one extreme, they were asking about $1.36 million that had gone through one of Alan's accounts that couldn't be explained. At the other, they were worried about two windsurfers and an inflatable boat that seemed to have gone missing. In the middle was a tantalising $100,000 in cash that Eileen's personal assistant had picked up from a bank in Perth, which Bond said had funded the family's living expenses for a while.

Bob Ramsay was clearly shocked by what his team was uncovering, and flabbergasted at the amounts of money that Bond had given away, and it must have seemed like a nightmare, for he was gradually discovering that Bond had divested himself of the $32 million in gifts and everything else of value, by either placing it in trust or someone else's name. It appeared that Bond had been planning for bankruptcy for many years. Yet, at this stage, Ramsay was still hopeful that he could overturn some of the transactions, and was probing and exploring to see how it might be done.

It was clear in these first few weeks that his relationship with Bond was going to be prickly at best. But if Bond behaved as if he had better things to do than answer Ramsay's huge list of questions, he did have other pressing matters to attend to. On 25 May 1992, his trial was due to start on a dishonesty charge relating to the rescue of Laurie Connell's Rothwells Bank in 1987.

Bond's alleged crime had taken place in the dark days of October just after the world's stock markets had gone into a tailspin. Two weeks after the crash, his old mate's merchant

bank faced imminent collapse as depositors rushed to withdraw their cash amid rumours that millions were missing.
Bond had been called back from Rome on a Friday night to
coordinate the rescue, knowing that Connell would be unable
to open the doors on Monday morning unless a $370 million
bailout package could be put together over the weekend.

Bond was a ball of energy as they raced against the clock,
and his salesmanship was vital in convincing Australia's rich
and powerful to pledge millions in a vast corporate telethon.
But in twisting the arm of another old mate, Brian Coppin,
Alan allegedly failed to mention the fact that he stood to profit
hugely if the Rothwells rescue succeeded.

Bond had gone round to Coppin's house at seven o'clock on
the Monday morning, with only a couple of hours left till the
bank was due to open, to tell him that the rescue would collapse unless he pledged his unconditional support. And Coppin
had reluctantly promised $15 million to keep it alive. But
according to the prosecution, Bond had omitted to tell Coppin
that he had negotiated a $16 million success fee for Bond Cor-
poration with Laurie Connell only hours earlier.

Had Brian known that Alan had a nice little earner lined up
he might well have decided not to risk his cash, but the prosecution needed only to prove that Bond knew about the fee
and then acted dishonestly by concealing it. And according to
Western Australia's Director of Public Prosecutions, John
McKechnie, there was no other way to describe Bond's
behaviour.

Despite being legally broke, Bond had assembled a defence
team comprising no fewer than three QCs that would have
given him little change out of $25,000 a day. And he had
clearly spent a great deal more on an army of solicitors to brief
them, because his legal bill for May and June 1992 would

come to nearly $700,000. But even this amount of money was not enough to get him acquitted. He was found guilty and sentenced to a maximum of two-and-a-half years in jail, which in practice meant he should be out on parole within twelve months.

There were gasps in the court when the verdict was handed down, and his now ex-wife Eileen burst into tears. Outside, she told reporters that Alan had taken it 'like the man he is', and soon afterwards a press statement from the family was issued to say that they could not understand either the verdict or the severity of the sentence.

Bond served his time at Wooroloo Prison Farm, fifty kilometres east of Perth. It is a minimum-security jail, with no bars on the windows or locks on the doors. But for all its free-and-easy atmosphere, it was a world away from the one that Alan was used to, in which there were limos and first-class travel, five-star hotels with marble bathrooms, and servants at his beck and call.

Like all the other inmates, he was sent to work for eight hours a day in the prison workshops or on the farm, ate his meals in a communal canteen with 200 other prisoners, and took his showers in a communal block that everyone used. His sleeping quarters were in one of six old tin-roofed buildings with rooms that opened onto long verandahs. And he had to share this bedroom too.

He later confessed that it was not an easy time for him. 'For the first few weeks in jail it was difficult because I was ill. It was very cold. I was in a dormitory with eight other people: four aborigines and four white people. The windows had been broken. It was about zero degrees at night.'⁴ His aboriginal cellmates stole his blankets, he said, because he was too sick to stop them, and it was then too cold to sleep. According to a psychiatrist's report in 1994, Alan was still preoccupied by the ordeal two years later:

> He was shattered by the unexpected incarceration. He was threatened. He was attacked by someone with a knife. He thinks recurrently of the experience ... He recalls it with distress and is tearful. He has tended to avoid discussion of the events, even with close family. He has a morbid fear now of prison ... the experiences of court represent a constant threat and reminder to him.[5]

Bond told journalists that prayer and a bit of business acumen helped him survive, and that he wrote letters for other prisoners to get himself 'a clean shirt or whatever it was that I needed: an extra orange, just simple things'.[6] But luckily for him, he did not have to serve his full sentence. Ninety days after he had been imprisoned, his conviction was quashed on the grounds that Laurie Connell's evidence could not be trusted, and a retrial was ordered (at which he was acquitted in November 1992).[7]

He walked free into the winter drizzle to be greeted by waiting camera crews and reporters, his normally plump face drawn, his eyes hollow, his usual rosy cheeks grey and unshaven. He seemed to have aged ten years and lost a lot of weight, and the old confident smile was gone. He struggled to complete a few sentences about his innocence, the unfairness of his treatment, and his desire to spend time with his family. Then he all but broke down and cried, and had to seek refuge in the dark blue Mercedes in which son John had come to collect him.

Alan had been ill in prison, and when he came out he went

straight to the old family home in Dalkeith, where Eileen nursed him back to health. He had suffered a heart condition for around five years and this had suddenly become more acute. After only two weeks in Wooroloo, he had nearly fainted from an angina attack that had given him a savage pain in his chest and right arm, and had been taken by ambulance to the Royal Perth Hospital, where tests had shown him to have a swollen heart and a leaking heart valve. He was now seen by a couple of heart specialists and booked in for open-heart surgery to fix the problem. His operation in February 1993 proceeded smoothly and without drama, and once again it was his ex-wife who looked after him. According to an old friend of the Bonds, Tony Weatherald:

> When he was ill Eileen used to go round every night and cook his meals for him, she'd go round and get breakfast for him, she waited on him hand and foot. Do you think she still loved him? Yes, of course she did. There was nothing she wouldn't do for him. When he wasn't with Diana, she was with him whenever she could be.[8]

In the aftermath of Alan's spell in prison and subsequent illness, Eileen clearly had qualms of guilt about divorcing him at a time when his world was falling apart. In 1994 she told author Susan Mitchell:

> I still feel I'm Mrs Bond ... He still is a prime consideration. What happened to Alan was grossly unfair and I didn't even want to add to his struggles. Had I known what was going to happen, I don't know if I would have gone on with it.

I don't think I would have piled that on top of
Alan as well as everything else.[9]

It was not clear, however, that Alan always repaid her in kind
or that she always felt so warm towards him. On one occasion
in 1993, Weatherald was on the telephone to Bond from a
London hotel while Eileen was in the next room, and was
asked to fetch her so Alan could give her some news: 'He was
laughing down the phone. He says: "I've gone and sold
Watkins Road, I think I've done a good deal on it too"'.

A few minutes later, according to Weatherald, Eileen came
back 'bawling her eyes out, saying: "What will that bastard do
to me next? He's gone and done it to me. He's gone and sold
my house. What am I going to do with all my furniture?"'.[10]

In the time that Alan had been in Wooroloo, Bob Ramsay
had been working hard to get money for the creditors, and in
November 1992 he won a major victory by gaining control of
Bond's $2.7 million superannuation fund. This had been set
up for him in September 1990, when he had been forced to
quit Bond Corporation, and had been designed to be proof
from attack. But for once Bond's legal eagles had failed to
work their magic.

One problem for them was that the law had been changed
since the fund was set up, and this had made it easier for
Ramsay to get his hands on the money. But Bond's trustee had
also persuaded the courts to strike down a special clause in
the trust deed that was intended to divert all monies in the
fund to Alan's family if he went bankrupt. And on top of that,
the court had overridden a special resolution of the fund's
trustees (made after Alan's bankruptcy) that the $2.7 million
should not go to Bond's creditors.

The victory promised to be a landmark decision, because

super funds had always been safe from creditors and spouses, but it was just the first round in what was bound to be a long battle, because Bond would now appeal all the way to the High Court and it would be two years before the outcome was confirmed.

Bond's tactics in this regard were the same as Field Marshal Haig's in World War One when he had waged trench warfare against the Germans. Just as Haig had believed in trading lives one for one until his opponents ran out of men, so Bond believed in trading dollars hundred for hundred until his pursuers ran out of money. As a result, Ramsay and the creditors faced constant legal actions and massive legal fees whenever they tried to do anything. Every point of fact and every point of law was disputed. In this case, even the date of Alan's departure from Bond Corporation had been contested, while the hearings had been moved from Melbourne to Perth in a manner that the judge described as 'totally unwarranted', apparently to make life difficult for Ramsay.[11]

But this was not the only legal battle brewing, for Ramsay was also taking a swing at Alan's lifestyle, using new powers known as the Skase amendments, that had come into force in July 1992. The aim of these was to prevent bankrupts from living the high life while their creditors got nothing. And they could well have been tailor-made for Bond, as the explanatory memorandum to the new legislation made clear:

> Some bankrupts manage to put their assets out of the reach of creditors, and to channel income away from themselves through the use of associated individuals, companies, partnerships or trusts ... These associated entities may, and usually do then provide the bankrupt with substantial non-cash

benefits, such as free or low-cost housing, motor
vehicles, boats or payments of expenses ... The
Bill tackles these difficulties.[12]

The new law set a limit of $24,000 on what a bankrupt was
allowed to earn as income, and defined this to include benefits
in kind. Above the limit, any bankrupt was now required to
hand over half to his creditors. Or so the theory went. But
Bond wasn't going to be constrained by this sort of nonsense.

When Ramsay first made an assessment of his income in July
1992, Bond told him that he was receiving only $22 a week,
from sewing mailbags or tilling the prison gardens, and was
spending some of that on soap. But now that he was out of
jail, he was obviously enjoying something nearer his normal
lifestyle. The Australian public was allowed a glimpse of this
when his younger daughter Jody got married in Perth in May
1993, and TV cameras were there to record the occasion. Alan
was snapped in the front seat of a huge white Bentley, dressed
in a black morning suit with dazzling white shirt. He beamed
at the cameras, his skin shining, his chubby face restored and
glowing with health. Eileen sat in the back, glittering with diamonds, her red hair piled high, with the two of them and their
grandchildren looking for all the world like Perth's answer to
the royal family.

The party at the house in Dalkeith, with smoked salmon and
champagne, was a relatively modest affair compared with the
extravaganza for Susanne's wedding back in 1985, when there
had been gold medallions for the guests and an orchestra float-
ing on the Swan. Nor was the cost anywhere near the
$750,000 that had reportedly been lavished on his younger son
Craig's reception, when revellers had been flown across from
the eastern states at the Bond family's expense. But the family's

shining white Bentley and the perfect-teeth grin were still not a good look for a man who was meant to be skint. This wasn't humble pie, it was lording it.

Nor was Alan slumming it when he wasn't at family functions. The boats and the Merc had gone, and he was no longer living at Watkins Road with its resort-sized pool and myriad bathrooms, but he had settled into a comfortable new house down on the beach at Cottesloe, where Diana was an increasingly frequent visitor. This had cost around $400,000 to buy and another $200,000-or-so to renovate, and had been provided by one of the Bond family cash boxes, the Green Place Trust, which allowed him to live there without paying rent. In his driveway stood a $60,000 Alfa 164, generously provided by his son Craig.

Bankruptcy hadn't forced him to stop travelling either. His son John had coughed up $14,000 for four round trips to Melbourne, so Alan was clearly still sitting up the front of the plane and staying in five-star hotels. And if all that weren't enough, he also had free office space in Adelaide Terrace and a secretary, provided by the family company Armoy.

For a man on his uppers it wasn't half bad.

Ramsay had assessed the cost of all these things and, in the style of all accountants, had come up with the remarkably precise figure of $206,129 that Bond now needed to contribute to his creditors, as half of his 'income' over and above the statutory $24,000. But like everything else, Bond merely announced his intention to fight the assessment in court. So this, too, was dropped into the pot with all the other legal actions.

Ramsay had in fact grossly underestimated what the various court cases were costing Bond, but when he did ask the question, it raised a fascinating line of inquiry. In the six months before his bankruptcy, Bond's legal fees had been running at the rate of $2 million a year. And since then the pace of legal actions had quite probably accelerated. So where had all the money come from?

The answer was that Bond's bills were being paid by a number of extraordinarily generous friends. Robert Quinn, a stockbroker mate from London, had coughed up $200,000 from a Swiss bank account at Credit Suisse in Davos. British entrepreneur Graham Ferguson Lacey, another old mate, had also kicked the tin, sending $150,000 from one of his Bermudan companies, Hemisphere Management. And a former Bond Brewing executive, Murray Quartermaine, had contributed $100,000 that he had borrowed from Armoy, which ran the Bond family's Alpha Trust.

But the lion's share of these legal fees had been picked up by a shadowy Swiss gentleman called Jurg Bollag, who had sent $600,000 from an account at the Zuger Kantonal Bank in Zug, Switzerland, on behalf of his Panamanian company called Juno Equities.

In August 1992, Ramsay wrote to Bond asking him who was paying his legal fees and why. Bond wrote back to say that he had no idea who had paid them in the past or who would pay them in the future, but that he 'hoped for support'. He claimed to be unaware that Quinn and Bollag had been so generous.

But finally, Bond was asked why Mr Bollag would want to spend a fortune on actions that Alan was fighting. Bond replied that Mr Bollag was a good friend. But as the investigators would discover, he was a great deal more than that.

6

Bondy's Banker

If the defendant (Susanne Bond) or myself required
money at any given time Mr Bollag would be
contacted and money would appear from
Switzerland.

Sworn Statement of Armand Leone, 23 May 1988[1]

The mysterious Mr Bollag had already hit the headlines a
month before Bond went bankrupt. Or, to be precise, he
had hit a young Kiwi photographer called Nigel Marple who
was trying to take a picture of him for the *Sydney Morning
Herald*.

The incident had happened in London on 11 March 1992
outside the Bonds' house at 14 Selwood Place, Chelsea, where
a journalist had already spotted Alan sitting in the front room.
Marple had gone down there in the hope of grabbing a picture,
but a tall man with grey curly hair had emerged from the house
instead and made his way towards a parked car, swearing at
the photographer as he did so, and telling him he had no right
to be there.

Nigel Marple had not the slightest idea who this angry man
was, and neither did the rest of the world at the time. But Jurg
Bollag had guaranteed himself instant fame by putting his

briefcase up to hide his face and then shoving it hard into Marple's lens. It had given the mild-mannered New Zealander a nasty cut on the nose that had 'bled like buggery'. And it had instantly identified Bond's philanthropic friend as a man who valued his privacy.

But Bollag's reluctance to be photographed was hardly surprising because it would soon become clear that he was sitting on assets worth up to $50 million that Alan Bond and his family enjoyed. For not only had he paid Bond's legal fees, he had also spent millions of dollars over the years on diamonds for Eileen, horses for Susanne, a yacht for Alan and an apartment for Diana Bliss, plus houses, ski lodges, farmland, paintings and country estates that Bond and his family now had the use of.

Alan's story would be that Mr Bollag was merely a generous friend, who had purchased these baubles with his very own funds, then selflessly handed them over to the Bonds to have fun with. But if you believed that, you would believe anything.

Bollag, for a start, did not appear to be particularly wealthy. He lived in a small town in Switzerland in a modern development with four or five similar houses. Like the others, his wasn't a waterfront property and had no view of the nearby lake. It was a comfortable brick-and-tile home in a suburban cul-de-sac that had probably been built in the 1970s for an accountant or a bank manager. It was what real estate agents called an executive residence. But it was not the home of a multi-millionaire.

Nor, if his tax returns were to be believed, was Bollag even a millionaire. These, amazingly, could be inspected at the local municipal offices, and revealed an annual salary of $170,000, which in Switzerland was no more than a decent living. His net worth in 1992 was a solid but unspectacular $550,000, which was well short of the magic million. And on that basis, he had just rendered himself completely penniless by paying Bond's lawyers' bills.

Clearly, there was something amiss. In fact either Jurg had been telling porkies to the Swiss taxman, or Alan was lying when he said that Bollag had bought all the houses, horses, paintings and jewels with his own money. But it had to be said that Bond's account was pretty incredible even without the evidence of the tax returns. For in 1989 Jurg had forked out £315,000 to settle Alan's bill at the top London jeweller Aspreys and had never asked for his money back. And in November 1990 he'd paid for Alan's new ocean racer *Jackaroo*. This was at a time when lending money to Bond was financial suicide, because his public company, Bond Corporation Holdings, had already collapsed into the arms of the receiver with a deficit of $4.5 billion, and death for Dallhold was bound to follow hard behind. Yet Bollag had splashed out $250,000 for Alan's brand new boat that was being built in Perth.

In both these cases, as with the legal fees, the cash had come from bank accounts in Zug that Bollag controlled. But the supposed 'sponsor' of the boat had been a Liberian company called Jupiter Services, resident in the West African city of Monrovia. It was a mystery what this outfit stood to gain from Alan's sailing activities, but it was even harder to explain why it hadn't got its money back when the project had been canned. The boat builder Skip Lissiman had written to Bollag to tell him that he had been instructed to pay the unused $55,000 to Alan Bond's account in Perth. And Bollag had not uttered a murmur of complaint.

But as investigators would discover, these were just two of at least a dozen examples of Bollag's baffling generosity, for which there was really only one sensible explanation: that all this money belonged to Bond.

In April 1992, when Alan went bankrupt, Bollag was a tanned, slim, fit-looking forty-eight-year-old who had known Bond for eight or nine years. They had met while Bollag was working in corporate finance at the Dow Banking Corporation in Geneva, which, like most of the other banks in the world, was then lending money to the Bond Group.

In November 1986, he had set up shop by himself in his hometown of Zug, to look after other people's money.[2] And there was no doubt that Alan Bond was his biggest client.

To run his new business, Bollag set up a company called JF Consulting, with the initials reflecting his first name, Jurg, and his wife's name, Florence. But files at the local corporate registry showed the company had at first been christened Crasujo Investments.

This name had been changed after only two months. And, when you thought about it, it wasn't hard to guess why. Crasujo formed an acronym for three of Bond's children: Craig, Susanne and Jody, or Craig, Susanne and John. Which made it pretty easy to divine whose money Mr Bollag was investing if it wasn't his own.

In fact, as investigators would soon discover, Bollag had declared Crasujo Investments in 1987 to be the owner of the Liberian company that would so kindly pay for Alan's boat *Jackaroo*. But that is jumping the gun. For first we need to explain how Bollag's name came into the public eye in 1988, as a result of a marriage that went drastically wrong.

Susanne Bond's wedding in Perth in November 1985 to the New York doctor Armand Leone had come with the trappings of a fairy-tale romance and all the glitz that money could buy. It had been Australia's version of *Dallas*, the next best thing to

Charles and Di. The caterers and the florists had been flown in from Melbourne, Prime Minister Bob Hawke had sent a telegram of congratulation, and there had been vintage Krug on tap.

But two years later, the marriage had fallen apart, and a bitter row had begun over who would get what, and in particular over who owned their valuable horseflesh. Susanne and her husband were both international showjumpers who between them had at least a dozen horses worth nigh on $3 million. But Susanne was adamant that some of the most expensive ones could not be included in the divorce settlement because they didn't belong to her or her spouse.

The full story of the fight over these animals involves bizarre tales of horsenapping on both sides of the Atlantic, as Susanne and Armand both tried to hang on to what they believed to be theirs. But events in the courtroom were even more intriguing to Ramsay and others who were trying to trace Bond's overseas assets, because in May 1988 Susanne swore in an affidavit to a New Jersey court that five of the couple's horses worth more than $1 million had been paid for by Bollag, through two of his offshore companies, Siren Company and Kirk Holdings. The ever-generous Mr B had supposedly bought them with his own money, then allowed Susanne to ride them because he was so keen that she should be selected for the Olympics.

Susanne's deposition, which explained how all this had come about, made it sound as though Bollag had been discovered almost by chance. As she told the story, she and Armand had travelled to Perth to talk to her father and Robert Pearce, the managing director of Dallhold Investments, about finding a buyer for a talented young horse called Puntero, that had already won a big competition in Europe.

I asked Dad would he be able to find a company that might be interested in investing in a horse. He said okay and then from there I left it in the hands of Robert. And Kirk Holdings purchased the horse.[3]

Puntero had duly been bought in October 1986 for US$325,000, with money telexed to the USA from an account at the Allied Irish Banks in Jersey, where Bollag's company Kirk Holdings was apparently based. Yet Bollag had never even bothered to look at the animal he was buying.

According to Armand Leone's sworn statement to the court, Leone himself had flown to Mexico with a trainer from Europe to inspect Puntero, and the horse had then been shipped directly to his father's farm in New Jersey, where it had remained. Bollag had never had anything to do with it.

Nor had he even given instructions for the money to be paid. These had come instead from Robert Pearce, Bond's managing director at Dallhold, who had authorised a firm of Jersey accountants to transfer the funds to an account at Paine Webber in New York. It was unthinkable that he would in fact have been able to do this, and do it by telephone, if Kirk Holdings had genuinely been Bollag's company. But that wasn't the only problem with this story, for Puntero's passport showed Armand and Susanne Leone to be the horse's owners, even though it had supposedly been bought by Bollag. And there was similar confusion with another top-class jumper, Ladino, that had been purchased for US$200,000 by Bollag's Siren Company. This time the passport declared that the horse belonged to Alan Bond and Dallhold Investments.

Leone was also quite scathing about the notion that Bollag

was just a generous family friend. His sworn statement to the court painted a remarkable picture of Jurg as keeper of the Bonds' money box—a man whose duties were:

> ... to transfer money at the request of the Bond family from various Swiss bank accounts held by the Bond company. If the defendant (Susanne Bond) or myself required money at any given time Mr Bollag would be contacted and money would appear from Switzerland.[4]

Leone's description of Kirk Holdings and Siren Company was no less damning. These, he told the court, were 'none other than Mr Bond's creative manoeuvrings'. Or to be even more blunt: 'offshore holding companies of Alan Bond's'.[5]

Back in 1988 when these allegations were made, it had not mattered to anyone but the taxman whether Bollag and his companies held assets for Alan Bond or not. And once Armand had accepted a settlement of $450,000, the smoke of battle had quickly died down. But in 1992 it had become a matter of huge importance to establish whether Jurg was really a man of gargantuan generosity, as Bond maintained, or took care of the Bond family millions, as Armand alleged, because if Bollag was just a front then all these millions belonged to Alan's creditors.

By this time, however, there were many more gifts from Bollag that Bond needed to explain away, because the records of Dallhold's art collection contained invoices and letters relating to two valuable pictures that Kirk Holdings had purchased in the 1980s, again with money from its Jersey bank account.

The first was a painting called *Natives in the Eucalypt Forest* by the famous Australian colonial artist John Glover, which had cost Kirk £425,000 in December 1984. The second was a portrait of the explorer Matthew Flinders, by a little-known French artist called Antoine de Toussaint Chazal, which had cost Kirk $492,000 in 1987.

In line with his absurdly generous attitude to these things, Jurg Bollag had allowed Alan Bond to ship both of them to Australia in Dallhold's name and hang them on his office walls in Perth. And there was little doubt that there were other artworks that the beneficent Mr B had bought for Bond, because a memo from Dallhold's managing director in December 1990 listed $10 million of Bond's artworks as being 'held offshore', all of which had gone missing by the time he went bankrupt.

Bond himself had sworn an affidavit in the New Jersey divorce proceedings to counter what he called the 'outrageous lies' being told about him and to hose down suggestions that he might be evading tax through these Jersey companies, and in particular he had tried to minimise Bollag's role. According to Alan's sworn evidence, Jurg Bollag was simply 'the manager of an investment company in Switzerland and an independent adviser on international management and finance'. Bollag, he emphasised, was certainly *not an employee of mine or any of the companies in which I own an interest*.[6]

But as with the horses and the paintings, it seems that Bond was again not telling the truth. Alan's former personal assistant, David Michael, who worked for Bond from 1985 to 1988, is adamant that Bollag's number was in the Bond Group's internal telephone book. And he is absolutely sure that Bollag was also on the payroll. Michael says he saw the letter of engagement in 1987 and remembers it vividly, because he was angry that Bollag was being paid so much. As he recalls it, the contract promised Bollag a Mercedes in Switzerland plus a salary of $250,000 a year. But, most significant of all, Michael recalls that it specified Bollag's duties, which were to manage Bond's personal financial affairs outside Australia. As a result, Bollag was sometimes referred to by the inner circle as Bondy's private banker.

Simon Farrell, who was Alan's executive assistant for several years, told Ramsay on oath in 1993 that he met Bollag many times in London at the two houses owned by the Bond Group in Belgrave Mews. 'If Alan was in England,' said Farrell, 'Jurg would more than often come and see him.' He added that, 'Alan put a great deal of weight in Jurg's advice to him. He thought he was very clever'. But Farrell was absolutely adamant that Bollag never did business with Bond Corporation. So did he do business with Bond on a private basis when he made these visits, he was asked? Yes, said Farrell, he assumed that he did.[7]

In 1994, Bond was examined on oath in the Federal Court by Francis Douglas QC, who asked him whether he could think of any reason why Jurg Bollag should pay $600,000 worth of legal fees that Alan had run up:

Bond: Yes, because he's a friend. I asked him to help.
Douglas: Even though these fees amount to hundreds of thousands of dollars?
Bond: Yes.
Douglas: He is that good a friend is he?
Bond: Yes.[8]

Bond also offered the explanation that Bollag had been his business partner in the Queensland Nickel Project, and stood to get a lot of money back if the nickel mine and its refinery could be prised from the jaws of the so-called SULA banks that had made Bond bankrupt.[9]

But this only dug Bond in deeper, because the story revealed yet another connection between him and Bollag that only made sense if it was Alan's money that Jurg was looking after.

The Queensland Nickel Project was often described by Bond as the best deal he ever did, yet he only fell into it by accident in 1983, when he bought a controlling share in a company called Mid-East Minerals, which he wanted for its gold mines.

The project comprised a huge mine at Greenvale in north Queensland, a refinery at Yabulu, and a rail link to the port at Townsville. But by the mid-1980s it had fallen into desperate straits, because the nickel price had plummeted, and it had racked up debts of $800 million on which it could no longer pay interest.

Bond's brilliant idea was to persuade the banks who had lent the money to sell him their debts for just 6 cents in the dollar. And he had then borrowed $50 million from another bank, Standard Chartered, to do the deal.

The terms of the agreement stated that Standard Chartered had the right to receive all cash flows from the nickel project up to the point where its $50 million had been repaid, after which the money would flow into Bond's private companies. But for some extraordinary reason, Alan had agreed to surrender his rights to this future cash flow to an offshore company fronted by his old friend Jurg for next to nothing.

As Bond revealed to the Federal Court in November 1991, Bollag's Metal Traders had been granted an option to acquire all the debts of the nickel project once Standard Chartered had been repaid, which would have the effect of diverting all the cash, tax-free, to the Isle of Man.

This option was going to cost just $3 million to exercise, but as Bond told the court, it could be worth as much as $700 million, because when the nickel price was high in the late 1980s, the project had been extremely profitable.

So why on earth had Bond given away such a hugely valuable asset? As usual, there was only one answer that made any sort of sense, and that was that Jurg was just acting as a front man for Alan Bond.[10]

Remarkably, Bond would go some way to admitting this in December 1994, when he told the *West Australian*'s Mark Drummond: 'There was to be a deal. It had been verbally agreed—it was never documented—that the benefits of the option deal would be shared between Bollag and myself in an offshore structure to be put together. And it would have been an offshore structure. There's no question about that. It was all offshore and we were going to make a lot of money out of it'.[11]

But it was most unlikely that Bollag would have received any of the money himself. Dallhold records show that Bond wrote in January 1991 to his friend Graham Ferguson Lacey to suggest that he find US$185 million to buy out the SULA banks. The letter proposed that Lacey could have a 51 per cent share of the nickel mine, with Bollag holding either 21 per cent or 36 per cent, as Bond's letter put it: '*On my behalf*'[12] (emphasis added).

Neither the original option deal nor the proposed arrangement with Lacey ever became reality, but each showed how Bond might have sent money offshore by the truckload without the taxman or anyone else finding out. If the Australian Taxation Office had tried looking in the Isle of Man they would have found no evidence to link Metal Traders to Bond, for its nominal owners were two obscure Jersey companies called Langtry Trust and Langtry Consultants.

In the late 1980s, Bond often boasted to people about all the money he had stashed offshore and how he would never be poor. One of those who has testified to this is the ex-chief executive of Bond Corporation in the UK, an Australian called John Richardson.[13]

Another is Bungo Ishizaki, the public face of a Japanese property developer EIE International, who did a lot of business with Bond in the 1980s. Ishizaki revealed in 1995 that Bond had offered to show him how to set up a family trust in Switzerland, and told him it would be completely safe from anybody who came after the money. 'They can't touch you,' Bond confidently assured him.[14]

But if it was indeed Bond's money that Bollag was looking after, as the evidence overwhelmingly suggested, how much was still around for creditors to chase, and was it now in assets or cash?

Part of the answer to this was in the English countryside, where John Lord, the liquidator of Alan's master private company Dallhold, which had gone bust in July 1991, was fighting for possession of a valuable stately home.

7

Lord of the Manor

Jurg used to laugh about Upp Hall because Upp Hall
was 'absolutely stolen. For what it cost us and the
way we got it, it's been one of the most beautiful
and satisfying deals'.

Bond friend, Tony Weatherald, 1996[1]

Upp Hall is an 'outstanding partly moated Elizabethan
Manor House' that sits in beautiful, rolling, green countryside less than an hour from London. The approach brings
you up an avenue of lime trees which, as the brochures point
out, is a classic introduction to a most impressive piece of real
estate.

The house itself dates from the fifteenth century and is of
Grade One historical interest, while the 'very fine sporting
estate' boasts a 'First-Class Shoot and Trout Fishing'. At
today's values, the freehold is worth around £5 million, or
about $12.5 million.[2]

Despite being only fifty-five kilometres from the West End,
the estate comes with a four-bedroom eighteenth-century
farmhouse, seven cottages and a magnificent listed tithe barn,
not to mention a tennis court, heated swimming pool, and a
sixty-metre-by-thirty-metre riding school, which Alan Bond's

daughter Susanne used to train her showjumpers. Oh yes, and 400 hectares of prime English farmland.

Since the early 1980s, this magnificent mansion has been the Bond family seat in Britain, thanks to a tenancy that Susanne claimed she was granted by her father back in 1985. But in 1992, when Bond went bankrupt, it was supposedly owned by Alan's good friend Jurg Bollag, out of reach of Bond's creditors.

Bollag claimed that he had bought Upp Hall from one of Bond's companies in 1987 for just under £2 million, yet had never bothered to live there because he had generously agreed that Susanne Bond should be allowed to occupy the house.

It seemed quite incredible that Bollag should have spent £2 million of his own money to buy a house for the Bonds to live in, and it was a story that Alan and Jurg would have found hard to sell to their mates in the public bar, but it was nevertheless the story that they chose to argue in court. And, of course, there were stacks of expensive legal documents to support their case.

The Upp Hall estate had originally been purchased in 1981 by a subsidiary of Bond Corporation called the Wydgee Pastoral Company, so it had been paid for at the outset by the shareholders of Bond's public company. But in 1985, as a director of Wydgee, Alan had generously granted his daughter Susanne the right to live there rent-free for life.

It's not at all clear how Bond thought he could justify giving Susanne the exclusive use of this asset, which had been bought with millions of dollars of other people's money, but in 1991 Susanne swore an affidavit for a UK legal action in which she claimed that she had been given the tenancy in exchange for using her showjumping activities to promote the Wydgee Pastoral Company's products.[3]

Now Wydgee has never quite become a household name in Australia or the UK—in fact, it's only ever owned a few pine trees on a block of sand north of Perth—so Susanne must have had trouble with the job. But this is hardly surprising because Wydgee had no products to promote, and she was never the world's most famous showjumper. She was on the fringe of the Australian team, rarely won on the international circuit and certainly never made the Olympics. And to cap it all, she didn't wear the Wydgee name on her horses when she competed.

Susanne claimed that her other duties in return for this tenancy were to manage the army of cooks, cleaners, housekeepers and gardeners at Upp Hall, and to entertain Wydgee's clients at pheasant shoots. But perhaps her most onerous task of all in running this lovely house was to provide for the care and training of her very valuable horses. Or should one say, Jurg Bollag's.

Had this scandalous deal come to the attention of Bond Corporation's auditors or shareholders, there's little doubt that they would have regarded it as pretty lousy value for the near-£2 million it had cost them. And that is why, it seems, the Upp Hall estate had been sold in 1987. By taking it out of the public company, shareholders would no longer have cause to complain. So the lease was transferred to Bond's private company Dallhold, which reaffirmed Susanne's tenure, and the freehold was sold to a company called Lindsey Trading Properties which had been set up specially by Bollag to do the deal.

Lindsey's home was a post office box in Panama, where its three Spanish-sounding directors hailed from the splendid law firm of Arosemena, Noriega & Contreras.

There were a number of things, however, that suggested the transaction was just a sham and that it was not really Bollag buying Upp Hall at all. First, his tax records in Zug made it perfectly clear that he did not have £2 million to his name, and certainly not to spend on others. Second, it made no sense at all for him to buy a hugely expensive property in the UK, when he lived in Switzerland and the Bond family had it locked up for life. And third, there were documents in Dallhold's records that actually appeared to accept that he was buying it for Bond.

These documents, which were discovered by the Dallhold liquidator, John Lord, described the 1987 sale of Upp Hall as a transfer from Bond *corporate* to Bond *private*. Crucially, they also specified that a Bollag company was to be the purchaser. In other words, they suggested that Bollag was again acting as a cover for Bond and his family so that the property was not in their name.[4]

And this was clearly what Susanne believed back in May 1988 when she gave evidence to a New Jersey court, during her divorce from Armand Leone, swearing on oath that Upp Hall was '*a rural property controlled by my family*'[5] (emphasis added).

Such, then, was the background in September 1991 when a legal battle over Upp Hall began in courts in Australia and the UK, with Bollag and his Panamanian company ranged against John Lord as Dallhold liquidator.

Dallhold's interest in the property was that its UK subsidiary had been granted a lifetime lease in 1987, during the sale to Bollag, which was potentially worth £1 million or more to the company's creditors back in Australia. This lease conveyed the right to farm the land at Upp Hall in perpetuity—and to occupy the house as well if Susanne Bond could be evicted—for as long as the company stayed alive.

But here was the problem: the lease would be worthless if

Dallhold Estates UK could be wound up (or killed), which is exactly what Jurg Bollag was trying to do.

The legal action batted back and forth between Sydney and London during 1991 and 1992 with the initial victories going to Lord. And in the process Jurg Bollag was forced to reveal some remarkable information. When Dallhold in Australia had hit financial difficulties he had provided large amounts of cash to pay the Bonds' bills at Upp Hall, including £2,500 for pheasants' eggs that Susanne had ordered for a party.

Between May 1989 and July 1991, he had in fact coughed up £373,000 in fourteen separate instalments from an account at the Zuger Kantonal Bank in Zug, Switzerland. And although this was in his name, it was a pound to a penny that the money belonged to Bond. Best of all, the bank account number, 00-736-488-01, was shown clearly on the transfers.

Amazingly, however, this crucial piece of information was never passed on to Bob Ramsay when Bond went bankrupt in April 1992, even though it would have been an invaluable lead in hunting down cash that belonged to Bond. Nor did the Dallhold liquidator himself try to crack open the account.

In defence of John Lord and his team, who were running the Upp Hall action, they were drowning in documents at the time and were dealing with a million separate pieces of paper. But this incident highlights one of the great problems that dogged the search for Bond's fortune, which was that information was often not shared between the three different teams of accountants and lawyers who were chasing him.[6]

Having won the first round of the legal battle for Upp Hall, which involved ensuring that Dallhold Estates UK stayed alive, Lord's next aim was to get Susanne Bond evicted from the house, and in September 1992 a new round of legal action began in the UK to achieve this. By this time the courts had been told that there was no written record of Alan granting her a life tenancy, and Justice Chadwick, who had presided over the British hearings, had been scathing about her claim, saying it was likely to be struck out.[7]

But even if he was right in predicting another victory for Dallhold, it looked like being a long hard grind to get Susanne out, because she and Alan would both swear blind that the promise had been made. And Susanne was now bringing her own legal action in which she claimed that Dallhold's agents had behaved so abominably that she deserved compensation. This would tie up the courts through 1993 and 1994 and, if necessary, for several years thereafter.

First of all, she said, they had made her pet Rottweiler go missing, causing her 'much consternation and distress'. Next they had brought people to view Upp Hall, suggesting that it might be for sale. And finally, and most shocking of all, servants of Dallhold Estates UK had entered the property on one occasion and prevented her 'from having access to the wine cellar thereof, thereby causing her distress and embarrassment in the presence of her guests'. The sum total of this was that she was demanding 'exemplary and aggravated damages' from the very company that had allowed her to live in the estate rent-free for the previous five years. The nerve of it was quite extraordinary.[8]

But so was the Upp Hall saga from the start. Tony Weatherald, who worked for Bond after he was made bankrupt, acting as a messenger between Bond and Bollag, told a journalist in 1996:

> Jurg used to laugh about Upp Hall because Upp Hall was 'absolutely stolen. For what it cost us and the way we got it, it's been one of the most

beautiful and satisfying deals. And they have got
no hope of ever getting it back off us'.[9]

According to Weatherald, 'Bollag always used to say *us*. He
didn't say Alan or the Bonds, he said *us*'. And this no doubt
explains why Lindsey Trading Properties made several other
generous contributions to the Bond family fortunes. In 1989,
when times were hard, Bollag's company lent Dallhold
£3 million to bolster Bond Corporation's share price, and in
1987 bought Alan's luxury ski lodge in Vail Colorado for
US$3 million.

Best of all, it lent $11.5 million to the Bond family trust
company, Armoy, in June 1990 to buy Dallhold's cattle and
sheep properties at Dandaragan, north of Perth. This ensured
that they stayed in the family, rather than going to creditors,
at a time when the National Mutual Royal Bank was calling
in its $7 million loan and Dallhold was on the brink of
collapse.

As usual, Bollag was quite astonishingly decent about it all.
At a time when the market rate of interest was 18 per cent, he
allowed Lindsey to lend money to the Bonds at 3 per cent, and
failed to take any security, even though farm prices were
falling.[10]

Nor did it seem that any of this money could be recovered.
The legal actions over Upp Hall dragged through the courts
during 1993 and 1994, with John Lord having to fight all the
way to the House of Lords to ensure that Dallhold Estates UK
did not get thrown off the property by having its lease termi-
nated. The battle to evict Susanne was finally ready to go to
court in late 1994, but by this time Bond was busy negotiating
a settlement with his creditors.

By then, it was just one of a number of legal actions that

Lord was planning against Bollag and the Bond family, but it was not going to come cheap. The Upp Hall case alone was forecast to cost £175,000, which creditors would have to gamble to win the prize.[11]

As so often with Bond, the battle turned into a high-stakes game of poker, where Alan seemed to have more nerve and more money than his creditors.

8

Millions Offshore

I let you get away with it last time but I won't let
you get away with it again. I can tell you now. If
you mention Bollag I'll sue.

Alan Bond to Paul Barry, June 1993

I n June 1993, I met Alan Bond outside the magistrates' court
in Perth where he was about to be charged on two counts
of fraud and two of deception relating to Manet's painting
La Promenade. This had been sold for a profit of some
$15 million that Bond had pocketed for his private company,
despite the fact that all its lease payments had been met by the
shareholders of Bond Corporation.

At the time, I was working on a program for the ABC's *Four
Corners* about Jurg Bollag and the huge amount of money and
assets that Bond appeared to have secreted overseas.

We were all waiting in the crush in a hallway, with a gaggle
of people from the press, while a housebreaker was being
charged by the magistrate, so I took the opportunity to ask
Bond whether he might like to be interviewed for our program.
It was a gratifying moment in some ways, because he immediately became quite agitated, hopping from one foot to

another and furiously trying to attract the attention of his son John and lawyer Andrew Fraser. 'This is the man who wrote that book,' he kept on saying to them, 'this is the man who wrote that book.' The book being *The Rise and Fall of Alan Bond*.

He then turned his attention to me to say: 'I know what you've been saying about George Bollag, and I can tell you, it's way off beam. It's just totally wrong'.[1]

I suggested that the best way to convince the public that we were mistaken was to come on *Four Corners*, so I made the offer again. But Bond decided it was simpler to threaten me instead, as he had done before publication of the book. I can't remember every word he said, but his parting shot is still etched in my brain: 'I let you get away with it last time but I won't let you get away with it again. I can tell you now. If you mention Bollag I'll sue'.

The crew and I spent the next three weeks or so following the money trail across Britain and Europe until we ended up in the middle of Switzerland in the mediaeval town of Zug, whose cobbled streets, pretty churches and sparkling lake make it look like the cover of a chocolate box.

For reasons that go back into history, Zug's laws are very different from the rest of Switzerland, and the local canton allows foreign companies to operate from here without paying any tax. As a result, it is a town with more companies than people, and is full of prosperous Swiss businessmen who have got rich by managing other people's money. It is also, of course, the home of Jurg Bollag, who appeared to be doing just that for Bond.

In the three days we were there, we checked out Bollag's tax records, searched the corporate registry and ate a few sandwiches at $20 a round, and then concentrated on trying to locate him. We phoned his home several times but got no reply, and went round there on three or four occasions with cameras at the ready, but always found the house empty. Finally, after too much hanging around, we decided to have one last try before going back to London. We didn't know whether he was even in the country, and there was no guarantee that we would get him by coming back to Zug a week later. So we were beginning to worry about what we would say to the office back in Sydney. It was going to look like a very expensive trip if we failed to find him.

We drove rather gloomily to within a couple of kilometres of the house, and then stopped in a lay-by for me to don a radio mike and to check that the camera was working, because there's no excuse for catching your quarry and failing to get the pictures, or missing the magic moment because you have no sound. Strangely enough, people like Bollag rarely hang around for 'take two'.

We knew his house was down a cul-de-sac where it would be hard to turn and even harder to hide, but we were pretty sure he wouldn't be there, so before we knew it, we had turned into his road and were looking over his fence from the big van that we had hired for the occasion. And there, to our immense surprise, sitting in a deck chair in the garden reading his newspaper, was the curly-haired gentleman who had last been seen bashing the *Sydney Morning Herald*'s photographer with his briefcase fifteen months earlier.

We just stopped. We were too shocked to do anything else. But in a couple of seconds we managed to drive a bit further down the road, park the van and regroup. We had spied an Alsatian in the garden that looked like it might cause problems, but there was a gate between Bollag and his back door, and provided he hadn't seen us and bolted, we should be able to film something over the top of it. So, cameras running, we walked briskly round the corner of the house and leant over the picket fence to say hello.

I am sure Mr Bollag was even more taken aback than we were, because the law in Switzerland is very unkind to snooping journalists, and to foreign journalists in particular, but his surprise rapidly turned to anger, as the transcript of our brief conversation makes clear.

PB: Excuse me, are you George Bollag?

JB: Yes.

PB: Paul Barry from Australian television. We're hoping to talk to you about Alan Bond who is a friend of yours, I believe.

JB: This is Sunday, please.

PB: I realise it's Sunday, would you ...

JB: Would you please leave?

PB: We'd like to talk to you ...

JB: You're on private property.

PB: We'll get further back. Can you please talk to us about Alan Bond?

JB: I'm calling the police.

PB: There are a number of assets, worth several million dollars, that ...

JB: Horse shit.

PB: It's not horse shit. What about Upp Hall, Mr Bollag?

JB: Go away. I call the police now.

Some five minutes later the Swiss police arrived and took us back to the station, but the exchange by then had been caught on camera, and to our relief they did not confiscate the film.

A couple of weeks later it was duly shown on the ABC's *Four Corners* in a special hour-long program that detailed Bollag's beneficence. This 'horse shit', as Bollag so graphically described it, was spread all over Australia's airwaves, as was the conclusion that Bollag was not just Bond's generous friend, but was in fact taking care of his millions.

Yet despite Alan Bond's very specific threat to sue us if we mentioned Bollag, and despite the fact that we had accused him of using his Swiss friend to hide his money from creditors, neither Bond nor Bollag sued me or the ABC. And one has to ask why they did not. To which the only sensible answer is that we had hit upon the truth.

But why, if we could get away with saying that Bollag was just a front man for Bond, could the people chasing Bond's assets not also win the game? Well, in a sense, that's what this book is about. But part of the answer is that it's easier to say things on television and defend them in an Australian court than it is to satisfy a judge in the UK or Switzerland, or a whole host of tax havens, that property and cash apparently owned by one person really belong to another and must be handed back.

The fact that someone lives in a house, rides a horse, drives a car and sails a boat without paying anyone else for the privilege would be enough to convince most people that those assets actually belong to that person, especially when there's a pattern to it all, as there was with Bollag. But when it comes to proving the proposition beyond a shadow of doubt, it can be hard, especially when the documentary evidence and the people who can testify are safely stowed in tax havens around the world.

As the Bond case demonstrates, it is relatively easy to set up corporate structures that are almost impossible for investigators to crack. In-flight magazines are full of ads for outfits that will establish and run offshore companies for a few thousand dollars a year. And their brochures typically make it clear that these are designed to beat the taxman or to hide assets from creditors. They recognise the need for secrecy, which they call confidentiality. And they emphasise that one of their conditions of business is that they won't disclose details of your transactions to anybody without your permission, unless their lawyers tell them they have a legal obligation to do so. The same secrecy pledge naturally applies to the local directors and lawyers they use in the various tax havens to act as your front men.

One of the biggest providers of these services, with a branch in Sydney, boasts that it has several hundred offshore companies ready to go within hours, in Belize, the British Virgin Islands, the Caymans, Niue (a coral island near Tonga with a population of 2,000 people), Anguilla (in the Caribbean) and about twenty-five other tax havens.

Different tax havens have different advantages, and some merely offer legitimate tax-saving routes into overseas investments. But if hiding your money is what you're after, then the British Virgin Islands, the Turks and Caicos Islands, Panama, Mauritius and the Seychelles are hard to beat. In these places, you don't have to tell the locals who really owns the company, so the authorities can't give your secrets away; there's no nonsense about filing accounts or needing local directors; and there are often secrecy laws to stop people talking if they do know your business. Tax havens like these are so tough to crack that most investigators don't even bother to go knocking. And if they do, they normally come away with nominee owners and dummy directors, and no hint of who the company really belongs to.

The British Virgin Islands and other super-secret havens also offer the ultimately hideable company, which has what are known as 'bearer shares'. With these, there is simply no record of who owns the company, because the shares belong to whoever is holding them at any particular time. These bearer shares can be passed round the table, from hand to hand, from wallet to wallet, safe to safe, and ownership passes from person to person as they move.

Often, companies in one tax haven are run from another, like Jersey or the Isle of Man, because these offshore financial centres have better banking and communications facilities, and use English as their business language. But serious asset-hiders also like to multiply the locations so that they have different pieces of the jigsaw in different havens around the world, which makes it more difficult for investigators to put the picture together. So while the company might be run from Jersey, for example, it could have its registered office in Liberia or Panama, its directors in the Isle of Man, its bank accounts in Liechtenstein and a power of attorney held by someone in Switzerland, who takes instructions from the real owner, who is somewhere entirely different.

The complexity of such arrangements is limited only by the trouble you wish to take to keep your money hidden, and the expense you are prepared to incur. But if you're really desperate to avoid discovery, the idea is to construct as many different cells as possible, so that they act like bulkheads in a ship. The investigators then have to break through each one before they can move on to the next. And at each bulkhead you can fight a legal action to oppose the release of information.

Normally, documents alone won't provide the proof one needs, and the only way to crack the puzzle is to crack the accountants or lawyers who are actually running the company. You will invariably need a court order to make them talk, but unless you can convince the authorities that you have evidence of a crime, you may well not be able to get one, especially in the smaller Caribbean or Pacific tax havens which rely on their reputation of being uncrackable to stay in business. And it's pretty hard to get the sort of evidence you need if you can't get into the tax haven in the first place. So it's Catch 22.[2]

Recently, however, life has become a bit easier for investigators. New anti-money-laundering laws enacted throughout Europe in the 1990s have forced people setting up companies and opening bank accounts to disclose who really owns the assets, and this includes a requirement that they disclose the real beneficiaries of discretionary trusts. And since the mid-1980s several of the more respectable tax havens have become keener to cooperate with overseas investigators of crime.

In particular, Jersey has been keen to be seen as an offshore centre that won't harbour criminals or foster fugitives. Since December 1992 it has even been prepared to assist foreign trustees in bankruptcy, such as Bob Ramsay, who are chasing assets on behalf of creditors. As a consequence, it was far easier to get information when Bond went bankrupt in 1992, than it had been in the early 1980s, when Bond's offshore structures had been established.

In those days, Jersey was still perfectly safe from prying eyes, and Bond could not possibly have guessed that his accountants would be forced to open their files or spill the beans on his private affairs. And he had no way of knowing that when the Australian sleuths eventually came knocking, the Jersey courts would be only too happy to help.

In fact, Bond's Jersey citadel was first invaded in August 1991 by a young investigator from Western Australia, Joseph Lieberfreund, who was looking for millions of dollars looted from Rothwells Bank by Laurie Connell. For the last half of that year and most of the next, this brilliant if bumptious accountant parked himself in London at the Department of Trade and Industry and worked full-time on the search for Laurie's millions. And in the course of his search, he stumbled upon traces of Bond's fortune, too.

The paper trail from Perth led him to an art dealer in the Cotswolds; an aristocratic bank called Coutt's in London, where the doormen wear tailcoats; and to a firm of stock-brokers called TC Coombs, who had been raided by the UK Serious Fraud Office on suspicion of laundering large amounts of money for Australian businessmen.

Most importantly, it then pointed him to Jersey, to the St Helier offices of a firm of accountants called Touche Ross where Connell had based his offshore empire. There, with the help of the Attorney General, who was in the process of prom-ulgating new fraud laws, and orders from the Royal Court of Jersey, Lieberfreund gained access to the secret files of a mul-titude of Panamanian, Liberian and British Virgin Islands com-panies that Connell had set up to hide his assets.[3]

This in turn led him to the St Helier branch of the Allied Irish Banks, where a number of these Connell companies kept their accounts. And what he found there must have almost knocked him sideways, for among the boxes of documents that the bank handed over were records of a company that acted as a postbox for a number of Touche Ross's Australian clients, including Alan Bond and his inner circle of executives. Touche Ross were understandably furious but were unable to put the lid back on the box.

The banking documents suggested that up to $50 million had been channelled through two dozen companies run by Touche Ross for Connell, Bond and his head honchos between October 1988 and July 1990. Exactly who owned this money, in what proportion, and how it had been earned (if indeed that was the right word) were a mystery. And Touche Ross were certainly not prepared to throw any light on it, because the court order compelling them to talk referred only to Laurie Connell's affairs.

But according to a secret report prepared for the Royal Commission into WA Inc, this much was sure: millions of dollars had been hidden in Jersey in offshore trust companies for Bond and his three most senior executives, Peter Beckwith, Peter Mitchell and Tony Oates. Typically, this money had been sent to the Channel Islands from Australia via banks in New York, Toronto or London to make the trail harder to follow.[4]

Jersey was therefore the next stop for the *Four Corners* team back in 1993, because the report not only suggested in general terms that Bond had money there, but also identified two companies we already suspected to have handled Bond's or Bollag's offshore millions: the horse buyer, Kirk Holdings (which we knew about from Susanne's divorce proceedings) and the legal-bill payer, Juno Equities (which we had discovered in files in the Australian Federal Court). Both, of course, were run by Touche Ross.

Jersey is only a few kilometres off the coast of France, but in some ways it's more British than Britain. In the summer at least, there are echoes of the archetypal dirty postcard, with fat women in thin summer dresses sprawled in deck chairs on the beach, and men in ties and knotted handkerchiefs. There's enough flabby white flesh on show to make you glad that St Tropez thongs are not yet in fashion there. The hotels in the main town of St Helier are also typically English, with whorly coloured carpets, reproduction antique furniture, fake horse brasses, and lounges that smell of beer and rancid fat.

But Jersey is also a charming place, with narrow winding streets, old buildings, and the occasional spectacular castle. And there's a glint about it all, which probably comes from the jewellery shops or the vast numbers of brass plates advertising the offices of accountants, lawyers, banks and offshore trust companies. Like Zug, the main game in St Helier is avoiding tax for the rich and secretive. And it's what continues to make the residents wealthy.

Apart from getting these touristy pictures, however, it was not clear when we arrived what we would be able to film, except an ugly modern accountants' office on a busy main road. But we decided it would be enlightening to phone a director of some of Bond's offshore companies, who turned out to be a delightful man named Francis Plaistowe. I still haven't the faintest idea what he looks like, since we never went round to his house, but over the phone he sounded like a jolly retired air-force officer, with sandy hair and a green tweed suit. In any case, he was more than happy to tell us what he knew, which was nothing, and to have a good chuckle about it all. Here was a man who acted as director to all sorts of companies, anxious to explain that he was merely a man of straw. It was a fascinating insight into the system.

> Yes, it's no good talking to me because I'm only a nominee director, that's all ... I mean, I'm just, you know, I just go in and sign papers ... I mean, I'm on lots of boards for Touche Ross ... All that happens as the nominee directors, you can imagine ... I mean when you've got a hundred of them or a couple of hundred of them or whatever, you just rely on Touche Ross ... so if anybody is going to end up in jail, it's Touche Ross not me. (laughs)[5]

Mr Plaistowe, it turned out, received a fee of £50 a company for the documents he signed, and never had the inconvenience of going to directors' meetings or anything like that. Typically, the papers would be sent en masse to his house, or he might go into Touche Ross's office to sign a heap of them. He was kind enough, anyway, to tell us that the man at Touche Ross who really looked after these companies was a partner called John Hatton-Edge.

Mr Hatton-Edge, however, was not keen to discuss anything to do with Bond, so we resolved to pay him a visit. Parking ourselves outside his luxury block of apartments early one morning, we waited to catch him going to the office. Sadly, he was still in no mood to talk. Viewers of *Four Corners* soon afterwards were treated to a shot of a plump, bald man peering crossly through the windscreen of a new black Porsche, which roared off into the dawn before we had had time to say hello. Further attempts to get him to talk about the companies that he ran for Bond resulted in him putting the phone down.

But if *we* didn't have the power to get Hatton-Edge to talk, Bond's trustee in bankruptcy Bob Ramsay certainly did, provided he could get the Royal Court of Jersey to issue an order compelling him to cooperate. And sure enough, by late 1993, he was already trying to do exactly that.

9

Jersey

Q: Did you ever instruct the partners of Touche
Ross on the island of Jersey that they should
accept instructions from Jurg Bollag?
A: I don't remember Touche Ross's name at all.

Alan Bond, Federal Court, May 1994[1]

In early November 1993, without telling Bond or his
lawyers, Bob Ramsay flew into Jersey's small island airport
to examine two partners of Touche Ross on oath, along with
the office manager who had looked after the Bond files.

The grilling was to be conducted in secret before the Royal
Court of Jersey, which had compelled the three individuals to
give evidence. The court had also ordered Touche Ross and
the Allied Irish Banks in St Helier to surrender all their files
on a string of companies and trusts that Ramsay believed to
be connected to Bond.

It looked certain to be a thrilling few days, not least because
Touche Ross's archive had coughed up a letter dated and
signed by Alan Bond, that had been sent in February 1987 to
the partners of Touche Ross, telling them to accept instructions
from four people in relation to his affairs. One of these, pre-
dictably, was Jurg Bollag.

This absolutely crucial document appeared to be the smoking gun that could lead to Bond's conviction for perjury and for hiding assets from creditors. For Bond had not only denied having any contact with offshore advisers, but had also denied having assets overseas, and had admitted to only one old bank account in London. And Ramsay was now about to gather volumes of evidence that he was lying on all three counts.

Ramsay had asked Bond in a letter on 11 September 1992: 'Have you had any dealings or contacts with solicitors, accountants or financial or other advisers in Jersey?'. To which Bond had replied in a letter of 5 November 1992: 'Not to the best of my knowledge in relation to my personal affairs'.

But the evidence that he had was overwhelming.[2]

The February 1987 letter showed that Alan Bond had in fact told Touche Ross to accept instructions regarding his affairs from his son John Bond, his personal solicitor Harry Lodge, his managing director at Dallhold, Robert Pearce, and his all too generous friend Jurg Bollag.

Geoffrey Davies, the Touche Ross partner who looked after Bond's offshore companies from 1979 to 1985, had only met Alan once, at Jersey airport, when he had touched down briefly to inspect the accounts of a trust company that had been set up for him. And John Hatton-Edge, for his part, might not have met Alan at all had he not bumped into him in the lift at Bond Corporation in Perth.

But despite their lack of direct contact, neither had the slightest doubt that Alan Bond was their client, and a very substantial one at that. In fact, reading between the lines, it seemed likely that Bond was the biggest client that Touche Ross Jersey looked after.

As to Jurg Bollag's role, they gave a variety of answers that all said roughly the same thing, which was that Bollag acted as Alan's front man. It was pretty ridiculous, of course, to suggest that he had bought all his houses, horses and paintings just to give to Bond. But here at last was first-hand confirmation that Bollag was merely managing Alan's millions.

Hatton-Edge described the Swiss banker variously as Bond's personal adviser, Bond's financial adviser and Bond's financial planner, emphasising that he did not regard Jurg Bollag as a man of substantial wealth in his own right. 'So,' Hatton-Edge was asked, 'did Mr Bollag control Mr Bond's personal affairs?' To which Hatton-Edge replied: 'Certainly the ones that we were involved in'.

Geoffrey Davies confirmed this account of Bollag's role on oath:

A: I think he generally managed his offshore affairs, advised Mr Bond on certain things and carried out the wishes of Mr Bond, perhaps for his family.

Q: So in relation to Touche Ross, did he control Mr Bond's personal affairs as you saw it?

A: Yes, I think that's very true.[3]

Davies was also asked:

Q: Would it be fair to say, Mr Davies, that you saw Mr Bollag as Mr Bond's alter ego?

A: Yes, probably. Yes.[4]

But it was clear that Bollag was not the only person to have fulfilled this role, because the Jersey companies had been set up long before Bollag had even arrived on the scene.

Touche Ross's files contained an earlier letter of instruction from Bond, written on 26 May 1982 on notepaper headed with Bond's name, that was once again signed by Alan himself. On this occasion, it was telling the accounting firm to accept instructions from Robert Ashley Pearce, the managing director of Dallhold, concerning 'any matters associated with me'. Davies recalled that Touche Ross had asked Bond to provide both of these letters so that they had formal instructions on file, as any professional lawyer or accountant likes to do.

Robert Pearce had visited Jersey three to four times a year to talk about Alan's affairs, either to get reports on what Touche Ross had done or to give new instructions, and he had been just as active as Bollag in running Alan's offshore finances. Hatton-Edge said he had met him a dozen times, usually in Jersey or London.

Then in late 1986, Bollag had taken over from Pearce. According to Davies:

> Sometime in 1986 George Bollag was introduced to us as an adviser to the client and someone who would be taking over the client's affairs from us . . . Early in 1987 we received a letter from Alan Bond requesting us to act on instructions from four people who included George Bollag. After that date instructions were normally received from George Bollag.[5]

Davies first met Bollag in January 1987 in London, where he briefed the new boy about the Bond companies and trusts that he was taking over and about the assets that each owned. Pearce attended this meeting too and accompanied Bollag to Jersey on several occasions thereafter.

Davies felt that Bollag had a more personal connection to Bond and his family than Pearce had done, and that the Swiss had ultimately taken far greater control. In fact, soon after Bollag arrived, the Jersey companies were moved lock, stock and barrel to Zug, and Bollag took over the running of most of the companies himself. Davies believed the explanation was that:

> Alan Bond wanted a dedicated person to look after his affairs and George Bollag was known to him as a banker who had many connections ... I believe that this was the prime reason why Alan Bond's affairs were moved to Switzerland.[6]

Until this happened in 1987, however, Bond's Jersey empire comprised around a dozen companies or trusts, most of which were registered in Panama, and had bearer shares that were held in a safe at Touche Ross's office. Sometimes these were accompanied by a formal declaration of trust to say who owned them. Other times they were just slipped into an envelope with the name of the owner scrawled upon it. In either case, Touche Ross always wanted to be quite clear.

But despite all this high-level secrecy, even an outsider would have been able to crack the naming code, at least to see that certain of these entities had a common origin. For the companies were typically created in twos or threes, with the company holding the assets normally owned by a trust which also had a trustee company to look after it.

And one of the endearing features of Touche Ross's naming policy was that Bond's companies were christened in pairs. Thus, the trustee for the Liberian company Kirk Holdings was a Panamanian outfit called The Enterprise—both names being drawn from *Star Trek*.

Similarly, Juno Equities was owned by the Jupiter Trust, both named after Roman Gods who were man and wife. Pegasus Investments, meanwhile, was owned by the Icarus Trust and, as any classical scholar could tell you, both these names were from Greek mythology—Pegasus being a winged horse, and Icarus the boy who stuck wings to his feet with wax, then perished when he flew too near the sun.

Among this plethora of companies, one seemed to have bankrolled most of the others, paying their fees and expenses, and lending them money. And this was the same one through which Bollag had bought the horses for Alan Bond's daughter Susanne and paintings to hang on Alan's walls.

Kirk Holdings had been set up in July 1984 and had flourished in Jersey for about three years. At its zenith, it had held five accounts in various currencies at the Allied Irish Banks in St Helier, through which millions of dollars of Bond's money had flowed.

Kirk was described by the Touche Ross partners as 'a large account' and a company with 'a great deal of money'. And certainly the funds rolled in and out of Kirk's bank accounts in early 1987 in quite astonishing amounts.

Without having access to all the documents, it's impossible to be precise about how much the company was really worth, but in a seven-month period from late 1986 to mid-1987, more than $30 million flowed into the company's accounts and $42 million flowed out again. As to who this money belonged to, Geoffrey Davies told the Royal Court of Jersey on oath: 'I do know that Kirk, as far as I am concerned, was for the ultimate benefit of Mr Bond and his family'.[7]

John Hatton-Edge, who took over the running of Kirk in 1986, agreed: 'I believed it was for the benefit of Mr Bond and other beneficiaries, probably in his family'.[8]

This company, remember, was not a huge multinational like Bond Corporation but a slice of Alan Bond's personal fortune that had not been declared to his trustee in bankruptcy. Yet the cash came and went in multi-million-dollar chunks, that were sometimes as big as $10 million. Typically, the money arrived via a network of British, American and Swiss banks. But where it had come from before that and where it went to afterwards was for the most part a mystery.[9]

On some occasions there were no banking documents to even hint at where the cash had originated. A letter from Kirk to the Allied Irish Banks in August 1986, for example, referred to a new sterling call account that had been opened to accommodate £5.285 million 'recently transferred to our account', but there were no clues to explain which bank or country it had come from. And it would probably have been a fruitless task for investigators to attempt to find out.

It is a feature of the international banking system that money can be sent round the world in a matter of hours, and done in such a way that the trail is impossible to follow. Most banks use something called the SWIFT system, which identifies the bank sending the money and the person ordering the transfer, but does not specify the account that it came from or where the money started its journey. So if cash is channelled through two or three different banks, it's a nightmare to track it back to its source, especially if any of the countries it passes through has strict banking secrecy laws.[10]

John Broome, who ran Australia's National Crime Authority until September 1999, knows a fair bit about money laundering, and believes that it's a snack to get money out of the country and hide it, even with laws that require banks to report big movements of cash. The world financial system, says Broome, is set up to handle huge international transactions with ease, and it's simply a matter of using these transactions to shunt money across the globe. You can, for example, buy shares in one place and sell them in another, then wash the proceeds through a couple of banks, and a couple of companies to rub out the traces. And the chances of being caught or having the money recovered are infinitesimal.[11]

Bond Corporation and Dallhold had no shortage of large international deals in which hundreds of millions of dollars were sent around the world. And it would not have been hard for bits to have fallen off on the way. No auditor or investigator could ever have followed all the trails or sifted through the hundreds of thousands of documents that accompanied this frenetic activity.[12]

And even when documents were examined it was often impossible to make head or tail of them. One celebrated money-go-round that Bob Ramsay investigated involved a Touche Ross company called Calpex which had been used in March 1987 to channel $4.5 million, or US$2.8 million, from Kirk Holdings in Jersey, via Dallhold in Australia, to Bollag's company Crasujo in Switzerland—which was the company apparently named after Bond's children.

This movement of money had been recorded by Calpex as a loan to Dallhold, and by Dallhold as a loan to Alan Bond.[13] But a year later, more than twice that amount of money, or $10 million, had been sent back to Jersey by Dallhold.

Now, what was suspicious about this was that Dallhold's records cast doubt on whether Dallhold had ever received any cash to repay, so it was conceivable that the entire transaction was simply a way of sending a large amount of money offshore by repaying a phantom loan. Ramsay's QC Francis Douglas put precisely this allegation to Bond in May 1994 in his public examination.

But the truth was that none of the investigators really knew what had happened. Nor could they find the $10 million, which was paid into an account at the Allied Irish Banks in London, set up especially to receive it, whence it disappeared into thin air.

It was usually a bit easier to see what had happened to money that had been despatched from Kirk's accounts in Jersey, because the bank had kept requisition slips indicating what most of the payments were for. And these showed the usual roll call of horses, paintings, diamonds, shares and the like.[14] But a large chunk of money had also gone to an account at the Arbuthnot Latham Bank in London, held in the name of Alan Bond, c/o Jurg Bollag. And this had also disappeared.

This Bond account had received US$2.75 million from Kirk in December 1986, along with specific instructions to the Jersey bank that: 'no mention of Kirk Holdings is made on the transfer'. Bond would be asked by Francis Douglas QC for Ramsay in May 1994 what he had done with this money, which was in an account that he had definitely not declared to his bankruptcy trustee. And Bond simply replied that he had no idea.

> Douglas: No idea? You receive US$2.75 million into your personal account and you've no idea what you did with it?
>
> Bond: No, I couldn't tell you the ins and outs of the accounts ...
>
> Douglas: So you've no idea what you did with that money?
>
> Bond: No, I don't.[15]

Other lumps of up to $5 million, which had been paid by Kirk into banks in the Channel Islands, could not be traced. But

Kirk's millions had gone to fund other companies in the network, such as Juno Equities, which was used in 1992 to pay Bond's $600,000 legal bills.

Juno Equities' main claim to fame before that point was that it had bought a £500,000 London apartment in which Diana Bliss had lived for four years without paying rent, rates or maintenance. It was a nice apartment too, just off the Fulham Road, in a block of solid redbrick maisonettes called Evelyn Gardens. And as Bliss admitted, she was very 'fortunate' to get it for nix.

So how had Diana come by this incredible stroke of luck if Juno Equities had nothing to do with Alan? Her explanation, which she gave on oath to Ramsay's lawyer Karen Coleman in June 1994, was that she had met Jurg Bollag several years before and had become friends with him. In 1987, on deciding to move to London to pursue her career in the theatre, she had told him of her plans. And lo and behold, he had replied that he was about to buy an apartment himself and needed someone to live in it.

Jurg's generosity, Diana claimed, had absolutely nothing to do with Alan. In fact, she was certain that she had not even told Alan she was looking for a place. Nor had it ever occurred to her that the sumptuous apartment might belong to him.

Now Diana was the daughter of a Methodist minister and had doubtless been told how important it was not to tell lies. But she was hard-pressed to explain truthfully why Bollag would let her have such a valuable flat for free.

She assured Karen Coleman that her tenancy had been just a temporary ad hoc arrangement until Bollag was ready to sell the apartment. But documents from Touche Ross's files showed that she had a sub-lease, which essentially gave her a rent-free tenancy for life. Shades of Susanne Bond and Upp Hall.

Diana swore that she had neither seen nor signed this lease.

She also swore that she had agreed to pay all ongoing costs like rates, maintenance and service charges. But, aside from the fact that Bollag could have commanded a small fortune by letting the apartment to someone else, documents from Touche Ross again suggested that this was untrue. Rate notices had been sent to her but had then been paid by Juno Equities in Jersey, on Bollag's instructions.

This she was completely at a loss to explain.

> Q: You did tell us earlier that you definitely paid
>   the rates.
> A: I made a mistake ... I can't recall this. I'm
>   confused as to what I paid.[16]

More documents from Touche Ross showed that Juno Equities had picked up at least three bills from the company that maintained the property, and had paid the service charges levied by the real estate agent. In fact, Miss Bliss was unable at the examination to provide evidence of any expenses that she had paid herself.

But she was able to reveal that she and her good friend Jurg had a mutual interest in theatre. And just as his love of horses had caused him to buy showjumpers for Susanne Bond, so he had been happy to put up £50,000 for Diana's first London theatre production, *Big Game*, losing roughly half of his, or perhaps Alan's, money in the process.

Diana's tale of the free £500,000 apartment was yet another chapter in the preposterous saga of Bollag's beneficence. But once again the facts suggested that this money really belonged to Alan. For Juno Equities had been lent the funds to buy the apartment by Alan's Kirk Holdings, and had never been asked to pay interest.[17]

In fact, Kirk had made other interest-free loans to Juno at around this time, which added up to more than £2 million. These were never repaid, even though Juno clearly continued to have plenty of money. This again suggested that Juno and Kirk belonged to the same person, which was Alan Bond.

Bond was asked many times about Kirk Holdings in his bankruptcy examination in May 1994, and on each occasion he claimed to know nothing about it:

> Douglas: I would suggest to you it was a company which you used frequently during the 1980s as a means of acquiring investments, painting, jewellery and other items of that nature.
>
> Bond: I don't recall the name of Kirk Holdings in the 1980s or 70s or whenever you assert that the company was formed.
>
> Douglas: It just strikes no bell at all.
>
> Bond: No, I'm afraid it doesn't.[18]

Shortly after Evelyn Gardens was purchased in 1987, almost all Bond's Jersey companies were closed down and money was shipped off to Switzerland by the bushel. In the space of seven months, some $5.5 million was transferred from Kirk's Jersey accounts direct to the Zuger Kantonal Bank in Zug. Alan's account at Arbuthnot Latham in London saw $750,000 fleeing to Switzerland two years later. And Zug now took over from Jersey as the money centre. When Upp Hall was bought in July 1987 by a new Bollag company, Lindsey Trading Properties, the funds were despatched from a numbered account at the Zuger Kantonal Bank, as were the funds that later kept Susanne Bond in pheasant eggs.

The company records at Touche Ross were also moved out

of Jersey as the Bond empire there was shut down and tidied up. It was obviously pointless to leave a paper trail there when investigators might come knocking. But Juno and its records did stay in St Helier, along with a company called Engetal Properties, which still owned a valuable asset in England.

The Bonds' house at 14 Selwood Place, Chelsea, which by the 1990s was worth around $1.5 million, had been bought in August 1982 and lived in by various family members during the 1980s. Susanne and her husband Armand had perched there for five months in 1987, and John Bond had lived there for three years with his wife Gemma, while working for a merchant bank in London.[19] Alan had also stayed there with Tracey Tyler on the occasions when they had visited London together, and had been holed up there just before his bankruptcy.

Alan maintained that the house belonged to Bollag, who let the Bonds live there rent-free (which seemed to be a common story), and in March 1992 he even issued a press release to deny that he owned it. But, if this was possibly true by 1992, it certainly hadn't always been so, because the house had been bought some four years before Bollag had started managing Bond's money and a year before Alan and Jurg had ever met.

What's more, there was a stack of documentary and oral evidence to suggest that Bond had owned the house himself. Eileen's personal assistant, Sue Park, certainly had no illusions and had written to a firm of solicitors to say that it was one of Alan's houses. Susanne Bond also had no doubts. During her divorce battle in 1988, when she had been so careful to say that her horses belonged to Bollag, she had sworn an affidavit describing Selwood Place as 'a home owned by my family'. And she clearly knew the house well enough to be sure, because she had signed the affidavit as she sat in the front room.[20]

The paper trail for Selwood Place also led inexorably to Alan Bond, despite his protestations to the contrary. Land registry documents showed the house had been bought by Engetal Properties, operated by Touche Ross in Jersey, whose partners gave sworn evidence that the company belonged to Bond. Engetal's nominal owner was a Panamanian company called Pegasus Investments, which in turn was owned by the Icarus Trust. And it was clear that this had also been established for Bond.

The legal fiction of the Icarus Trust, as set out in a twenty-six-page deed unearthed from Touche Ross's files, was that the assets had been settled by a Jersey resident called John Charles Sauvary, and could now be distributed to anyone under the sun. But this was just a pretence. Sauvary was a front man acting for Touche Ross and the assets were certainly not his, as he reminded trustees in his 'Letter of Wishes' in January 1983:

> I confirm that it is not intended that I or my family should obtain any benefit from the Settlement, and that it is intended that it should be principally for the benefit of Alan Bond ... and his family.[21]

Sauvary's letter also instructed the trustees to consult a man called Harry Lodge about any investment or distribution decisions. And this was even more intriguing. For more than twenty years, Harry Lodge had acted as Alan Bond's personal solicitor, in which capacity he had drafted his wills and held power of attorney to execute documents, until Bond was made bankrupt in 1992.

But even more to the point, until 1989 he had been the senior partner at Parker & Parker, Perth's biggest law firm, who were still acting for Bond in the 1990s. Yet this firm was now helping Bond deny the existence of the very offshore empire that Lodge had helped set up.

What's more, they were accepting a large part of their fees from Swiss bank accounts controlled by Jurg Bollag, who had run Bond's offshore finances for several years.

To put it mildly, Parker & Parker had a major ethical problem.

But Harry Lodge had an even bigger problem, because in July 1993 he had been examined on oath in Perth by a lawyer acting for Bob Ramsay and had tried his damnedest to deny knowing anything about Bond's financial affairs, and in particular about Jersey.

10

·Trouble With Harry

Q: So you had no involvement with the setting up
of any trusts for Mr Bond?
A: No, not at all ...

*Bond's family lawyer, Harry Lodge, on oath,
July 1993*[1]

Despite his denials, it was Harry Lodge who had sounded the trumpet to establish Bond's offshore empire in the first place. Or so Geoffrey Davies told Jersey's Royal Court in November 1993:

> A: I first became involved with Alan Bond and his affairs when I was instructed by Harry Lodge, who was then a partner in Parker & Parker, resident in London, to form a company called Pianola in 1978 or 1979.
>
> Q: Was he the family lawyer? Was that his role?
>
> A: I had that impression.[2]

Harry Lodge had phoned Davies out of the blue in 1979 and arranged to fly down to St Helier from London. Soon afterwards, on his instructions, Touche Ross had set up a Jersey

company called Pianola and an accompanying trust, the
Juniper Trust, so that Bond could own a £1.5 million property
in Belgrave Mews without risking UK Capital Gains Tax. The
funds to set up these two entities had been sent over from
Parker & Parker's client account in Perth.

Harry Lodge had been asked about Juniper four months
earlier by Ramsay's counsel Peter Macliver, and had denied on
oath having anything to do with it.

> Q: Was this Juniper Trust of Mr Bond's something
>   that you had set up?
> A: No, I had not set it up ...
> Q: So you had no involvement with the setting up
>   of any trusts for Mr Bond?
> A: No, not at all ...
> Q: You didn't instruct anyone to set up that trust?
> A: No, no.[3]

Lodge had then been asked several times about the Icarus
Trust and had said variously that it didn't ring a bell, that he
was not familiar with it, knew nothing about it, and had never
heard of it. In fact, he denied all knowledge of it:

> Q: And the Icarus Trust. Are you familiar with
>   that trust?
> A: No, no ...
> Q: Is that not one of the trusts in respect of which
>   you were a contact?
> A: No, I'm sure it wasn't. But if it was, I've never
>   heard of it.[4]

But in Jersey in November 1993, this testimony was directly

challenged. For not only was Geoffrey Davies pointing the finger at Lodge, but Touche Ross's files contained a letter that Harry himself had signed in January 1983 instructing the trustees of the very same Icarus Trust to consult him at regular intervals about who the beneficiaries should be, how the funds should be invested, and how income and assets of the trust should be distributed. And on the bottom of this letter, Lodge had added a message in his own handwriting that said: 'After the date of my death or upon my earlier advice to you that I can no longer continue my consultation duties, please consult with John Bond'.[5]

Since Ramsay's investigators had been unaware of this treasure trove when they examined Lodge in Perth in July 1993, they had not given Bond's lawyer nearly as tough a time as he deserved. But they had uncovered one valuable piece of evidence to throw at him.

In October 1984, Lodge had gone to Jersey for a second time to update the arrangements he had made for Bond and to monitor progress. And on that occasion, he had scribbled four pages of notes of his conversation with Geoffrey Davies on Touche Ross's notepaper. These jottings mentioned all Bond's key companies, including Kirk, Juniper, Pianola, Icarus, Engetal and The Enterprise, and referred to houses, bearer shares and transactions that Lodge appeared to have discussed in detail.

This incriminating document had been tucked away in Parker & Parker's files during the 1980s in a folder labelled 'Bond A: Reorganisation Private Affairs'. But it had been discovered by Bob Ramsay's team shortly after Bond's bankruptcy. And it now proved to be at least a partial cure for Harry Lodge's amnesia.

Lodge had at first disclaimed any knowledge of Alan Bond's

financial affairs offshore, and had affected not to know whether he had any. He had also specifically denied having set up companies for Bond offshore or giving instructions to others to do so. And when asked about the October 1984 meeting, he had claimed that he couldn't remember it.

But when his handwritten notes were placed in front of him he was forced to summon up his powers of recall. Yes, he had been to Jersey. Yes, it could have been on 26 October 1984. Yes, he'd popped down on the plane in the morning with one of the Bond Corporation executives. And yes, he had met with the accountants from Touche Ross in St Helier. But he couldn't remember why he had made the trip, although he was rather partial to the local asparagus.

Certainly, he agreed, the four pages of notes were in his handwriting. But he didn't know why he had headed them 'A. Bond'. And as for the Panamanian trusts, Liberian companies and Isle of Man shareholders whose names he had jotted down, well, he couldn't recall what that had been about at all. Except that he was quite sure he had had nothing to do with establishing them.

He was aware, he admitted, that several of Bond Corporation's directors had set up trusts in Jersey to hold their offshore assets, and now that he thought about it, he recalled overhearing that one called Juniper had been set up for Alan Bond. But he hadn't done it himself. He was quite certain about that.

So why had he gone down there? Here Lodge's efforts to find an excuse were like a schoolboy trying to explain why he didn't have his homework.

First there was the palaver with checking his passport to see whether he had been in the UK at the time. Then there was a long blank look at his notes, which had meant nothing to him at all. And now there was a lame effort to explain why he might have gone to Jersey in the first place.

A: Well, I think I went down with one of the
    Bond directors to talk about his affairs.
Q: Sorry, to talk about whose affairs? Mr Bond's?
A: No, no. I didn't go down to see him about Mr
    Bond, because I had nothing to do with that—
    that trust concept of theirs—maybe he was just
    telling me. I mean he did tell me that Mr Bond
    had flown through on his aeroplane once . . .
    But I don't know whether he was filling me in
    just because I came from here. He knew that I
    did work for Bond. I just made notes of it in
    case anyone asked me.[6]

Gradually the details began to come back to him. Yes. He remembered better now: one of the Bond directors, Peter Mitchell, had said he was going down to Jersey, so he had decided to go along for the ride and have a spot of lunch. Plus he could meet his old friend Geoffrey Davies (whom he had practically denied knowing a few minutes earlier). And that was really about all that happened. They'd had a brief little meeting, a bit of lunch and tootled off back to London again.

Yes, but what about these notes? How had they come about? Had he gone along with Mitchell to talk about Bond's affairs?

A: No, not at all. No not at all.
Q: Well, this first sheet of yours is headed
    A. Bond.
A: Mm.[7]

.

Well, why on earth had an accountant in Jersey told him all these intimate details about Bond's affairs if he wasn't acting as Bond's lawyer, hadn't gone there to talk about Bond, and had nothing to do with it anyway? Well, that was a hard one. But Lodge had to speculate that Davies was telling him all this because he knew that Lodge came from Western Australia. And he had jotted it all down, meaningless as it was, just in case anyone in Western Australia should ever ask him what these jolly nice Jersey chaps were doing for Alan.

Harry Lodge OBE retired from legal practice in 1989, but is well known about town as a respectable, conservative gentleman, and pillar of the local Liberal party. In 1995, his role in setting up Bond's offshore empire was exposed by the author of this book in *The Australian* newspaper, along with his protestations that he had had nothing to do with it. Shortly afterwards, he wrote to the newspaper to complain. But all he succeeded in doing was to admit most of what he had so strenuously denied on oath two years earlier.[8]

By the time he wrote to *The Australian*, Lodge had recalled that he had been to Jersey in 1979 to set up the Juniper Trust and Pianola for Alan Bond. He remembered, too, after all these years, that he had visited Jersey in October 1984 and had taken notes of a conversation with Davies 'concerning mutual clients'. He also accepted that he had consented to act as someone from whom the trustees of the Juniper Trust, the Icarus Trust, and possibly others could take instructions. His vindication, he made it clear, lay in the fact that he had never been consulted.

Memory, of course, is a funny thing, especially as you grow older. But Harry Lodge must consider himself lucky that he was not pursued under section 77C of the Bankruptcy Act, which makes it an offence punishable by up to twelve months in prison to withhold information from a trustee in bankruptcy. For, in initially denying on oath that he had anything to do with the Juniper or Icarus trusts, he had arguably done just this.

It is possible, however, that Lodge knew even more about Bond's offshore affairs than he was prepared to admit to *The Australian*. In the mid-1980s, for example, he went to a series of meetings with Bond's tax adviser from Price Waterhouse, Geoff Mews, and Bond's managing director at Dallhold, Robert Pearce, to discuss Bond's personal financial affairs.

Lodge also billed Dallhold in November 1988 for: 'Attendances and advices on ... Mr Bollag concerning financing of Mr Bond's art collection'.[9]

This was barely three years before Bond denied, whilst Parker & Parker were still acting for him, that Kirk Holdings or Jurg Bollag had ever bought or paid for any paintings on his behalf.

Lodge was also heavily involved in the drafting of Bond's will or wills, and in January 1987 prepared an internal memo for Parker & Parker concerning Alan Bond, in which he wrote:

> Consideration should be given to the possibility of making wills in other jurisdictions and confining our present will to dealing only with Australian assets. For instance, there could be a will in the United Kingdom, one in the United States and one in any other place that might seem appropriate.[10]

Harry Lodge would quite probably also have seen a file note prepared by Anne Duncan of Parker & Parker on 8 September 1987 in which she recorded that Alan Bond had indicated to her that he had: 'Some concern that his will made no mention of his international assets'.[11]

To answer Bond's concerns, Parker & Parker subsequently advised Robert Pearce at Dallhold that further wills should be prepared for property held outside Australia. And on 15 October 1987, Pearce replied that separate wills would be drafted. Sure enough, Bond's subsequent Australian will, which was found in Parker & Parker's files in 1992, stated clearly:

> ... this will ... shall affect only my real and personal property in the Commonwealth of Australia, and shall not affect any of my real or personal property in any other part of the world other than the Commonwealth of Australia.[12]

Bond was asked on two occasions by Bob Ramsay during 1992 whether he had a will that covered his overseas assets, and on each occasion replied that he had neither a will nor assets offshore. He also denied having bank accounts overseas, with the exception of one at Arbuthnot Latham in London in the name of Dallhold (which was not the account in his own name, c/o Jurg Bollag, that had secretly received several million dollars from Kirk Holdings).

Bond's denials about bank accounts, overseas assets, offshore companies and wills were certainly made while Parker & Parker were still acting for him. Even if his answer relating to offshore wills was in fact correct, it is very hard to see how they could have been satisfied that Bond had no offshore assets or bank accounts, particularly since they received hundreds of thousands of dollars from a Swiss bank account held by Juno Equities to pay Alan Bond's legal fees.

After the Jersey evidence became public in May 1994, Parker & Parker must surely have known the history of Juno Equities, Touche Ross, Bond's Jersey companies, and Harry Lodge's role in setting them up—assuming that they didn't already know via Lodge himself or their own records. Yet they continued to act for Bond and echo his denials even after this date. And to charge large amounts of money for doing so.

To put it mildly, it was really quite remarkable.

11

Zuggered

Please ensure that this transfer is made through
London and make no mention of Kirk Holdings
or Jersey.

*Instruction to Allied Irish Banks, St Helier, to
transfer money to 'Jane' account at Zuger
Kantonal Bank, Switzerland, October 1987[1]*

There was one big problem with the treasure chest that
Bob Ramsay had discovered in Jersey, and that was that
the money was no longer there. Not to mention the fact that
by November 1993 the trail to Switzerland was six years old.

In a world where millions can be switched from country
to country in a matter of hours, the $42 million that had
moved out of Kirk's Jersey bank accounts in 1987 could
have been scattered to a hundred different places since then.
And there were precious few physical assets for Ramsay to
put his hands on. Most of Susanne's horses had been sold;
Kirk's valuable paintings had been spirited out of Perth to
an unknown destination; Upp Hall was being fought over by
the liquidator of Dallhold; Di Bliss's apartment had been
turned into cash in 1992; and the house in Selwood Place
had been sold in mid-1993 for £600,000, which had disappeared into the ether.[2]

So, despite their triumph in Jersey, Bob Ramsay and his team of asset tracers, led by Karen Coleman from the big Sydney law firm Mallesons, were still a long way from recovering any money for the creditors.

The obvious next step, of course, was to contact the banks in Switzerland, because a lot of money that had left Jersey had gone to Zug. But as Ramsay had already discovered, getting them to help was a great deal harder than getting cooperation from banks in the UK or Jersey. In fact, it was a complete nightmare.

Ramsay had originally sought their assistance back in May 1992, only six weeks after being appointed. On discovering that $800,000 had been wired from accounts in Zug and Davos to pay Alan's legal fees, he had written to the two Swiss banks involved, asking them for details of all accounts they held for Bond, and telling them to freeze all funds so they couldn't be moved.

Credit Suisse in Davos, which had sent $200,000 to Perth in October 1991 on behalf of Alan's American stockbroker friend Robert Quinn, wrote back almost by return of post to tell him that they did not recognise foreign bankruptcies in Switzerland, and would not disclose any details of their clients' affairs even if they did.

The Zuger Kantonal Bank, which had sent $600,000 on behalf of Bollag's Juno Equities in April 1992, gave him equally short shrift, telling him to come back when he had a court order.

It's worth saying that Bond's bankruptcy might have taken a very different course if the Swiss banks had agreed to help at this stage, because the trail was still fresh and money was still there. It's also worth noting that British or American banks would probably have been happy to help. But the Swiss seemed to be shocked that he had even thought it worth asking.

In any case, it was abundantly clear that they would neither reveal details of the accounts nor hand over money, so in September 1992, Ramsay set about getting a court order to compel them. And here he discovered that getting the Swiss courts to assist in a civil action, as opposed to a criminal prosecution, was almost impossible too.

The first stage in this arcane legal process was an application to the Federal Court of Australia to issue confidential Letters of Request to the Swiss courts asking for assistance. Affidavits were duly sworn, detailing Bollag's many and varied acts of generosity and recounting the tale of how the Swiss banks had refused to help. And soon afterwards, the letters were zipping off to Europe via Australia's diplomatic bag, in conditions of great secrecy so that Bond did not find out.

Within weeks, the British courts, whom Ramsay had also approached, were signalling that they were happy to cooperate, and by May 1993 the Jersey court had fallen in line. But the Swiss proved to be much more reluctant. In theory, they were willing to assist foreign legal actions, but in practice, as Ramsay now discovered, they were really only prepared to help the police, and even then it took ages for anything to happen.

By November 1993, a year had passed, but the Swiss request had still come to nought. And since Ramsay was in Jersey, which was only a couple of hours by plane from Zurich, he decided to make a direct approach. Fresh from learning about Bond's offshore empire, he now had a wealth of evidence to convince the Zuger Kantonal Bank that Jurg Bollag had indeed been laundering money for Bond.

So when he got into the manager's office at the Zuger

Kantonal Bank, which was one of the ugliest buildings in that pretty town, he was able to demonstrate that Bond's Jersey company Kirk Holdings had transferred several million dollars to accounts at the bank that could actually be identified. One of these was numbered 00-700-843-00 and held in the name of Treuhand Konto Trust Account, while a second was numbered 00-736-488-01 and code-named 'Jane'—crucially, this latter account was the one that Bollag had used in 1991 to fork out £373,000 for expenses at Upp Hall—so the circle of money going from Bond in Jersey to Bollag in Switzerland, and back to Bond appeared to be complete. This 'Jane' account had received only a small amount of money from Jersey in 1987, but the bank had been instructed to send it through London and to make sure that no mention of Kirk Holdings or Jersey was made on the transfer.[3]

Ramsay's evidence was arguably sufficient reason for the Zuger Kantonal Bank to break its client's confidence, and he was hopeful that they would allow him access to the vaults, if only to gather documents that would show where the money had gone next. But the manager was still unmoved by what Ramsay and his Swiss lawyer, Dr Bernhard Vischer, laid out before him, even when he was shown the multi-million-dollar deals that Bollag had done for Bond, and was led through tax records, which showed that either Bollag had been lying to the Swiss tax authorities or the money belonged to someone else.

His only reaction was to tell his unwelcome visitors that Jurg Bollag was one of his bank's valued customers, a Swiss national, and was innocent until proved guilty. Once again, he advised Ramsay that if he wanted any information about the bank's clients he would need to produce a Swiss court order. Whereupon he showed them both the door.

Ramsay was annoyed to be given such a frosty reception,

but he could hardly have been surprised, because secrecy is the rock on which the entire Swiss banking system is founded. And it is why at the beginning of the new millennium the country has almost three thousand billion dollars on deposit, or roughly half the world's privately managed assets. It is also why Switzerland still serves as a safe haven for corrupt dictators, drug runners and corporate crooks.

Today, the official Swiss Government line is that such people are neither welcome nor entirely secure. But it still remains a criminal offence, punishable by a hefty prison sentence, to disclose details of a customer's identity or banking transactions. And this restriction applies to both present and past bank employees, who essentially must carry their secrets to the grave.

Even now, the only legal excuse for bankers, lawyers or money managers like Bollag to break the code of secrecy is if they have *evidence* that the client has engaged in criminal activity. And some still take the view that they have no need to blow the whistle unless the courts convict their client or order them to tell all.[4]

In the early 1990s, before anti-money-laundering laws were introduced, it was still possible for a Swiss bank manager not to know who his real clients were. Until July 1991 one could open a Swiss bank account using the notorious Form B, and have a fiduciary or lawyer like Bollag act as a front man, without telling the bank who really owned the funds. But since 1991, this supra-security level has not been available, and Swiss banks have been required by law to know whose money is in their vaults. So when Bob Ramsay was sitting in the manager's office at the Zuger Kantonal Bank, there would unquestionably have been a piece of paper in the bank's files or a record on the system that revealed who Bollag was acting for.[5]

Ramsay's problem, however, was that he had very little chance of getting hold of the evidence if the bank refused to give it to him. Breaking into the records by hacking into the bank's computer system was certainly not an option, even if Ramsay wanted to consider it, because Swiss bank security was unbreakable. To get past the first level, which merely got you in the front door, you needed an ID and a password from an authorised bank employee. To get past the second level into the private account database, you needed an ID and a password from someone at branch manager level. And to get to level three, where you could access individual account details, you needed the ID and password for the exact person in the bank responsible for the individual or company you were after. Even if you could find out who that was, and bribe, force or blackmail them to help, you would almost certainly be caught by the twenty-four-hour security that monitored entry into these areas. In other words, it wasn't worth thinking about.[6]

But there was one line of attack that seemed to offer possibilities, and that was for Ramsay to pose as Bond or, to be more precise, to get Bond to order Bollag and the Swiss banks to return all documents and assets to him. Ramsay certainly had the power to force Bond to do this for, in Australia at least, he now controlled Bond's assets and was Bond for most legal purposes. As he put it, somewhat indelicately, he could now do anything on Bond's behalf except sleep with his wife.

So, a month after being shown the door in Zurich, Ramsay drafted a letter from Bond to Bollag which the Federal Court ordered Alan to sign. This instructed his friend Jurg to hand over all assets, monies and documents he was holding on Bond's behalf, and to give Ramsay a complete history of anything that he had previously held for Bond, including its current whereabouts. Further to that, Bollag was instructed to hand over all details of trusts, companies and bank accounts, along with details of any sub-contractors Bollag might have engaged to hold assets for him on trust for Bond. And even that wasn't the end of it.

The letter also told Bollag to order all banks with accounts of which he was a signatory to hand over details of any transactions relating to Bond's affairs. Finally, it instructed Bollag himself to meet Ramsay's representative in Switzerland before 31 December 1993.

Sadly, however, this clever idea fared no better than any of the others. Bollag merely wrote back some six weeks after the deadline had passed to say that he was forbidden by paragraph 271 of the Swiss penal code from disclosing any such information, adding that Ramsay's Swiss lawyer was not allowed to act for a foreign trustee in bankruptcy. Of course, he added, he would comply with the request if he was forced to do so by a Swiss court. But in the meantime, Ramsay could go fry.

A similar letter from Bond to the Zuger Kantonal Bank, ordering them to divvy up all documents and money, was returned to sender. Ramsay subsequently sent along a lawyer to argue the case, but his pleadings fell on deaf ears.

So by January 1994, it was once again back to first base and the tricky task of persuading the Swiss courts to order the banks to cooperate. And here things were still looking grim.

By this stage of the 1990s it was perfectly possible in theory for Swiss banks to be compelled by a local court to supply details of their clients' business, provided that evidence could be shown of money laundering, insider trading, fraud or criminal activity. Even more theoretically, it was also possible to get a court order via a civil suit that had originated overseas. But it was devilishly difficult to provide sufficient evidence to convince a Swiss court to take such exceptional action, and it was bound to be enormously expensive, because Switzerland has a different legal code to the one that Anglo-Saxon countries use, a different language, and a different attitude towards a rich person's right to privacy.

At the very least, the banks would be likely to oppose the action by fighting against any court order and then appealing; and at some point Bond and Bollag would inevitably be asked to join the fray. So at best it would be a long, hard, bruising battle that would take several years to fight.

There was, however, another course of action open to Ramsay. He could begin proceedings against Bollag in the Swiss courts, on the basis that Bollag was controlling assets to which Ramsay, as Bond's trustee in bankruptcy, was entitled. This would aim at securing a declaration from the Swiss courts that the assets should be returned. And in early 1994, this was the way that Ramsay decided to go, with some hope at this stage that it might succeed.

In the meantime, though, there was the exciting prospect of being able to question Bond on oath about the evidence obtained in Jersey. Alan had, after all, denied in letters to Ramsay that he had bank accounts offshore, even though there were four at Arbuthnot Latham in London, five in Jersey that belonged to Kirk Holdings, and at least one in Zug that appeared to have inherited his money. He had also denied having assets overseas, yet had clearly owned companies in the mid-1980s that contained many millions of dollars. And finally, he had denied 'to the best of my knowledge', as he put it, having ever instructed lawyers, accountants or other advisers outside Australia. Yet he had instructed Touche Ross in 1982 to take instructions from Robert Pearce about his affairs, and in 1987 to accept directions from Bollag, Pearce, John Bond and Harry Lodge.

Bond was still blissfully ignorant of what the investigators had dug up in Jersey, because everyone involved in the process had been sworn to secrecy. So if they could ever get him on the stand, it looked like providing hours of fun. Ramsay's power to examine Bond was backed by the sanction of twelve months in prison for anyone who withheld information or lied on oath. So it was hard to see how Bond could avoid telling the truth.

But it never paid to think you had Alan beaten. He was determined to avoid answering questions at all costs. And in the meantime, he had a friend who was doing his utmost to create a diversion.

The beginning of the end. Forced out of Bond Corporation, September 1990.

Hey you! Bond's good friend Jurg Bollag waves his finger at the camera ... then attacks the photographer with his briefcase. The fracas took place outside Bond's London house in March 1992, a month before Alan's bankruptcy.

Distraught … Eileen Bond is led away from Perth District Court by a security guard after Alan received a 30-month jail sentence in May 1992.

It's in the bag. Bond was allowed out of prison to appeal against the Rothwells conviction in July 1992.

Crying in the rain. Bond faces the cameras after his release from Woorooloo Prison in August 1992.

Brain-damaged? Depressed? Alan and Eileen in top form at daughter Jody's wedding in May 1993, where Alan told reporters he was fit and well after his heart operation.

We're winning. Alan Bond and lawyer Andrew Fraser.

Bond leaves court after being charged with a $15 million fraud over Manet's painting *La Promenade*. He stops to warn me, 'If you mention Bollag, I'll sue'.

Upp Hall, the Bonds' $12.5 million English country mansion.

Susanne and Craig Bond at Susanne's wedding, July 1993.

Graham Ferguson Lacey, who helped pay Alan's legal fees.

12

Lucky Jim

Multi-millionaire at 21, broke at 23, multi-
millionaire at 27 ... lost $10 million at 29-30;
on the way up again.

Jim Byrnes, Who's Who in Business in Australia
1992[1]

Whil en Jim Byrnes first met Alan Bond in 1993 he was
only thirty-five years old, but he had already lost
several million dollars of other people's money and claimed to
have lost a few million more of his own.

He had been bankrupted for the second time in June 1992,
just two months after the banks had put Bond under, but in
typical fashion that no doubt recommended him to Alan, he
hadn't let it affect his lifestyle. He continued to drive two
Rolls-Royces—a lilac Corniche convertible for when the sun
was shining, and a blue hardtop for when it wasn't—which
were owned by a convenient family trust that kept them away
from his creditors. 'I've been rich, I've been poor, I've been in
jail,' he told a journalist, 'but I've always had a Rolls-Royce.'[2]

Before his latest financial difficulty, Byrnes had managed
to get himself into the pages of *Who's Who in Business in
Australia* with the following entry: 'Multi-millionaire at 21,

broke at 23, multi-millionaire at 27, just under $20 million in assets; lost $10 million at 29–30; on the way up again'. But now he was heading down once more, having borrowed $8.5 million to invest in property just as the boom was ending.

In many ways, Jim Byrnes was cast in the same mould as the man he was now enlisted to help, for he was a great charmer, storyteller and attractive rogue. And while you had to wonder whether anything he told you was true, you somehow didn't care if it wasn't, because his tales were so entertaining that it hardly mattered. Doubtless, this was why he had got so far in life and why finance companies continued to lend him millions when they should have known better.

It helped, of course, that Jim was a good-looking fellow who could have been mistaken for a successful boxer or a famous footy player. He was a big man with even bigger Italian suits and a chubby almost babyish face. But with his close-cropped hair and wire-rimmed glasses there was also an unmistakably studious air about him, as if a bouncer had been cross-bred with an art dealer. And in a way this hybrid summed up his character, for Jim cultivated a hard-man image to help him in business, and had a genuine love of art and antiques, even if he was occasionally accused of omitting to pay for them.

Jim also loved food, wine and pretty women, but his passion in life was cars, which were constantly getting him into trouble. In his time he had driven a red Porsche cabriolet, a Mustang convertible, a red Corvette and a Jag, as well as a number of Rollers and Bentleys. And he had been famous for his gold Mercedes coupé with the number plate HIT ME, in which he had not surprisingly been stopped by police in Kings Cross who asked to see his licence. Jim had been forced to admit that he didn't have one and had promptly been convicted in July 1992 of driving while disqualified for the third time in three years, for which he was given 100 hours community service and disqualified yet again, this time for six months.

Byrnes's and Bond's paths first crossed in early 1992 before Bond was made bankrupt, when Jim rang out of the blue to offer Alan assistance. By this stage, Byrnes had gathered so much personal experience of dealing with angry banks and creditors that he was putting it to good use by earning a quid as a debt consultant. And there was certainly no bigger debtor in Australia than Alan Bond.

Some fifteen months later, it was Bond who got back in touch with Byrnes to ask for help, and this collaboration proved to be much more fruitful. Jim was now advertising in the *Australian Financial Review*, telling people with financial problems that he could get rid of their debts 'for less than 10 cents in the dollar'. But he had also been recommended personally to Bond by someone that Alan had met in the bar at the Sheraton Wentworth Hotel. Jim had helped this man settle with his creditors, and had supposedly done a great job.

Some of Byrnes's methods were a bit cruder than Bond's, and they were not always successful. In fact, two of his smaller clients were convicted in 1997 of defrauding their creditors after following Jim's advice to remove $55,000 from their ailing business and park it in their children's bank accounts.[3] His two strengths were that he had an encyclopaedic knowledge of the bankruptcy laws and could drive his pursuers to despair. During attempts to make him bankrupt in 1992, one of the lawyers acting for the finance company that had lent him $8.5 million filed a wonderful affidavit setting out the way in which he had managed to delay proceedings. He had told this young woman over the phone that she and the finance company were wasting their time, and would never get anything out of him:

> I don't think I will have any problems in stalling this matter for at least three years. I am a professional staller. I've read the Bankruptcy Act and I can make approximately 27 applications by way of instalments before I will ever be bankrupted ... Even if you get this matter listed before a Registrar again, I will produce an air ticket to say I am going overseas. You won't be able to get this matter heard. So why fight?[4]

A little later, the lawyer had asked him where he had got the money for the red Porsche that he was still driving around town, despite his massive debts and, indeed, his lack of licence, to which he had replied: 'The car's not mine. It's a friend of mine's and I'm trying to sell it for him. I'm not stupid you know. I don't have anything in my own name'.

When Byrnes wasn't fighting off bankruptcy or driving expensive cars, he seemed to spend most of his time in court. In fact it was a miracle that he had time for business, because he was forever fighting with bankers, builders, tenants or acquaintances, or being prosecuted by the police. In early 1992 he got into a fight with a bank over a Jaguar belonging to a friend who was behind with the payments. Jim tried to extract $12,000 from the bank for telling them where they could find the missing car, and almost ended up in jail as a result. He was ultimately made to pay the bank's legal fees, even though he wasn't a party to their court case, and was then singled out by the judge for a most unflattering assessment of his character:

Mr Byrnes was evasive, prevaricated, gave conflicting evidence and, as any observer of him in the witness box would have found, was an untruthful witness ... I have not the slightest doubt that Mr Byrnes is a thoroughly dishonest man who would say whatever he perceived to be convenient to his own interest.[5]

Alan Bond could be forgiven for not having read this particular judgement when he signed up Byrnes to act as his emissary, but he could hardly have been ignorant of Jim's colourful history, because it was a favourite topic of the gossip columns in Sydney's tabloid newspapers, and Jim had worse stains on his record than telling porkies in court or making a fool of the bankruptcy laws. Four months before teaming up with Bond, he had been charged with fraud in relation to a stolen $30,000 cheque, and around the same time, a process server had sworn an affidavit that Byrnes had attacked him physically as he tried to deliver him a bankruptcy notice.[6] Even worse, as a young man in the 1980s, he had acquired convictions for aiding and abetting a malicious wounding, stealing a motor vehicle and supplying heroin.

Byrnes's explanation of this episode in his life was that he had been young and naïve and had taken the fall for a drug deal that he had never been involved with. Still, he had been sentenced in 1986 to five years in prison, of which he served two, after time off for good behaviour, in Sydney's Long Bay and Silverwater jails. There, he once again claimed to have turned adversity into triumph, by coming out on day release to run the family car yard in Sydney's auto alley, Parramatta Road. In doing this, he said, he had made a fortune, buying the car yard and a house for his parents, borrowing $500,000, and getting himself a Rolls-Royce Silver Shadow, complete with chauffeur, to drive him to and from his prison cell. 'So not only am I a Rolls-driving bankrupt,' he boasted, 'I was also a chauffeur-driven prisoner.'[7]

The official history of the Byrnes car yard was a little more tarnished than this. Records at the New South Wales Consumer Affairs Department show a raft of complaints from customers about the cars, and the business eventually crashed, owing large amounts of money to a finance company called Custom Credit. But you had to agree that Jim's version of the story was a great deal more fun.

Before bonding with Bondy, Byrnes's main claim to fame had been his brief marriage to the singer Jackie Love, who had been famously photographed in 1986 at the opening of Bond's Observation City, kicking up her heels between Alan and his mate Laurie Connell. She was taller than both of them, as well as blonder and more beautiful, with long, slim legs that one critic had labelled the loveliest in Australia. And in March 1992, after a whirlwind romance, she and Jim had tied the knot.

For the first few weeks, Byrnes rang the papers regularly to tell them how smitten he was with his new bride: 'I love that girl, I'd do anything for her. I'd die for her'.[8] And Jackie was equally enthused, telling another journalist in an exclusive interview: 'Jim is warm, generous and caring. He's a sweety'.[9]

But before a year had gone by, Jackie had fled, with grand piano, waterbed and clothes, and Jim was again hitting the phones to tell the papers how he felt: 'I am totally devastated,' he told the *Telegraph Mirror*, 'I am in a rage one minute, and I am upset and crying the next.'[10] The next day he was front page news, with a passionate plea for Jackie to come back. 'If I could say anything to her, I would say I love you, I'll always love you, and I won't stop loving you.' Yet somehow he also couldn't help adding his views on what might have gone wrong, telling her she had to choose between him and her mother, and then giving her a free personality assessment. 'Sometimes she can be warm and loving, but sometimes she can be as cold as a mackerel,' said Byrnes, adding philosophically, 'sometimes you go to bed with a warm and loving person and you wake up with a fish.'[11]

One of the problems, it seemed, was that Jackie had been shocked to hear about Jim and his exploits. And to be fair, it must have been a rapid education, for not only had she discovered he had a criminal record and financial difficulties, but she had also collected him from hospital after he had taken a beating from a creditor who believed in more traditional methods of debt collecting. Not-so-lucky Jim had been sitting in his North Sydney office one morning in June 1992 when a couple of blokes had barged in and beaten the bejasus out of him. He had woken up an hour later in the Royal North Shore Hospital to find a couple of teeth missing, a huge black eye and several large lumps on his head, which was how he had appeared in court a few days later to be finally made bankrupt.

Byrnes reckoned, however, that his battle scars were a plus when it came to helping Bond, because he was 'a corporate street-fighter ... a no-holds-barred type of guy, and that's what Alan needed'.[12]

By this time, Bond had spent a huge amount of money on lawyers fighting court cases, and apparently felt he was getting nowhere. He was also desperate to get Ramsay off his back and to get out and do deals again. Never the most patient of men, he wanted his passport back so he could travel, and he wanted to be free of all these pesky people inquiring into his affairs. And Byrnes offered him another opportunity of getting all these things to happen.

In June 1993, Byrnes flew to Perth at Bond's expense and agreed to a deal in which he would approach Alan's major creditors to get support for a settlement of around $6 million, which was less than a hundredth of what they were owed. In return, Byrnes would get all his expenses paid and would receive a fee of $100,000 if he could get Bond released from bankruptcy.[13] On top of that, if he could persuade creditors to settle for less than $6 million, he would get 10 per cent of the shortfall. Byrnes happily signed the inevitable confidentiality agreement and then rang the *Australian Financial Review* to tell them that a compromise between Bond and his creditors was now looking likely. When asked by the paper what he stood to gain from any settlement and why he had become involved, he replied that he was doing it for love and was 'not drawing a cent in fees', which was a bit loose with the truth, to put it mildly. But truth, as we know, was not Jim's strongest point.

By the end of the month Jim had already made half-a-dozen phone calls to the Hongkong Bank alone, and sent several faxes to its chairman Willie Purves in Hong Kong, telling them that seven big creditors who were owed $100 million were now keen to settle with Bond for around one cent in the dollar. He was also badgering Don Argus, chairman of the National Australia Bank, with a similar story that creditors were eager to work out a compromise. And in each case he tried spinning the line that the banks had already got all their money back from Bond and shouldn't be chasing him for more.

The banks and big creditors mostly told Byrnes they weren't interested, but this did not discourage him. Jim simply stuck to the principle that all great pants men employ, which is that if you ask enough girls to come to bed with you, you are bound to find one who says yes. And sure enough, the Commonwealth Bank eventually came across. Typically, Byrnes had been chasing big debts and going straight to the top in his attempt to get satisfaction, but this time he found someone working late in the bank's collections department and used his immense charm to persuade him that this was an offer he could not refuse. The bank was owed only $14,000 on one of Bond's credit cards, and Byrnes was able to smooth talk them into handing it over for a measly $400. Crucially, he was then smart enough to get the offer accepted in writing, in case the unfortunate fellow's superior attempted to backtrack.[14]

When Byrnes phoned Parker & Parker to tell them the news, they were apparently incredulous, because Byrnes had been told to deal with the big debtors, like the Arab Bank and Tri-continental, who were owed hundreds of millions of dollars, and he had come back with one of the smallest debts on offer. But it was hardly a defeat, because Jim's $400 purchase would now give him access to all creditors' meetings. So the lawyers rapidly prepared a weighty legal document for the Commonwealth Bank to sign.

The bank's senior managers, meanwhile, opened their morning newspapers to discover the appalling truth of what had happened. For Jim had not only told the press that he had bought the debt, but had spun them the story that the Commonwealth Bank was coming to Alan Bond's rescue. Naturally, the bank was desperate to get out of the deal, but the written offer of acceptance made it impossible for them to renege. So after a bit of chest thumping by lawyers on both sides, the bankers were forced to live with the consequences. They had undoubtedly spent far more in management time and legal fees than the $400 that Byrnes had paid them, and they had bought themselves a heap of bad publicity to boot, but Byrnes for his part now had standing as a creditor, which would allow him inside the citadel where he could do his best to wreak havoc.

Byrnes was fond of quoting from the famous Chinese text *The Art of War* by Sun Tzu, which advised you to defeat your enemies by creating confusion, and he now set about doing just that, by attacking Bob Ramsay and attempting to sow discord among Bond's creditors. To this point they had been united in their desire to chase Bond's offshore assets, and convinced that Ramsay was doing a decent job, but Byrnes was hoping that when he had finished they would be bickering among themselves and worrying that the trustee was wasting their money.

This strategy made perfectly good sense, because Ramsay could only make progress in Switzerland if creditors continued to pay for his investigations and legal actions, and if the whole process of Bond's bankruptcy could be made sufficiently difficult and frustrating, those creditors might well lose patience and give up. Thus far, almost all the bills had been paid by Tricontinental, who were keen to press on, and by the Hongkong Bank, who were much less so. And Byrnes now tried to make it more difficult for both of them by suggesting to other creditors that the two banks might gobble up all the spoils.

Meanwhile, he also tried to take Ramsay's eye off the ball by jumping up and down and making a nuisance of himself, at which he was a master. In early July he fired off a letter listing eighty-six questions to Ramsay about the way he was running Bond's bankruptcy, and demanding immediate answers. Some of these questions were aimed at discovering how close the investigators had come to finding Bond's offshore assets, and asked Ramsay to tell where he had been, whom he had hired, how much money he had spent, what he had spent it on, who had provided it, how much money remained, whether he had found or seized any property or money, and what if anything he was still looking for. But some of the questions were just plain mischievous.

Not surprisingly, Ramsay replied that he was not prepared to discuss the progress of offshore investigations because it was vital that they remained secret. And he brushed off most of the other enquiries by saying that he simply did not have the time to deal with them. But then the skirmishing began in earnest.

Byrnes wrote back to say he was extremely dissatisfied with Ramsay's conduct and had no option but to complain to the Official Receiver, the Inspector-General in Bankruptcy and the Attorney General. He also sent letters to the Australian Taxation Office, who were owed some $23 million by Bond, criticising Ramsay's management of Bond's affairs. And then, to spice things up even further, he wrote to the Hongkong Bank to tell them that Ramsay had taken a secret commission, or to put it bluntly a bribe, from the ABC's *Four Corners* in exchange for supplying information to them. This was complete nonsense and Byrnes was soon writing to Ramsay to apologise—yet it all helped to stir the pot.

At the first creditors' meeting he attended in September 1993, Byrnes came armed with his list of eighty-six questions, and harried Ramsay and the Hongkong Bank for two hours, finally declaring his intention to report Ramsay to the Attorney General for failure to carry out his duties. Byrnes recalls with a chuckle that people yelled at him to sit down and threw their papers onto the floor in annoyance, which was exactly what he had hoped to achieve.

Byrnes's behaviour made Ramsay so angry that he wrote to the Attorney General's Department asking them to change the law to prevent people from infiltrating the ranks of creditors by buying up debts. He also fired off a letter to Parker & Parker asking them who had put Byrnes up to the purchase and where his money had come from. But it was all to no avail. There was nothing that could be done to get rid of him.

Whether Byrnes really succeeded in weakening support for Ramsay or was just a minor irritation is hard to discover. In the long term, he almost certainly did make a difference, but in late 1993 things still seemed to be going well for Bond's creditors—except in Switzerland. Their legal right to Bond's $2.7 million super fund had been upheld by the Appeal Court in November, and the Administrative Appeals Tribunal had confirmed in August that Bond was indeed liable to pay creditors half his notional income. In fact, the tribunal had even increased the amount that his mates would have to find for 1992–93 to $345,000, because Bond had spent far more on legal fees than Ramsay had dared to imagine. So it looked like the new law was working well.

In late 1993, Parker & Parker, John Bond, Jody Bond, Jurg Bollag and Graham Ferguson Lacey were therefore served with demands from the Official Receiver to pay up on Bond's behalf.

All that now remained was to force Alan Bond to tell the Federal Court (as the law said he must) about the money that Bollag was hiding in Switzerland, and Ramsay would be home and hosed.

Surely victory was now in sight.

13

Brain Damage

He has experienced public and private shame,
humiliation, guilt and public harassment ... he is
overeating, he suffers persistent insomnia ... he
contemplates suicide.

Dr William Barclay on Bond, February 1994[1]

B ob Ramsay had originally sought a Federal Court order
to examine Bond on oath in December 1992, on the
grounds that Alan had given him unsatisfactory answers to a
whole series of key questions.

In particular, Bond had denied having overseas assets, overseas bank accounts or an overseas will, despite a mass of
evidence to the contrary. A series of letters had then been
exchanged in which Ramsay had produced more and more
material to suggest that Bond was lying, but the obfuscation
and denials had continued, and finally the two men had met
face to face in Bird Cameron's offices in Melbourne, where
Bond told Ramsay point blank: 'I will not have any discussion
with you or answer any of your questions on an on-the-record
basis'.[2]

The Federal Court had immediately ordered Bond to
undergo a section 81 examination in which he could be forced

to answer Ramsay's questions or be thrown into prison—either for contempt of court or for offences against the Bankruptcy Act which carried a maximum penalty of twelve months jail.

This examination would also put him in danger of perjury charges that could see him behind bars for five years if he gave false answers. So in theory he would have only one way out, which was to tell the truth and admit that Bollag was hiding millions of dollars for him in bank accounts in Switzerland.

The problem was that it looked like being a nightmare to get Bond into the witness box. The scheduled examination in February 1993 had been cancelled because he had been rushed into hospital for open-heart surgery. And now in November 1993, as Ramsay tried to nail down a new date, Bond and his lawyers were arguing that he was mentally unfit to take the stand because he had lost his memory.

Initially, their pitch was that Alan's amnesia had been caused by brain damage suffered during his heart operation. Later, the blame was shifted onto depression and anxiety. But either way, the aim of it all seemed pretty transparent. With the bankruptcy more than halfway through its normal three-year term, Bond would be able to escape interrogation completely if he could just keep Ramsay at bay for a year or so. And medical arguments about the mysteries of Bond's brain were quite capable of lasting that long.[3]

The basis of the case was that Bond's brain had been damaged when his aorta had been clamped for two-and-a-half hours to divert blood around his heart while surgeons fitted a new heart valve. In roughly one case in ten, the experts said, this caused small bubbles of air, or micro-embolisms, to enter the brain. And this, they argued, had happened to Bond.

But there were huge problems with this scenario. First of all, this type of brain damage was usually very minor. Second, it was pretty crazy to suggest that Bond could have forgotten that he had hidden millions of dollars offshore. Third, his operation had gone smoothly and been judged a success. Fourth, and worst of all, the public had not been given the slightest sign that there was anything wrong with him after his operation. Indeed, the evidence suggested that he had been bursting with health.

Three months after his heart operation, Alan had been filmed at his daughter Jody's wedding looking a million dollars. His face had been plump, his skin rosy and shiny, and there had been a huge smile on his face. And he had actually told a TV interviewer happily that he felt 'very well'. Rest, he said, had done the trick.

At around the same time he had been photographed by *Woman's Day* on the beach near his home, and judged by observers to be in great shape:

> He looks a little trimmer, more taut, and he's obviously feeling terrific. Fallen tycoon Alan Bond, who underwent open-heart surgery in February— an operation doctors predicted would take six months to recover from—appeared to be sparking on all cylinders as he took a brisk walk and a paddle on the beach near his home in Cottesloe, WA, recently.
>
> ... As our exclusive pictures show, his glowing tan is back—along with the smile and style with the ladies. And there's definitely more pep in his step.[4]

Lee Tate, the man who sneaked the photographs, reckoned Bond was 'his normal robust, chatty self'. Alan, he said, had been dancing around the beach like he was 'spring-heeled' and had then swum 500 metres in the surf. 'He just can't help himself.'

A month later, in June 1993, when Bond was charged with a $15 million fraud over Manet's painting *La Promenade*, he again seemed to be in tip-top mental shape. He walked briskly and cheerily into East Perth Magistrates' Court, looking as feisty as ever. And when I approached him outside the court-room, he had no difficulty remembering me or in threatening me with a lawsuit.

Three months after that, on the tenth anniversary of his America's Cup win, he was quite well enough to give long interviews to Perth's *Sunday Times* and Channel 9. He told them he had gaps in his memory about the victory, as most people would ten years after the event, yet looked perfectly fit and well. Channel 9's reporter, Liam Bartlett, came away convinced that the energetic entrepreneur was in top form, and later told Ramsay's lawyers: 'The interview with Bond lasted about one-and-a-half hours. Mr Bond seemed to be his normal self and sharp as a tack mentally'.[5]

Around this time, an enthusiastic Bond was seen roaring round Sydney with Diana Bliss, attending a series of highly public opening-night performances. In early December 1993, a Sydney gossip columnist reported him to be 'looking dangerously well' outside the Sheraton Wentworth, brandishing a fistful of dollars to anyone who could find him a cab, and announcing to anyone who would listen: 'I've a plane to catch. Doesn't anyone round here want to work?'.[6]

Yet despite this apparent rude health Bond and his lawyers were claiming that he was too sick to instruct them, and that his memory was so shattered that he could not possibly take the stand in court.

Bond had first started to complain that he was losing his memory back in April 1993, when he had told his GP that it was getting so bad that he had become lost driving round the streets of Perth. On a couple of occasions, he said, he had forgotten the names of old friends. His GP had referred him to a top Perth neurologist, Dr William Carroll, who diagnosed Bond as having a *mild* form of brain damage presumed to be caused by a micro-embolism. But Carroll had emphasised that an electroencephalogram (EEG) of Bond's brain showed 'only very minimal changes', while a high-tech Magnetic Resonance Imaging (MRI) scan showed 'no major structural lesions'. He had also advised Bond that his condition was likely to improve, and told him that it was not serious enough to merit treatment. Finally, he had reassured Alan's lawyers that it would not prevent Bond from briefing them.[7]

Shortly afterwards, Alan took himself to a forensic psychologist in Melbourne who made his living by giving expert evidence in court cases. Tim Watson-Munro saw Bond six times in the next four months and concluded that he was anxious, depressed, fragile, vulnerable, suicidal and suffering from cognitive and memory impairment.

In October, this same psychologist was asked by Bond's lawyers to give an opinion on whether Bond was mentally fit to face a trial or a section 81 examination. He wrote back to say that it would be beyond Bond's 'level of emotional and cognitive capacity' to brief counsel and that it might seriously worsen his condition if Alan was forced to go into the witness box:

> Given his poor capacity to recall and his current tendency to muddle even simple logical sequencing, I suspect that he would have immense difficulty in

coping with both examination-in-chief and cross-examination, and that should he be placed in a stressful situation in the witness box, there will be aggravation of cognitive deficits to the point of him possibly breaking down.[8]

This of course was exactly what the lawyers were looking for. Better still, the good doctor told them Bond had little chance of a quick recovery:

I believe it is unlikely that there will be any significant improvement in his functioning for at least six months and, regrettably, if the suspected brain damage is confirmed, Mr Bond's current level of reduced cognitive functioning may well prove to be permanent.[9]

Even more usefully, Watson-Munro reported that he had submitted Bond to an intelligence test that revealed his IQ to be only ninety, or lower than average for the population at large. And on this evidence, he concluded, Bond must have been so severely brain-damaged by his heart operation that his IQ had dropped at least thirty points.

This was a pretty remarkable allegation for Watson-Munro to make, but it was even more remarkable that he did not have a jot of evidence to support it. He had not looked at the ECG showing Bond's brain damage to be minimal. Nor had he obtained previous IQ-test results for Bond as a comparison. Instead, he had assumed that no one with an IQ as low as ninety could possibly have run a large multinational corporation, and had then swallowed a series of stories about Bond's childhood brilliance which were an absolute fantasy.

Alan had boasted to the gullible expert that he had studied five languages as a child, excelled at mathematics, taken accountancy at night school and been so proficient at sign-writing that he had completed his apprenticeship eighteen months early. But none of these tall tales was true.

Poor Alan had in fact suffered an inglorious childhood in the UK and Australia, in which he had been neither smart nor popular, and had later invented a more colourful history in which he had achieved great success. In the various versions that Bond had offered to interviewers over the years he had boasted of winning a Latin competition at the age of eight or of being sent to a school for exceptionally gifted children, and had always awarded himself an outstanding level of achievement in books and business.

In truth, however, young Bond had not been so much a brilliant student as one of the dullest. In 1949 he had failed his 11-Plus exam in England, which was an IQ test pure and simple, and had been despatched to a secondary-modern school, where the least intelligent children ended up. Even there he had obviously been no star pupil, because his fellow classmates remembered him as 'thick'. He had also played truant.[10]

Alan had certainly not studied five languages at that school or any other, and his first Australian employer, Fred Parnell, judged famously that he 'could hardly speak English'. As Fred recalled it, Alan's spelling as a fifteen-year-old apprentice sign-writer had been 'just dreadful'. On one occasion he had left a note to say that a customer in 'South Terris' wanted 'two moor signs'; on another, an angry shopkeeper had complained that Bond had painted the word 'business' wrongly on his shop front.[11]

Nor had Alan's command of the written word improved in

the 1990s. Five months before the heart operation had supposedly damaged his brain, he had been asked by Bob Ramsay whether he was a beneficiary of any trust, and had written back to say that he was possibly a beneficiary of some associated with his 'familey', as suggested in his 'statment' of affairs, but he couldn't be sure because he didn't have 'copie's' of the documents. When asked about details of his salary at Bond Corporation, Alan had told Ramsay to consult the 'scheduals' or, as he later put it, the 'scheduale'.[12]

It was quite possible, of course, that Bond was dyslexic, but that didn't alter the fact that his brilliant career, which had so impressed Watson-Munro, was a tissue of lies. His claim that he had completed his signwriting apprenticeship in record time was also a fiction. Bond had in fact been asked to leave by Fred Parnell because he was taking too many days off and was suspected of poaching Fred's customers.

What Bond also hadn't told Watson-Munro or anybody else was that he had notched up a lengthy criminal record as a juvenile. At the tender age of fourteen, young Alan had been convicted for stealing and unlawful entry and sentenced to two years in a juvenile institution. And four years later, as an eighteen-year-old, he had again been convicted of unlawful entry after being arrested as he attempted to break into a house in Fremantle. The *Western Australian Police Gazette* of 1952 even carried a segment devoted to young Bond's burgeoning career as a delinquent, complete with fingerprints and mug shots of Alan in his school uniform.[13]

Watson-Munro could have discovered much of this by reading *The Rise and Fall of Alan Bond*, but this would have rendered his 'expert' evidence less favourable to his client. Instead, he had taken Bond's stories at face value.

The other 'expert' writing sick notes for Bond in late 1993

was a Perth surgeon called John Saunders, who was also one of Alan's personal friends. Saunders was neither a psychiatrist nor a neurologist, nor even Bond's regular doctor, so his qualifications to talk about Bond's brain were not immediately obvious, yet he was able to state confidently that Bond was so ill that he might *never* be able to go into court:

> From the information before me and personal observation, I do not believe that Mr Bond has the ability to fully and adequately instruct anyone in relation to the proceedings against him. As to when he may be fit to do so, only time will tell. It is now ten months since his surgery. There seems to be no improvement in these problems and no likelihood of any improvement in the foreseeable future.[14]

Saunders's main claim to being an expert on Bond's mental state was that he had known him for many years and now saw him in a distressed state. But it was remarkable that any court could have even considered him to be an expert on brain damage, depression or amnesia, because he was clearly none of these. Yet he was allowed to deliver the killer punch for Bond's lawyers by stating that there was 'no doubt' that Bond had suffered brain damage and that this appeared to be the cause of his memory problems.

The first opportunity to try out this 'expert' medical evidence came in December 1993 when Bond's lawyers went to court in Perth to ask for his trial on the $15 million Manet fraud charges to be delayed. Their star witness, Watson-Munro, was flown across from Melbourne at Bond's expense to tell the magistrate that his patient was suffering from stress, anxiety and depression, had contemplated suicide, and was 'fragile and vulnerable'. Bond, said Watson-Munro, was also possibly suffering from brain damage, and was now so cerebrally challenged that he would 'have difficulty running a corner store'. On hearing this, the magistrate, Graeme Calder, understandably delayed hearing of the charges until July 1994.[15]

Bond did not attend court that morning, so did not hear the claims that he was suicidal. But Perth's journalists certainly did, and there was therefore a huge crowd waiting for him down in Fremantle, where he had agreed to show the media round the replica of the *Endeavour*, which Bond Corporation had helped to build. Most had agreed not to ask questions about his court case, but a young journalist from Channel 9, Ros Thomas, was keen to get a grab from him and felt herself to be under no obligation to keep off the subject.

Ros had been drinking in a Perth wine bar with Alan Bond only a couple of nights earlier, and he had not struck her as remotely likely to top himself. He had been extremely talkative and interested in her, which may have had something to do with the fact that she was a gorgeous young blonde woman. And he now greeted her like a long-lost friend:

> He came out of the door and saw me and, I'll never forget it, he gave me this big smile and then I thought, 'Right, time to ask the questions'. So I started talking to him as he was walking. I just remember saying, 'Mr Bond, why would your defence counsel say you're suicidal? What would give him that impression? Is it something you've told him?'. He didn't say a word. He had a grimace on his face. The smile had vanished and he was starting to look pretty peeved.[16]

Ros Thomas was not only convinced from her own encounter with Alan that there was nothing much wrong with him, but had also heard stories of him jogging on the beach and living it up in restaurants. So she figured he might be faking it when he appeared grey and listless in court. Besides, this was the biggest news of the day because his criminal trial had just been put off for six months. She kept walking beside him as they crossed the car park, asking why he hadn't responded, until suddenly he lost his temper in spectacular fashion:

> I was walking and saying to him 'Are you going to answer my questions Mr Bond?'. I must have said it about four or five times, and he just turned around and grabbed the mike and just pitched it, and it went flying over two or three cars. I thought he was going to punch me or slap my face but he just threw the mike and kept on walking. Then he got into the car, slammed the door and drove off. He didn't say a word to me that whole time, he just spat it.[17]

Bond's efforts to use brain damage as an excuse to stay out of court did not, however, get such an easy ride from his would-be bankruptcy examiners. By the end of 1993, Bob Ramsay had assembled his own team of experts to probe Bond's brain and was getting ready to fight the issue in the Federal Court. Meanwhile, Justice Sheppard, who had been hearing all matters relating to Bond's bankruptcy, appeared to be losing patience. In December 1993, a week after the Perth magistrate had accepted that Bond was too sick to stand trial, Sheppard ordered him to be examined by two neurological experts chosen by Ramsay.

On 7 January 1994, Bond therefore presented himself at the Perth consulting rooms of a neuro-psychologist called Michael Hunt, who was acknowledged to be a leading expert in assessing brain-damage victims.

Hunt may well have suspected that Bond was malingering, or perhaps he just probed deeper than Alan's doctors had done, but he soon managed to upset his patient. Before an hour was up, the once-great entrepreneur started to shake, complained of a splitting headache, burst into tears and declared he couldn't go on. As he fled from the building, he was approached by a process server and flew into a rage. Later, he explained why he had snapped:

> I was upset . . . I wasn't well at all. I felt awful. He started yelling at me. I lost control of myself and went for him to push him away, to get him to leave. I started shaking in a frenzy . . . I was quite out of control, I went for the guy, I got so angry.[18]

Two days later, Bond went back to Michael Hunt to finish his assessment and, unwittingly, to complete a task designed to catch people feigning brain injury. Called the 15-Item Test, it is normally presented to the subject as being difficult and demanding, even though it's actually extremely easy. The test consists of five groups of three letters or numbers, such as ABC, 123, abc, i ii iii, followed by a group of three shapes, which one has only ten seconds to memorise. Even people with serious brain damage are apparently capable of completing it with ease, yet Bond allegedly managed to recall just ten of the fifteen items, leading Hunt to wonder whether Alan was faking his amnesia or, as his affidavit put it, whether he might have 'a desire to appear impaired in terms of his memory'.[19]

Hunt was not absolutely sure that Bond was putting it on, but he was convinced that brain damage was not his problem. There was no sign of injury on the brain scans and the pattern of his memory loss was not typical of brain-damage victims. Bond's problem with memory, said Hunt, if indeed he had one, came from lack of concentration and attention.

Ramsay's other expert witness, a neurologist called Dr Wally Knezevic, agreed with this diagnosis, emphasising that he could find no physical evidence of brain damage, and pointing out that he believed Bond's cerebral function to be quite normal:

> I performed the Mini Mental State Examination. He scored 30 out of 30. This is a screening test which did not detect any obvious abnormalities of registration, orientation, attention and calculation recall or language. Furthermore, throughout the interview and examination which lasted one and a half hours, he did not demonstrate any evidence of significant intellectual impairment. On more detailed testing with memory, language and comprehension, he did not demonstrate any significant abnormality.[20]

Knezevic then addressed the question of whether Bond was fit to testify and decided that he was. Finally, he had a swipe at Dr John Saunders, whose evidence he declared to be of no relevance since the doctor had no qualifications in this field.

On this basis, Bond's chances of convincing the Federal Court to hold off his bankruptcy examination for a second time did not look good. But when the matter came to court in Sydney on 9 February 1994 there was a dramatic new development. Bond had been rushed into the Mounts Bay Clinic in Perth the previous day, suffering from a 'severe major depression', or as the *Sydney Morning Herald* put it, he had been struck down by 'Skase syndrome'.[21]

The Federal Court now heard that Bond's psychiatrist, Dr Dennis Tannenbaum, had informed Bond's lawyers that Alan was 'in obvious distress'.

> He appears to have difficulty in recalling even people he knows well . . . He feels that the future is hopeless. He feels that he has failed more than the average person . . . He feels that he is being punished and is disappointed in himself and tends to blame himself for everything that has happened . . . His irritation has extended into agitation and rage and he has lost his temper a number of times. He repeatedly feels he is unable to go on.[22]

A few days later, a second psychiatrist, Dr William Barclay, confirmed the diagnosis of major depression, suggesting that it could be accompanied by organic brain damage, and concluding that Alan would get agitated, stressed and possibly fly into an uncontrollable rage if he had to face cross-examination.

> He has experienced public and private shame, humiliation, guilt and public harassment . . . he is overeating, he suffers persistent insomnia . . . he contemplates suicide and has considered a method of ending his life. He suffers physical symptoms of anxiety . . . he experiences a high degree of shame and guilt. He has a sense of hopelessness about the future.[23]

Barclay asked Bond whether the situation had got to the point where he had seriously thought of killing himself, to which Bond replied:

> A: Yes it has. I got as far as actually a couple of
>   months ago going for a long swim off the
>   beach. I thought I wouldn't bother getting back.
> Q: What changed your mind?
> A: I was surprised I was still swimming. I kept
>   going a long time. I started thinking about my
>   grandchildren.[24]

Barclay had found Bond to be in a bad way during this interview. There were long silences, he had difficulty concentrating, and was frequently on the verge of tears. But if Alan had at last let life get on top of him it was hardly surprising, for even if he was found innocent of the fraud charges being brought against him, he would probably face a year in court to clear his name. And should he be found guilty, he had a long spell in jail to look forward to. On top of that, his empire had collapsed, his marriage had broken apart, and he was constantly pursued by police and press. He had gone from prince to pariah in the public's mind.

Given all these pressures, it was perfectly understandable that he said he sometimes woke in the dead of night, cried easily, didn't want to go out, felt tired, couldn't concentrate, and had lost his enthusiasm for life. In fact, it would have been quite extraordinary if he had not felt like this.

But depression was not the issue. It was whether Bond was mentally capable of instructing his lawyers and of dealing with questions about whether Jurg Bollag had hidden $50 million for him in Jersey and Switzerland. And there was evidence that

Bond was quite alert enough to do both things easily.

In the Mounts Bay Clinic, for example, while supposedly in the depths of despair, he cheered himself up by making phone calls in the middle of the night. Perhaps it was the wonder of Prozac, or possibly it was just insomnia, but in six days in hospital he managed to make seventy-nine phone calls, including a couple to Russia, which suggested strongly that he was still doing business in spite of his many afflictions.

And his improvement continued apace. Just two days after being released from hospital, Bond was seen enjoying himself at a Perth restaurant, and a few days after that he was photographed on the beach at Cottesloe with Diana Bliss, looking 'a picture of health'. According to *Woman's Day* journalist Ian Dougall, he outpaced Di as they swam 200 metres in the surf together, and then swam on while she rested. It was one of those wonderful pieces of writing that includes a paragraph written by lawyers to say that of course there has never been any suggestion that Mr Bond is anything but genuinely ill, yet opens with a sentence like this:

> Alan Bond, who only weeks ago was hospitalised and described as a physical and mental wreck, unable to appear at a bankruptcy hearing, appears to have made a miraculous recovery.[25]

Despite this latest embarrassing revelation, Bond's lawyers told the Federal Court they now had 'clear' new evidence of damage to Alan's brain, the severity of which could not even be assessed until February 1995 (or roughly when Bond's bankruptcy was due to finish). Meanwhile, they said, his major depression was so serious that he would be unable to take the stand even if the brain-damage argument were rejected.

As a consequence, Bond's section 81 examination was again postponed, as was the question of his fitness to face court, which was set down for hearing in mid-April, when a phalanx of twenty-seven experts would line up to do battle.

The first skirmish came on 12 April, by which time Bond's brain damage seemed to have worsened still further. His lawyers now alleged, via a new doctor, that his IQ had dropped by a massive sixty points—from genius level of 150 to near-dolt of ninety. This, said Alan's QC, Tony Howard, had diminished his powers of memory, speech and conversation to such an extent that his doctors believed there was 'a very real question' as to whether he was capable of 'going on at all' in these proceedings.[26]

But before battle could be joined in earnest, Justice Sheppard fired his own warning shot at Bond's army of experts. First of all, he told them he wanted to see Bond for himself; second, he warned that it would be the court (ie, him) and not the doctors who decided whether Bond was fit to testify; third, he had taken evidence from brain-damaged accident victims before and found them to be perfectly capable of answering questions; and fourth, he wished Bond's lawyers would make up their minds whether brain damage or depression was the main reason for Bond's supposed incapacity.

Then he lobbed in the grenade by warning Bond's lawyers that he would not suppress any of the medical evidence that they put forward.

A week later, the battle was over before it had even begun. Bond's adjutants came back to court to run up the white flag. Bond, they said, had now recovered from his depression and would answer all questions put to him. He would no longer argue he was too brain dead to appear, because he did not wish intimate details of his mental health to be revealed in public.

This sudden capitulation looked like total victory for Ramsay and common sense. But in fact it was no such thing, for the court had still not ruled whether Bond was fit to answer questions.

The last thing Ramsay wanted was for Bond to turn the interrogation into a farce by claiming that his memory had failed him, so he asked Justice Sheppard to declare that Bond was mentally capable of taking the stand.

Sheppard declined to give it. He also quit the battlefield, leaving his deputy to referee the contest as Ramsay and Bond shaped up for the most important fight of the bankruptcy. It is customary for judges to leave section 81 examinations to a registrar, but it was a shame that Sheppard chose this absolutely crucial moment to step aside, because his registrar would turn out to be nothing like as tough as he needed to be.

14

Remember Me?

A witness, who having been sworn, deliberately
evades questions by some device may ... be guilty
of contempt. One such device is a feigned inability
to remember.

Justice Brooking[1]

It had taken sixteen months to get Bond onto the stand, but
as soon as he walked into a packed Court 18B at Sydney's
Federal Court, it was obvious that it had all been a waste of
time.

The former America's Cup winner and one-time billionaire
stumbled up the steps looking dazed and confused, as if wan-
dering from the wreckage of a bomb blast. Once in the relative
safety of the witness box, he sat crumpled and listless, a sad,
sick, broken man. From time to time he stole a look around
the courtroom or popped a pill into his mouth, but most of
the time he simply stared into space. His lawyers said he was
on Prozac, but his demeanour suggested he'd been hit with
Largactil, a drug that's notorious for its use on troublesome
prisoners and is widely known as 'the liquid cosh'.

This, of course, was the tragic figure that Bond's lawyers
had told the court to expect, a man whose brain was so

damaged that his IQ had plummeted by sixty points, who was so depressed that he couldn't read more than a couple of sentences without losing the plot.

Even when the simplest of questions was asked of him, he often took ages to answer, then did so in a whisper that was barely audible. Sometimes he would pause for up to a minute as he stared vacantly into space, apparently trying to turn the tumblers in his brain to unlock the information. Watching him as the clock ticked by, you wondered whether he even remembered that he had been asked a question. It was, by turns, pathetic, painful and ridiculous.

This Bond was absurdly different from the bouncing beach ball who had been seen in public only weeks before or the man who had romped in the surf at Cottesloe and given interviews to Channel 9 about his yachting triumphs. As Peter Smark from the *Sydney Morning Herald* acidly observed:

> Gone were the smile, the bounce, the healthy glow; his hair was sparser and carelessly done, the trademark Rolex had been replaced by a cheap plastic number, the dark suit and silk tie were chosen carefully enough to be wholly respectable, but he seemed slumped into them, somehow shrunken. From this man who has sold projects, concepts, vast acreage and, above all, himself all his life, yesterday one would have bought little on offer. The old confidence seemed wholly gone. On show there seemed to be a man who had lost almost everything.[2]

At the end of the proceedings, Bond would be asked by his lawyer to tell the court how sick he was, but hour by hour his demeanour said it all. He had been depressed, had undergone major surgery, had suffered several strokes which had seriously interfered with his memory. 'There are spots that I can remember quite clearly,' said Bond, 'and others that I just can't remember at all.' Conveniently, everything about Jersey and its network of offshore trusts and companies was right off his radar. 'It is the 1990s now,' said Bond. 'I don't remember anything. It's just too long ago.'[3]

It was not just the details that escaped him, it was the very principle that he couldn't be sure of. Four or five times he was manoeuvred into a specific denial, or forced to adopt the formula that he did not believe something to be so. But a hundred times or more he simply repeated the mantra that he could not recall.

It was clear from the start that Ramsay's barrister, Francis Douglas QC, was in for a difficult time, and that Bond was not going to roll over and cooperate. But he must have felt that he had surprise on his side, for Bond had no idea about the wealth of evidence that Ramsay had gathered on his trip to St Helier. He did not know, for example, that the two partners of Touche Ross had given evidence on oath that they had run companies and trusts for him containing millions of dollars. Nor could he have guessed that Douglas had uncovered a paper trail showing Bond to be the beneficiary of trusts and the owner of undeclared bank accounts. Finally, and perhaps best of all, he would not have suspected for a moment that his interrogator would be holding two letters of instruction to Touche Ross from 1982 and 1987 that Alan himself had signed.

Douglas started off by enquiring whether Bond recalled Bob Ramsay asking him in November 1992 whether he had ever had contact with solicitors, accountants or financial advisers in Jersey. Bond had replied at the time: 'Not to my knowledge in relation to my personal affairs'. So did he still hold to that answer, he was asked? He agreed that he did.[4]

Soon afterwards, Douglas put the first key question to Bond directly on oath, and elicited the following exchange, in the style of dozens that would follow:

Douglas: Did you at any time during the 1980s give instructions to any other person for the setting up of an offshore trust in relation to your personal affairs?

Bond: I don't recall.

Douglas: Is it possible that you may have done that and you do not now recall?

Bond: I think if you have some information you might show it to me. It might refresh my memory but I can't recall.

Douglas: Do the best you can Mr Bond.

Bond: I can't remember anything.

Douglas: You cannot remember it?

Bond: No.

Douglas: The question I put to you is, is it possible that you may have done so but you do not now recall?

Bond: I just don't remember.

Douglas: You do not remember?

Bond: No.

Douglas: Do you think you might have?

Bond: I just don't remember.

Douglas: You have no recollection at all.

Bond: No I don't.

Douglas: You have no recollection at all of giving any

> instructions to any other person for the setting
> up of an offshore trust in relation to your
> personal affairs during the 1980s?
>
> Bond: I don't remember.[5]

Were Alan Bond to be reincarnated as a squirrel, he would be
a very thin one. Not only could he not recall where his nuts
were hidden, he had forgotten whether he had any.

Bond was next asked by Douglas whether he had given
instructions to his family lawyer Harry Lodge or to the Dallhold managing director Robert Pearce to set up offshore trusts
or companies for him, or whether he had told any overseas
advisers to accept instructions from those people. Once again,
Bond could not remember. He had dealt with hundreds of
thousands of transactions, he said, and his personal affairs had
been interwoven with those of Dallhold and Bond Corporation, and it was all too long ago.

Well what about Touche Ross in Jersey, he was asked. Had
he told Touche Ross in the early 1980s to accept instructions from Robert Pearce regarding his personal affairs? This
drew a complete blank. The name Touche Ross rang no bells
at all.

> Bond: I don't remember Touche Ross at all.
> Douglas: You do not remember Touche Ross at all.
> Bond: No.[6]

After a couple more attempts to get an admission from Bond
by rephrasing the question, Douglas then tried to get a denial:

> Douglas: So, Mr Bond, what I'm asking you is this. Do
>   you deny ever having dealings with Messrs

> Touche Ross on the island of Jersey in any
> capacity during the 1980s?
>
> Bond: I just don't remember the name Touche Ross
> at all.
>
> Douglas: Not at all?
>
> Bond: No.[7]

Douglas then produced the letter that Bond himself had signed in 1982 telling the partners of Touche Ross to accept instructions from Robert Pearce, in relation to (as Bond had put it) 'any matters associated with me'. But this didn't jog his memory either:

> Douglas: Just let me show you a letter. Do you agree
> with me that that is your signature?
>
> Bond: Yes, that's my signature.
>
> Douglas: And do you agree with me that on 26 May
> 1982 you instructed the partners of Touche
> Ross & Co at St Helier, Jersey, in the
> Channel Islands, to accept instructions from
> Robert Ashley Pearce concerning any matters
> associated with you?
>
> Bond: That's what this document says.
>
> Douglas: That document having been put before you,
> do you now recall signing it?
>
> Bond: No, I don't.
>
> Douglas: Do you recall what it was about?
>
> Bond: No, I don't.
>
> Douglas: You do not know?
>
> Bond: No, I don't.
>
> Douglas: You have no recollection?

Bond: No, I don't.

Douglas: And seeing that letter does not assist you in
           any way in refreshing your recollection as to
           what dealings you may or may not have had
           with Touche Ross on the island of Jersey
           during the 1980s?

Bond: No, it doesn't.[8]

Similarly, Bond had no memory of his second letter dated February 1987, in which he had told Touche Ross to accept instructions from Robert Pearce, John Bond, Harry Lodge and Jurg Bollag (as he had put it) 'in relation to my affairs', although he could hardly deny that he had signed it or dispute what it said.

Bond protested that 'my affairs' and 'any matters associated with me' could easily have meant Bond Corporation or Dallhold—which was hardly credible—then returned to the story that he could not remember Touche Ross, and certainly could not recall ever having contacted them.

This pantomime continued for most of the first morning in court and resumed after the lunch break, with Douglas asking Bond specifically about Jurg Bollag:

Douglas: Did you ever instruct Touche Ross in Jersey
           to accept instructions from Mr Jurg Bollag in
           relation to your affairs?

Bond: I don't remember the name Touche Ross at
           all; it hasn't come back to me over lunch.

Douglas: See, what I want to suggest to you is that
           after early 1987 Touche Ross used to act on
           instructions from four people on your behalf,
           including Jurg Bollag.

Bond: I have no knowledge of that at the present
           time.
Douglas: Would you deny it?
Bond: I don't remember anything about it.
Douglas: But do you deny it?
Bond: I don't remember.
Douglas: So you are not able to confirm or deny that
           fact. Is that what you're saying?
Bond: I just don't remember.[9]

Then, finally, we arrived at the essence of Bond's position:

Douglas: Mr Bond, what I am putting to you is
           this ... from 1978 through until 1986 there
           were many companies and trusts which were
           set up in relation to your personal affairs by
           Touche Ross on the island of Jersey, and
           they administered many millions of dollars on
           your behalf on the instructions firstly, of
           Mr Harry Lodge up until 1982 and from
           1982 through to 1986 on the instructions of
           Mr Pearce and that you knew about that fact
           at the time?
Bond: I have no recollection of that. I don't know
           whether that is correct or not.
Douglas: Would you deny it?
Bond: I have no recollection of it.[10]

What a strange life it must have been. Here were two partners
of a firm of accountants in Jersey swearing on the Bible that
they had administered millions of dollars for Alan Bond until
the late 1980s. And here was Bond swearing in court on a

similar oath that he just could not recall whether these millions were his. It really beggared belief.

What was also incredible was that Bond seemed not in the least excited to discover he had so much hidden wealth. Douglas at one point produced a letter from the settlor of the Icarus Trust, John Charles West Sauvary, who was writing to Touche Ross's tame trustee company in 1983 to tell them that the assets in the trust were: 'principally . . . for the benefit of Alan Bond . . . and his family'. Douglas then asked Bond whether news of this windfall came as a complete surprise to him:

> Bond: Yes, it does.
>
> Douglas: It comes as a complete surprise that this trust was set up for your benefit and the benefit of your family in Jersey in 1983.
>
> Bond: Yes, it does. I've never seen it before.
>
> Douglas: Do you accept that that trust was in fact set up for your benefit and the benefit of your family?
>
> Bond: I don't know.[11]

It has always seemed to me that one of the key qualities of successful tycoons is an extraordinary nerve and a capacity to swear that black is white, without apparent difficulty. And Bond certainly had this ability in spades. He also revealed himself, as the examination went on, to be a master of the red herring and the irrelevant half-truth. Time after time, Bond would succeed in diverting the flow of Douglas's enquiries, and time after time a huge effort would be needed to paddle back to the original question. A judge in Victoria, Justice Beach, once famously described the process of getting to grips with one of Bond's corporate transactions as 'like dealing with a large and slippery octopus', and it must have been the same for Douglas trying to deal with Bond himself. Reading the transcript five years later, it is hard to see how he avoided losing his temper or screaming in frustration, yet he remained patient and persistent 99 per cent of the time.

In the middle of the first afternoon, Douglas produced a trump card that he had probably hoped would make Bond chuck in his hand. This was the 230-page transcript of the Jersey court examination of the two Touche Ross partners who swore they had looked after Bond companies. As soon became clear, their testimony was backed up by a huge number of banking documents from the Allied Irish Banks that showed the transfer of millions of dollars belonging to Bond. Bit by bit, the outline of this story was now unveiled, with glimpses of paintings and houses and horses and bank accounts that Bond and his family had enjoyed. The story of Bollag was also revealed—of how he had arrived on the scene in late 1986 or early 1987 to take over the running of Bond's personal affairs and had moved the companies to Switzerland.

The huge detail of these revelations and the very fact that the Jersey accountants had talked must have been a huge shock to Bond, yet it was still not enough to get him to admit anything, least of all that Jurg Bollag controlled his money.

> Douglas: What I want to suggest to you is that Mr Bollag has under his control many millions of dollars which belong to you personally and which is used by him on your behalf to finance property and other investment transactions, both internationally and here in Australia.
>
> Bond: I don't believe that to be true at all.[12]

Douglas: The true situation is that you tell Mr Bollag what to do, Mr Bollag tells Touche Ross what to do and Touche Ross does it, and you distance yourself from these transactions because you want to be able ... to deny having anything to do with these companies or their assets because you do not want them to become available to your trustee in bankruptcy.

Bond: Well, that's a figure [*sic*] of your imagination and that's not supported by the facts.[13]

Later, Douglas asked about Bollag's company JF Consulting, which had changed its name in January 1987 from Crasujo, and suggested that this had been done because the name was dangerous, since it was clearly based on the names of Bond's children: Craig, Susanne and John or Jody.

Bond: I think that's a figure [*sic*] of your imagination. I don't know how you can possibly get the names of children into the word Crasujo.

Douglas: Well, it's not difficult really, is it Mr Bond? C.R.A.—Craig, S.U.—Susanne, J.O. John or Jody.

Bond: But then we could have—Bond T-shirts were named after me because the name Bond was used.

Douglas: No one will dispute that Mr Bond because they were around well before you came to Australia.

Bond: All I'm saying is that it's just a collection of letters that I don't think has any relationship.[14]

Towards the end of a gruelling first day, Douglas produced his second trump card: Harry Lodge's handwritten notes from 1984, which mentioned Engetal, Pianola, Icarus Trust, Kirk Holdings, and a raft of others. Once again there were houses, horses and paintings that these companies had owned, and there was the fact that Bond's personal lawyer had been taking notes about them in Jersey as he sat in Touche Ross's office.

Maybe it was because he had by now spent almost six hours in the witness box, or maybe it was the line of questioning, but Bond cracked for the first time. On the verge of tears, his voice wobbling with emotion, he challenged Douglas to remember what he was doing in 1987, asking him what he would make of bits of paper 'thrown' in front of him and how much he would remember:

> Bond: I don't have that ability, and I've told you
>   that ... I am getting very upset.
> Registrar: I can see that.
> Bond: And I've had enough, frankly ... I've had
>   enough and I don't need to go on anymore.
> Registrar: Just take it easy there, Mr Bond.
> Bond: I don't want to sit there and be tricked by
>   somebody that takes two lines out of
>   something, and it is just not fair on me.[15]

And with that, Round One came to a close, and battle was adjourned for the day.

Next morning, Douglas came straight back to the subject of Kirk Holdings, which had been the most important company in Bond's Jersey empire.

> Douglas: I would suggest to you it was a company

which you used frequently during the 1980s
as a means of acquiring investments, painting,
jewellery and other items of that nature.

Bond: I don't recall the name of Kirk Holdings in
the 1980s or 70s or whenever you assert that
the company was formed.

Douglas: It just strikes no bell at all.

Bond: No, I'm afraid it doesn't.[16]

Bond's failure to recall Kirk Holdings was harder to accept than his other memory lapses, not least because he would have learnt all about the company from *Four Corners* in July 1993, just ten months earlier. This had exposed Kirk as a Bollag company that had bought paintings and horses and held millions of dollars in Jersey bank accounts. And given that Bond had threatened to sue over this program, one would have thought that he would have watched it closely. Kirk had also been discussed in the press several times since, and Bond had actually sworn an affidavit about the company in 1988 during his daughter Susanne's divorce proceedings. He had told a New Jersey court that Kirk owned two of his daughter's showjumpers, Nicky and Puntero, and Bollag had sworn a statement at the same time admitting that Kirk was run by him. These statements were both quoted back to Bond by Francis Douglas, but he still maintained that he could not recall swearing the affidavit, had never heard of the company, could not recall anything about it and did not know who owned it.

Bond would also have known about Kirk because it had once paid him a large amount of money. On 12 December 1986, US$2.75 million had been sent from the company's account in Jersey to Alan's personal account at the London merchant bank

Arbuthnot Latham, with explicit instructions from the Jersey end that no mention of Kirk Holdings should be made on the transfer. Douglas reminded Bond of this, asking him why such secrecy had been needed and what he had done with the money, to which Bond replied: 'I have no idea'.

> Douglas: No idea? You receive US$2.75 million into your personal account and you've no idea what you did with it?
>
> Bond: No, I couldn't tell you the ins and outs of the accounts . . .
>
> Douglas: So you've no idea what you did with that money?
>
> Bond: No, I don't.[17]

Bond repeated his various denials about Kirk Holdings some thirty or forty times until Douglas finally tired of the charade and at last voiced what others in court had been waiting for:

> Douglas: I want to suggest to you, Mr Bond, that you are deliberately and consciously lying to me.
>
> Bond: You said that yesterday and I got very upset . . . so I think if you want to call me a liar, I am calling you one.
>
> Douglas: And I also want to suggest this, that you are deliberately feigning a lack of recollection of these matters because you do not wish to admit to any interest in these trusts or companies which were set up in Jersey on your behalf during the 1980s.
>
> Bond: I object to that. You have had documented medical evidence from Professor Cala[18] and

from other eminent neurologists which show
quite clearly that the strokes that I had are on
the right side of my brain and I have gone to
great length to do the best I can in my
memory and you know that to be so because
you have had the benefit of looking at the
documents together with other psychological
reports which would support that I have done
the very best I can. There are some things I
just don't remember and I have tried to tell
you that.[19]

Since Bond's apparent loss of memory had become the central
issue in this examination, I decided to subject Bond to my own
practical test. We had only met once before, which was the
same number of times that Bond had been to Jersey, but I had
made a couple of programs about him for the ABC and written
his unauthorised biography, so I was sure that he would know
who I was. I had not bargained, however, for the electric
manner in which he would react to me. As he arrived at the
hearing for the third and last day, I walked up alongside him
with the cameras running, and handed him a business card,
saying as I did so: 'Mr Bond, Paul Barry from *Four Corners*,
remember me?'. Bond stared at the card as if it was a snake,
then dropped it onto the pavement and ground it into the
tarmac with his shoe. 'So you do remember me?' I asked. 'Keep
right away from me,' he replied. 'Keep right away from me.'[20]

Parts of Bond's memory were obviously working, even if
Jurg Bollag and Jersey were covered in a convenient fog. But
the court apparently had no desire to probe the obvious question of whether he was faking amnesia about subjects that
might incriminate him. Instead, Registrar Howard listened

sympathetically to Bond's lawyer complain about the outrageous way in which his client had been impeded on his way into
court, and then asked the same lawyer to warn members of
the media not to harass Mr Bond again in this manner. And
after that, the charade of Bond's failure to recall was allowed
to resume.

On the third day of proceedings, however, Alan's mask of
memory loss slipped for just a moment, when he suddenly displayed a dazzling command of detail. Bond was asked by his
own lawyer to explain why he had considered giving Bollag
a hugely valuable option that would have sent $100 million a
year tax-free to Jurg's company in the Isle of Man (see page
58).

Suddenly, the brain-damaged zombie was replaced by the
1980s dealmaker, with a head full of numbers whose signifi-
cance he obviously understood, even if no one else could:

Bond: Well, there was a profit already made in
Queensland Nickel because the Queensland
Nickel debts were acquired as a billion dollars
of debts by Standard Chartered with his
assistance. He had an option for $3 million
over those debts, providing Standard &
Chartered were paid out $100 million. So the
whole of Queensland Nickel would have gone
to the hands of George Bollag and it is in that
context that he had agreed with me verbally,
because we hadn't finally documented,
although there may have been structures
attempted to be put into place, that we would
share the net gain, because there was no point
in having a billion dollar debt in one group

and paying that. Now that debt was paid down to $50 million. Mr Bollag could have arranged the $50 million to pay out the Standard Chartered Bank, but at the request of myself and Michael Cross he was convinced to allow the Hongkong Bank and Tricontinental to take a first security and he would take a second position. But it was on the understanding that they would have a long-term loan. He would not have given that consent for a six-month loan because he was entitled to the whole of the debts that went prior to the Hongkong and Tricontinental debt, so he gave up his position in the expectation that the $300 or $225 million loan as being provided by the Hongkong Bank and Tricontinental could have been serviced and the loan could have been repaid back and he stood to gain half of that amount of $350 million at least.[21]

This did not appear to be a man who was so brain-damaged that he had forgotten whether he had stashed millions of dollars overseas. But I doubt whether anyone who watched Alan Bond's examination for those three days in court, or read about it in the press, actually believed his claims of brain damage and amnesia. So why on earth did the Federal Court let him get away with his ridiculous performance?

Certainly, the court had plenty of power to punish him, either under the *Bankruptcy Act 1966*, which makes it an offence to refuse to answer questions in a section 81 examination, or via the wider law of contempt, which allows judges to throw witnesses in jail for refusal to answer questions.

And, crucially, the case law on contempt contains a famous example where a Victorian Supreme Court judge threw a witness in prison in 1978 for claiming that he had lost his memory. As Justice Brooking told the court:

> A witness, who having been sworn, deliberately evades questions by some device may similarly be guilty of contempt. One such device is a feigned inability to remember. The witness who deliberately evades questions by falsely swearing that he cannot recall interferes with or obstructs the due administration of justice just as much as the witness who openly and directly refuses to answer those questions ... A court must have the power to punish for contempt the liar who parries questions with a pretended inability to remember.[22]

Interestingly enough, Brooking's witness had marshalled four doctors to testify that his concentration and memory were impaired. One said he was suffering from acute anxiety; another said this anxiety had possibly impaired his memory; a third insisted his symptoms were genuine; and a fourth ventured that his memory was probably impaired by depression. Brooking, however, was swayed by none of them.

> My own assessment of (the witness) is that he is a sly and thoroughly untruthful person, well capable of misleading members of the medical profession for his own purposes.[23]

There was, as everybody now knew, a range of medical

opinion about how mentally incapable Bond had become by May 1994. Psychiatrists hired by his lawyers said he was depressed and brain-damaged; experts hired by his trustee in bankruptcy said there was next to nothing wrong with him and that he was malingering.

But no one was in a better position to judge Bond's mental state in mid-1994 than the friends who were doing business with him. Jim Byrnes, who saw him regularly at the time, says simply that Alan's 'brain damage' was all an act. Bond would be fine one moment as they walked down the street together, then suddenly slump his shoulders because he had spotted a camera. Between court appearances, he says, Bond exhibited extraordinary command of detail in a whole series of business deals. He concludes bluntly: 'There was nothing wrong with him'.[24]

Another Sydney businessman, Neil Cunningham, who did business with Alan Bond throughout 1994, is equally adamant that Bond was not brain-damaged. Cunningham says that heart surgery may have made him marginally less sharp than he had been before, but only by a matter of five per cent or so. And he sums up Bond's claims of ill health and memory loss as 'a pantomime'.[25]

Luke Atkins, yet another who did business with Bond in late 1993 and early 1994, simply laughs at the suggestion that there was anything wrong with him. In fact, to the people around him, Alan's performance obviously was a huge joke. And, remember, these were not Bond's pursuers or adversaries but business partners and friends.

Justice Brooking was not the only judge to think that the legal system needed to be protected from liars. In backing his decision on appeal, the High Court of Australia referred to a case from 1953 when a bankrupt called Charles Coward had been jailed for a similar contempt. Coward had been 'examined up hill and down dale for weeks' over his financial affairs and had eventually been hauled before a judge who had asked a series of questions himself and then concluded that: 'A substantial part of the answers ... represented in my opinion a shuffling and fantastic attempt to conceal the truth about the bankrupt's dealings'. The judge had sent Coward to jail and told him he could come out when he was prepared to return to the court and give some 'proper answers'.[26]

Sadly, no such judicial bravery was to be seen in the Bond case, even though Bond now proceeded to repeat the trick with the Dallhold liquidator John Lord, turning this examination into a farce as well, by claiming that he had forgotten almost everything.

Three times, Bond said he was too sick to continue and needed to see a doctor, complaining that he was suffering chest pains and dizzy spells. And three times the examination was interrupted. Eventually, John Lord agreed to postpone the hearings for a month, and finally he abandoned them altogether.[27]

Weeks later, he must have cursed his decision, because it became clear how busy Bond had been during the week of the hearings. Telephone records from the Sheraton Wentworth Hotel, subpoenaed by Bob Ramsay, showed that the 'ailing' entrepreneur had spent his time outside the courtroom making calls to Switzerland, the USA, the UK, India, Pakistan and Singapore. He had also made two dozen calls to a businessman in Australia with whom he was setting up a gold deal.

In the week of the Dallhold examination, when he had appeared so pale, uncertain, incoherent and incomprehensible, Bond had sent eight faxes and made sixty-five international calls at a cost of some $1,360, including one costing $66.50

to a phone box at Zurich railway station, six lengthy calls to the Zurich Hilton and one to a number in Zug that the Swiss authorities identified as the Zuger Kantonal Bank. It was as if he magically recovered as soon as he left the court, then became afflicted again once he took the stand.

Yet not even this revelation was enough to cause the court to march him back into the witness box and make him answer the questions properly. Nor was it enough to cause anyone to threaten him with jail for contempt.[28]

The insolvency laws in Australia are among the most powerful weapons in this country's legal arsenal. Based on the tax acts, they give liquidators and trustees in bankruptcy the same sort of powers that the taxman possesses—to seize documents and examine people on oath. But even the toughest laws only work if they are properly enforced. And throughout Bond's crucial examination on oath, the Federal Court had palpably failed to enforce this one.

Instead, Bond had been allowed to make a public fool of the justice system with his claims of brain damage and memory loss. And the court had neither insisted that he answer the questions nor punished him when he failed to do so. Thus, the best opportunity to locate and recover Bond's fortune had been allowed to slip away.

Quite simply, Bond had been allowed to get away with it yet again.

15

Faking It

We'll blow up your car. We'll get you one day. It can happen any time. You could be dead any minute.

Threat to witness in Bond trial, 1994[1]

Fresh from their success in deflecting questions about his business affairs, Bond and his lawyers now tried to give the ill-health argument yet another crack in the hope of getting his trial on the $15 million Manet fraud charges put off a second time, or even for good. And once again, Alan put on a command performance.

When the hearing opened in Perth on 26 May 1994, he arrived at court looking dazed and disorientated and had to be ushered to a private room by his psychiatrist Dr Tannenbaum. An hour later, his lawyer Tony Howard QC told magistrate Ivan Brown that Alan might well collapse if he had to give evidence. He had supposedly vomited on being told he had to come to court and was showing signs of an incipient stroke. As a consequence, his psychiatrist wanted to re-admit him to the Mounts Bay Clinic immediately for observation and treatment. The magistrate had been told initially by Bond's lawyers that Alan was too ill to come to court, but had insisted on seeing for himself. Now he clearly had no option but to send the entrepreneur off to hospital and continue the hearing without him.

Shortly afterwards, Bond emerged from court to confront the waiting news media looking like a man who had seen a ghost. Supported by his lawyer on one side and his doctor on the other, the once-great dealmaker was apparently unable to walk unaided and had to be helped along step by step. His coat was ill-fitting, his face grey and crumpled. He looked, as he had in Sydney three weeks earlier, like a man laid low by sickness and ill fortune.

Together with the evidence that his doctors would give in his absence, this might well have been enough to send Bond's Manet trial the same way as his crucial bankruptcy hearings. But unfortunately for him, the scene was being watched on the television news on the other side of Australia by a man who knew Bond well. And when he saw Alan looking so ill he almost fell off his chair in amazement. Lionel Berck had been with the stricken entrepreneur only thirty-six hours earlier in the Whitsunday Islands and had seen absolutely nothing wrong with him. There, in the hot Queensland sun, Bond had been walking, snorkelling, climbing a rocky creek bed, and bouncing around like a five-year-old. And mentally he had been in tip-top shape.

It seemed inconceivable that his health could have deteriorated so dramatically in less than two days. But the only other explanation for Alan's sudden collapse was that it was an act, and an Oscar-winning one at that. And before long Berck and his partners would be rushed across to Perth to suggest that to the court.

Nine months earlier, Bond had agreed to buy an island

called St Bees from Berck's family for $6.5 million, and they had been deep in discussions ever since. During all that time, when his doctors were swearing on oath that he was seriously brain-damaged and depressed, and incapable of adding two and two to make four, Bond had been nutting out the details of a grandiose plan to turn St Bees into another resort like Hamilton Island.

There was nothing wrong with this as a business proposition, for St Bees had coral reefs and eight or nine fabulous beaches of brilliant white sand, and was well suited to tourist development. But as a bankrupt, Bond wasn't allowed to run a company or handle millions of dollars, and his doctors and lawyers had sworn many times that he was mentally incapable of doing any such thing.

However, as Lionel Berck, his son Peter, and their business partner John Urch soon testified, the Alan Bond they had dealt with was a very different person from the pathetic brain-damaged specimen that his psychiatrists had been describing.

As each told Perth Magistrates' Court in June 1994, Bond had first visited the island the previous October, two weeks before Dr John Saunders had pronounced him unfit to brief his lawyers. He had flown into St Bees with Diana Bliss and a Sydney solicitor, Warwick Colbron, arriving by hired helicopter at noon, and within three hours had asked a series of pertinent questions, knocked the price down by $3.5 million and shaken hands on a deal to buy the island. Then without further ado, he had boarded the chopper and headed off again.

So had he appeared brain-damaged, John Urch was asked? Absolutely not, Urch replied. Bond had been as sharp as a tack, taken copious notes, led the negotiations and been in command of large amounts of detail.

Only two days after closing this St Bees deal, Bond had been examined by Tim Watson-Munro and diagnosed as 'fragile, suicidal and depressed'. The psychologist had also identified a thirty-point fall in Bond's IQ and had later testified in court that his charge was so badly brain-damaged that he couldn't run a corner store. So, he was now asked by prosecuting counsel, was this diagnosis consistent with the evidence given by Berck and Urch? Well, no, said Watson-Munro, he had to agree it was not.

In the four months after this first trip to St Bees in October 1993, Bond had met the owners of the island three more times, eventually beating the sale price down further to one-third of what they had been asking. Berck and Urch, who had dealt with Bond on each occasion, told the court that they felt he was not sick at all and had been 100 per cent fit. In fact, he had impressed them as the most formidable businessman they had ever met.

Urch's evidence in particular was hard to challenge, because he had kept a diary of his every meeting and phone conversation with Bond, in which he had also recorded the daily weather report and exchange rate for the Australian dollar. In the magistrate's view, he was 'a gem of a witness' whose evidence and diaries could be relied on.

These diaries, which Urch had been keeping since the age of fifteen, laid out the negotiations blow by blow, day by day and week by week, and showed Bond to be a man who asked a lot of good questions, who appreciated the financial, legal and technical issues involved and who could redraft a sale agreement to order. This Bond was no sorry, shambling nervous wreck who could not remember the names of his ocean racers. He was an energetic, aggressive businessman and the toughest talker John Urch had ever encountered.

The negotiations to buy St Bees had continued throughout

the period in which Bond was limping in and out of court and breaking down in doctors' surgeries. And the climax in February 1994 had come when he was supposedly at his psychological nadir, just before he was rushed into the Mounts Bay Clinic for six days of treatment. On this occasion he had met Urch in Sydney and rewritten the sale contract on two sheets of foolscap paper. Thereafter, he had continued to deal with legal matters concerning St Bees from his hospital bed in Perth, when he wasn't busy phoning Switzerland, Austria and Russia. In other words, he had continued to do business with the Bercks and others, while swearing on oath that he was suicidally depressed and so brain-damaged that he couldn't brief his lawyers or remember his offshore millions.

Alan had also left a physical record of his activity on St Bees in the shape of a huge phone bill. The Bercks' normal telephone account ran to two pages and could be paid from petty cash, but after Bond had been there they received a demand for $3,000 with a list of sixteen pages of mainly international calls, to Southeast Asia, England, Canada, America, Russia and other places besides.

This account of course, had only covered those times that Bond and his fellow visitors had used the Bercks' phone instead of the mobiles they all had brought with them. Diana Bliss had apparently been on a mobile phone constantly, both on her own account and, according to Lionel Berck, for Alan.

A:	At one stage I think there was nine people there and something like thirteen or fourteen phones. She kept phoning and passing the phone on to Alan and then she'd be off with another one calling somebody else and then that one would go off to Alan. She was organising.

Q: So she'd get people on the phone for Alan?

A: Yep.[2]

Lionel Berck's son Peter also gave important evidence about Bond's physical and mental state before his vaudeville appearance on the first day of the Manet hearing, when he had apparently been so unwell that he had had to be carried off to hospital. Bond had bushwalked, snorkelled, jogged along the beach and helped launch a metal dinghy on the island only two days earlier, said Berck. He had then asked Peter to book him a 6.00am flight back to Perth for 25 May, saying that he had to appear in court the day after. According to Berck, he had not been in the least bothered by the prospect of appearing.

There was no question that this first-hand evidence was dynamite, for the court had been subjected to a week of mind-boggling detail about MRI scans, ECGs and cerebral blood flows, and to teams of experts asserting that Bond was either perfectly well or shockingly sick. And this was hard evidence that there was nothing wrong with the man.

Up to this point, Bond might well have escaped facing trial. Now the magistrate Ivan Brown had no hesitation in deciding that the entrepreneur was fit enough to take the stand. The evidence of Berck and Urch had been crucial, he said.

Sadly, however, he did not go the next step to rule on whether Bond was faking his ailments to avoid facing justice. The best he could say was that he found the evidence of the medical experts 'conflicting' and 'indecisive' and was glad he did not have to make a diagnosis. He was prepared to accept that Bond probably had minor brain damage, though not to the extent that he or his doctors had suggested, and was inclined to believe that Bond was suffering from 'reactive depression', which in simple language meant only that he got upset when he came near a courtroom. But he was not prepared to take Bond to task.

And so another great opportunity was lost. If one believed the evidence of Urch and Berck, as the magistrate did, one could hardly avoid the conclusion that Bond had wasted court time, treated the law with contempt and made fools of a string of medical experts. But once again, he was not to be punished for it, nor even warned. Even a tongue-lashing would have been something, but instead there was silence.

There was also silence at the time about the fact that one of these vital witnesses received death threats. On Urch's second day in the witness box, his son had fielded a phone call at his Sydney home in which a man threatened to kill Urch and his family if he continued to give evidence against Bond. And John himself later received similar threats.

> A: They'd say, 'We'll blow up your car. We'll get you one day. It can happen at any time. You could be dead any minute'. My wife left the house for a while. I went down to the police station ... they would drive up and down my street and check.
>
> Q: So they never found out who made the calls, never traced them?
>
> A: No, no. My son who does security work around town he said he thought he knew the voice.[3]

The police discovered where one of these calls had come from. Modern technology makes it a snack to do a trace, unlike in the old black-and-white movies where the caller needed to be held on the line. But it had come from a phone in a public place to which any number of people might have had access, so they were never able to track down the culprit.

However, it is hard to see how anybody unconnected with the hearings could have known Urch's name. He had been flown over to Perth by the police in conditions of great secrecy, and his name had been suppressed by order of the court.

Death threats apart, the story of how Urch and Berck came to give evidence at all is quite extraordinary. Essentially it came down to the enterprise of a man who was then in charge of a team called the Bond Task Force.

Tim Phillipps had spent fifteen years working for the fraud squad and the Australian Securities Commission (ASC), but with his close-cropped hair, wire-rimmed glasses and sharp suits he looked less like a cop than a high-powered political adviser. At the tender age of thirty-five, he was in charge of a team of around twenty investigators trying to bring charges against Bond for the biggest fraud in Australian history, in which some $1,200 million had been removed from Robert Holmes à Court's old flagship company, Bell Resources.

Back in 1988, as Bond Corporation and Dallhold had lurched towards insolvency, Alan and his head honchos had gained control of Bell on the cheap, appointed themselves directors and siphoned off the cash from its coffers in a vain attempt to keep the Bond empire afloat. These millions had then been lost when the Bond ship inevitably sank with all hands.

Since then, various teams of investigators from the Australian Federal Police (AFP) and the Australian Securities Commission had spent almost six years trying to bring Bond to trial. And Alan's alleged ill health, come May 1994, threatened to put all this work at risk, for if his lawyers were able to persuade the court that he was too sick to answer the Manet charges, there was every possibility he would also avoid a far longer and more complicated trial on fraud charges relating to Bell.

Around this time, the Bond Task Force was being bombarded with phone calls from people claiming to have seen Bond in sparkling good health in cafés, restaurants and on the beach, or to have driven him round town in a taxi. And while none of these fifty-odd witnesses could really be used in court, Phillipps was encouraged to believe that it was worth following Bond's movements to see if they could prove that his illness was a sham. So for three weeks a team of twelve people from the Australian Federal Police kept Bond under twenty-four-hour surveillance while five members of the Bond Task Force chased up the leads. And before long they stumbled upon St Bees.

Phillipps won't say exactly how they got the information, but they had an informant whose identity they wished to protect, so their discovery presented them with a terrible dilemma. If they rushed Berck and Urch into court they would burn the informant and blow the surveillance operation. On the other hand, if the court did not hear their evidence, Bond might escape trial, and six years work would be wasted. Luckily, at the last moment, Tim Watson-Munro spared them the choice by telling the court that Bond had been to St Bees Island to rest on doctors' advice. This gave them the excuse they needed to follow the lead, and Phillipps himself jumped on a plane to Queensland, hired a helicopter to fly to St Bees, and took statements from the Bercks and Urch.[4] The witnesses were then rushed across to Perth and hustled into court, which allowed two twelve-hour hearing days so that they could complete their evidence.

According to Phillipps, the AFP's surveillance operation turned up a lot of other information suggesting Bond was not sick, which the police felt unable to use in court. One such suggestion was that Bond's shambling state had been induced by drugs that he was taking.

Strangely enough, this explanation was remarkably similar to the one that Bond used to London's *Daily Telegraph Magazine* in November 1994, when asked to account for his dramatic recovery, which allowed him to look 'sparkling' almost as soon as the bankruptcy examination finished. Bond told the *Telegraph*'s aptly named Paul Spike that it was the drugs he had been prescribed that made him look so ill. As soon as he stopped taking them, he said, he had instantly got better.

By the time he spoke to the *Telegraph*, Bond was openly in great form, showing no signs of either sickness or brain damage. 'During the three days I spent in Perth in Bond's company, I saw no evidence of memory loss,' Spike told *Telegraph* readers. 'He was able to cite many exact sums, including what his parents paid for their first house back in 1953.'[5]

But even in July 1994, when Bond finally faced the start of committal proceedings on the Manet fraud charges, which was only a month after his collapse in court, his health appeared to have undergone quite remarkable improvement. As the *Sydney Morning Herald* eagerly observed:

> The former America's Cup hero strode into court, vigorously reorganised the Bar table furniture and engaged his solicitor, Mr Andrew Fraser, in busy discussion. While waiting for the case to start, Bond read documents and made notes.[6]

So had Bond's doctors been duped all along?

Tim Watson-Munro was asked in June 1995 about Bond's return to health and said that he could quite understand why someone should raise the question of whether Bond had really been ill. 'All I can say is I stand by my opinion,' he told the *Bulletin*, 'I don't resile from it at all.'[7]

Alan's friend John Saunders was also quite confident that he had made the right call, even though he had said in December 1993 that there was no doubt that Bond had suffered brain damage, and even though he had specifically told Bond's lawyers, 'There seems to be no improvement in these problems and no likelihood of any improvement in the foreseeable future'.[8]

Seven months later, Saunders apparently had enough faith in his mate's mental abilities to consider engaging in a speculative gold deal with Bond. Asked whether it was possible for a friend to give unbiased evidence, he replied, 'It's difficult, but it's possible', adding that it all came down to honesty.[9]

Whether it was his or Alan's honesty he was talking about wasn't clear. But truthfulness had never been Bond's long suit, and he had never cared much about the rules either—which was why, in 1994, he was defying the law by continuing to do business while still a bankrupt.

16

Money, Money, Money

Alan said to Jim, 'Give Luke some money'. Then Jim
took $10,000 cash out of his pocket and gave it to
me ... Now this was ten o'clock in the morning and
we were in a crowded restaurant.

Luke Atkins with Bond and Byrnes in 1994[1]

In his double-breasted suit and striped business shirt, Luke
Atkins looked prosperous, conservative and almost avun-
cular, much like an English merchant banker.

And when he first met Bond in October 1993 in Sydney's
Ritz Carlton Hotel he was a banker of sorts, in that he was
the co-owner of a flashy new outfit called Asia Pacific, which
had just put up its shingle in North Sydney, styling itself a
boutique investment bank.

Asia Pacific's shop front looked impressive enough, with
deep carpets, antique furniture and expensive fittings, but it
had only been in existence for a matter of months when
Alan Bond walked through the door, and in a previous incar-
nation it had struggled to pay the rent and keep the phone
connected.

Yet in 1994 it became the nerve centre for a whole series of
bizarre business deals (in addition to St Bees) that Bond was

trying to put together while still a bankrupt and supposedly too sick to concentrate on even the simplest business matter.

The story of these would-be deals is just like a B-movie script, with a bunch of crazy ideas and even crazier characters, and it may well be that none ever came to fruition. But the tale is worth telling because it paints a picture of the people that Bond was doing business with and the rainbows he was chasing. There were gold and diamond mines that others had long ago abandoned, secret shipments of osmium-187 which is used in missiles, letters of credit from obscure banks in Panama, cargoes of tinned tomatoes to Odessa and even a proposal to buy US$25 billion worth of Russian roubles. And Bond apparently was excited by all of them. Indeed, as Neil Cunningham, one of his backers on St Bees, puts it, 'The weirder it was, the more he liked it'.[2]

It must be said that Bond was forced onto the fringes because most respectable banks and businesspeople refused to deal with him—he was, after all, still a bankrupt and still facing criminal charges for fraud, and the memory of him losing billions of dollars of other people's money was still fresh in the mind. But even so, he could hardly have chosen a less auspicious bunch of people to do business with.

There's a type of businessperson known as a fax jockey, because they fire off endless faxes offering incredible deals on Vietnamese cement, Russian steel or EU sugar to anyone with more money than sense, and Bond was like a magnet to them all. They had heard he had hidden millions of dollars in Switzerland and had figured he would not complain to the police if he lost it.

Luke Atkins therefore found hundreds of 'unrepeatable' offers spewing out of the fax machine at Asia Pacific for the attention of Alan and his chums.

One of Bond's mates would ring and say, 'I've just talked to this man and this fellow's big. His brother-in-law's the second-in-command to the man who polishes the shoes for General Wiranto in Indonesia, and what we're going to do is market shoe polish in Indonesia. And this fellow Bill is going to ring you at ten o'clock tonight and tell you where to send the fax'. And I'm thinking, 'I've gotta do my washing, I've gotta do my ironing, I've gotta go down to Woolies and I've gotta have two business plans ready by Friday and it's Wednesday night and the bloody fax roll's out'. I tell you, we used to replace fax rolls like they were going out of style.[3]

Helping Alan to marshal this avalanche of crazy and not-so-crazy opportunities was one of his old mates from Perth called Roger Bryer, a small-time entrepreneur who made his money finding deals for the big boys. In the past, Bryer had worked with Peter Briggs, a gold-mine promoter in Perth who had done time in jail for tax fraud in the late 1980s, but he had also acquired a sort of record for himself by leaving a remarkable trail of corporate wreckage in his wake. In 1994 he was listed by the Australian Securities Commission (ASC) as a director or ex-director of fifty-three different companies, of which no fewer than forty-six had been struck off or were on their way to the corporate graveyard.[4]

Like Bond, Bryer had a salesman's charm, which was no doubt how he kept recovering from such setbacks. And, like Bond, he had arranged his affairs so that he could survive almost any disaster. While his wife reportedly drove a Rolls-Royce and lived in a fancy house, Roger apparently had no assets to his name. His sole possessions appeared to be two mobile telephones that he kept constantly at his side, while his diet seemed to consist exclusively of cigarettes. As to where he came from and how old he was, it was hard to be sure. The ASC's records showed that Roger Maurice Bryer of Burke Drive, Attadale had been born in Perth on 23 June 1942, or in Melbourne on the same date, or in Liberec, Czechoslovakia, on 27 January 1947, depending on which version of his life you wanted to believe.

Bryer represented himself to Atkins as the Australian arm of a company called Tri Kal International, which hailed from the mining boom town of Calgary in Canada and claimed to be a big international development company. Tri Kal was almost as much of a mystery as Bryer, for it was behind with the rent on its modest-sounding fourth-floor office suite, and its landlord kept faxing Atkins in Sydney for $70,000 he was owed, even though Atkins had no connection with the company.

The Calgary telephone directory showed no trace of the company in either the business listings or the Yellow Pages, and none of the Canadian stock exchanges had ever heard of it. Nor did the name Tri Kal ring a bell with reporters on Calgary's local paper.

On closer examination, the company turned out to have its registered office in the Isle of Man, a tax haven in the Irish Sea, which was also home to the Bond/Bollag company Metal Traders. This was also a sign that Tri Kal might not be quite as substantial as it purported to be.[5]

Tri Kal's shareholders, according to Luke Atkins, or the people who would share the spoils (if any of its deals came off), were Alan Bond, Roger Bryer, Jim Byrnes and a Canadian accountant and ex-professional ice hockey player called Gerry Sklar, famously described by one of Bond's business partners as 'an eskimo in cowboy boots'.

Asked how he can be sure that Bond had a share in Tri Kal's

deals (which Sklar and Bond denied vigorously when documents were seized from Bond's home in 1994 by the Australian Federal Police (AFP)), Atkins says:

> They stated it, they wrote it, they sent a number of cards, they set it out on the whiteboard, with Bond saying who would look after his share ... and that was always clear to me from day one.[6]

Bond, however, had every reason to deny it, because the law forbade him from doing business while still a bankrupt.

In late 1993, Atkins was sent to the USA and Europe to assess a range of projects for Tri Kal which included a development in Denver, an investment banking operation in Texas and a casino in Las Vegas. His mission was to report on whether any of these Tri Kal deals was worth pursuing and to advise on whether they could be financed. But it seems to have been a bizarre experience. In Houston he was welcomed into a beautiful office full of flowers and expensive furniture, only to return the next day to discover that it was completely empty. In New York and Rome he dined in magnificent restaurants with Italians who ran cleaning businesses and carried guns. And in Zurich he sat for three days in a hotel room waiting for a phone call that never came.

The meetings were set up by Bryer and Sklar, but Bond told him what to say when he got there.

> Alan came to the office and said, 'Okay, we're going to do this, this, this and this, and we will pay the accommodation and airfares'. And 'this' was everything from a waste-disposal tender in Mexico to building low-cost housing in Texas.[7]

Bond, it seems, always called all the shots.

> He would decide on what, when, where, why, and
> what deals he liked and didn't like. He would write
> on a whiteboard or on pieces of paper, 'No, I don't
> want to do it that way, I want to do it this way,
> this way, this way. This is the best way to do it.
> This is the way to present it to people'.[8]

As far as Atkins knows, none of the deals that he discussed on
the trip (or at any other time) ever came to anything because
Bond and Tri Kal never came up with the millions of dollars
that were needed to make them work. Tri Kal was always
relying on others to produce finance, and for some reason it
never eventuated. It was a very frustrating time.

On a smaller scale, however, Tri Kal had plenty of money,
which paid for business-class airfares and five-star hotels all
over the world. And so did Bond, despite the fact that he was
supposed to be penniless. Atkins recalls being taken to lunch
one day by Alan at a restaurant opposite Asia Pacific's offices
in North Sydney:

> We walked across the road and everyone stopped
> and stared. Then we sat down and people came
> across and said, 'You're my hero, Bondy' and all
> that. We had lunch and at the end he pulled out
> of his pocket a huge roll of bank notes and pulled
> off fifty-dollar notes to pay for lunch. He then put
> the roll back in his pocket and we toddled off. You
> know, 'We've all been working hard and deserve
> a break'. As a charismatic character you can't beat
> him, he's unbelievable.[9]

On another occasion, when Luke complained to Bond that none of Tri Kal's deals was coming off and that he hadn't been paid for any of the work he had done, more cash materialised.

> He just said, 'Ha-ha, well come down to breakfast
> and meet someone'. So we went down to Bondi, and
> Jim Byrnes turned up and parked his Bentley out the
> front, and we had breakfast. And Alan said to Jim,
> 'Give Luke some money'. Then Jim took $10,000
> cash out of his pocket and gave it to me. And Alan
> said, 'Look, that's a loan to keep you guys on your
> feet. Now pay for breakfast'. Now this was ten
> o'clock in the morning and we were in a crowded
> restaurant full of people and Jim gets a roll of notes
> out of his pocket and just counts out $10,000. Then
> Alan and Jim went over to Jim's car and drove off.[10]

Many of the deals that attracted Bond's interest around this time were in the Eastern bloc, where the breakup of the Soviet Union had left genuine opportunities to make a killing. Here, Bond and Tri Kal found themselves dealing with a colourful Ukrainian called Vladimir D'Jamirze, a dashing young man with a ponytail and pencil-thin moustache who looked like a Cossack.

It was Vladimir D'Jamirze, in fact, whom Bond was so busy telephoning from his room at the Sheraton Wentworth in Sydney in May 1994 when he was supposedly too ill to undergo examination in the Federal Court. Vladimir had been staying at the Airport Hilton in Zurich, trying to set up a number of deals involving millions or even billions of dollars, and Bond had been in constant contact by fax and phone, even though he claimed to be too sick to remain in the witness box.[11]

Prince Vladimir D'Jamirze, as his business card described him, lived with his elder brother Victor in a vast cluster of redbrick houses in Sydney's western suburbs, along with five other brothers and assorted sisters, wives and offspring. Their Kennedy-style compound was protected by high security gates and crowned by a huge satellite dish, which distinguished it somewhat from the neighbouring fibro cottages, but the D'Jamirzes would have stood out in any environment, for they were hardly a run-of-the-mill family. They claimed, for example, to have presented a jewel-encrusted icon of the Madonna, worth $5 million, to the Patriarch of the Orthodox Church in Moscow to celebrate 1,000 years of Christianity in Russia, and to be on first-name terms with several high-up ministers in several former Soviet republics.

The D'Jamirzes described themselves as business brokers who could smooth the path of those who wanted to trade with Russia, and they had obviously made a decent living at this over the years, but in 1994 their record did not inspire confidence. One of their companies, Curly International, had planned to fly Russia's version of the space shuttle out to Australia, piggybacked on a huge Soviet cargo plane. A second company, Antonov Airlines, had tried to run cargo between the USSR and Australia in a private partnership with the Soviet Defence Ministry. But both had gone down in flames.

In fact, at the height of their dealings with Bond, five of the D'Jamirzes' eight companies had crashed to earth and Victor and Vladimir were on the verge of being made bankrupt. In February 1995, they were also banned from being directors, promoters or managers of any Australian company for three years because they had 'demonstrated their incompetence and lack of understanding of the duties of a director'.[12]

The deals that the two brothers were attempting with Alan

Bond appeared to be even more ambitious than the ones that had got them into strife. The most modest involved buying a valuable collection of Russian violins for US$7.5 million; the next was a promise to procure US$2 billion worth of diamonds, gold and osmium-187 from the Ukraine; and the third and best plotted the exchange of 3 trillion Russian roubles for US$25 billion. One has to say that when projects like these come off, the architects are acclaimed as geniuses. Sadly, the D'Jamirzes did not appear to fit into this category.

When I met Vladimir in 1999 in a café in Parramatta he certainly did not look like a billion-dollar businessman. He was dressed in jeans and a red T-shirt, and was wearing leather sandals. His trademark ponytail was still in place but his hair had turned grey. A tiny mobile phone rang constantly at his side, and every few minutes he broke off our conversation to answer it, reassuring callers that their various deals would work out.

I suggested that most of the projects he had attempted with Bond looked crazy, and he smiled a gentle, charming smile. 'These are the ones that make big money,' he said. 'If one of these deals had come off we would have made a profit of US$4 billion.' But judging by his account of the task involved, it would have been a miracle if any of them had succeeded.

In mid-1994, according to Vladimir, he and Bond attempted to buy and sell vast quantities of a radioactive isotope called osmium-187, which is used to make stealth bombers and missiles undetectable to radar. This precious substance was then worth around $200,000 a gram, according to Vladimir, yet he claims he was able to buy it from his Ukrainian contacts for a third of the price.[13] The snag, however, was that it was almost impossible to find a buyer, for osmium-187 is a strategically important material that can only be sold legally to a small club of 'friendly' countries like the UK, the USA and Japan, and then only to buyers with a valid end-user certificate.

This little problem had not deterred this odd couple from having a shot at the US$4 billion jackpot, and in 1994 Vladimir laid out US$3 million of his family's money to kick-start the deal. This was enough, he says, to grease a few palms in the Ukraine and secure a five-gram sample of the stuff, which was then delivered to a bonded warehouse in Germany for inspection by buyers. Bond, meanwhile, apparently claimed to have a customer and, according to D'Jamirze, produced a piece of paper that looked like a valid end-user certificate.

Vladimir says that he and Bond spent several months trying to stitch the osmium-187 deal together, and that he and Roger Bryer based themselves in Zurich for several weeks in mid-1994, trying to make this and other deals happen.[14] Bond, however, was no arms dealer. Nor did he have access to the US$2 billion which was needed to buy the ten kilograms that was on offer, so the deal fell apart and Vladimir lost his US$3 million.

According to Vladimir, the rouble deal also ended in dis-appointment—he smiled coyly when asked about the violins—but Alan produced enough ready cash to indicate that he might have access to several million dollars offshore.

Private documents seized by the AFP in raids in September 1994 suggest the same thing. They show that Bond instructed Roger Bryer to set up three British Virgin Islands companies to handle the D'Jamirze transactions, and to open Swiss bank accounts for each of them at the Banque Indosuez in Zurich.[15] Various sums of money then bounced in and out of these (and other) Swiss bank accounts in lumps as large as $2 million.

In May 1994, for example, when Bond was supposedly too sick to answer questions about Dallhold in the Federal Court, he was faxing Vladimir from his Sydney hotel room to say that US$1.24 million had been transferred to a Swiss account in the name of a company called Shannon Worldwide. Soon afterwards, he was signing a contract guaranteeing to pay Vladimir and Victor D'Jamirze US$3 million 'before the close of banking hours in Zurich' on 25 May 1994.[16]

Further documents seized by the AFP from Bond's house in Cottesloe show $1.7 million moving from the Banque Indosuez in Lausanne to the Swiss Bank Corporation in Zurich in mid-1994, apparently in connection with one of the D'Jamirze deals. Significantly, this money had started out from a bank account in the name of a company called SIDRO Anstalt at the Private Trust Bank in Vaduz, Liechtenstein, suggesting that this could be the latest hiding place for some of Bond's off-shore millions, last sighted leaving Jersey en masse in the late 1980s.

Liechtenstein, which is one of the world's most secret tax havens, sits in a small, steep valley between Switzerland and Austria, less than two hours from Jurg Bollag's home town of Zug. Its 30,000 citizens are still ruled by a prince, yet it is hardly the land of fairy-tale castles that its romantic Ruritanian image conjures up. Its capital, Vaduz, is a drab little town at the end of a bus route, whose heart is dominated by a large concrete car park and an even larger concrete bus station.

Tracing money here is a nightmare because Liechtenstein laws do not require the banks to know whose fortunes they are holding, and Liechtenstein's corporate records give no clues to the ownership or wealth of the thousands of companies that use the principality as a bolthole. When I examined SIDRO's file in May 1999, all that I could glean was that the company had been set up in April 1987 to own and administer assets outside Liechtenstein. Its registered office was a law firm in Vaduz's main street, rejoicing under the name of Dr Dr Batliner & Partners [*sic*], where two lawyers acted as the company's directors.

But there is a mass of evidence to link SIDRO and its millions to Alan Bond. Indeed, a trusted friend of Alan's, the late Tony Weatherald, was adamant that by the early 1990s it had become Bond's offshore money box. In 1996 he was asked about the company by Jamie Fawcett, a freelance journalist and investigator.

> Q: Have you ever heard the name SIDRO Anstalt?
> A: Yes.
> Q: In relation to what?
> A: To matters pertaining to Alan's private trusts and also set up by George Bollag.[17]

Tony Weatherald was a business battler who was hired to work for Bond in late 1992 but had known him for almost twenty years. According to Luke Atkins and others, he was constantly at Bond's side during his bankruptcy.

> Tony was a cross between a courier or bag man and a long-term confidant of Bond ... He never contributed to the substance or structure of any discussion ... He'd toddle about with documents and cash, here and there, here and there, here and there.[18]

Weatherald acted as a go-between for Bond and Bollag. He told Fawcett that he had ferried some documents to London for Alan in 1993. These related to a diamond mine in Colorado, into which Bollag had poured a lot of Bond's money, and the sale of some shares in a major US company. All had been signed by Bond so that Bollag could use SIDRO to complete the transactions on Bond's behalf.[19]

A Perth geologist called Greg Barnes has also linked SIDRO to Bond. In February 1993, the day before Alan went into hospital for open-heart surgery, Bond allegedly offered to buy Barnes's consulting business and some Austrian gold-mining leases, using SIDRO as the purchaser. Barnes was asked on oath by one of Ramsay's partners in January 1995 how the Liechtenstein company had been brought into the picture.

A: Well ... it was Bond and Kitarski [then working with Bond] deciding they were going to use SIDRO ... They sat opposite me and they said, 'Which company shall we use for this?' They went through a whole list of companies, most of which are names I've forgotten, and decided that SIDRO was the one to use ...

Q: And you've no idea how they would be aware of SIDRO?

A: I just assumed they owned it.[20]

Barnes was almost certainly right. Documents seized by the Australian Federal Police include a fax from Jurg Bollag to Alan Bond on 18 February 1993, asking Alan and Tony Weatherald to agree the wording of a letter that Bollag would send to Barnes on SIDRO's behalf.[21]

Greg Barnes met Bond twenty or thirty times in the space of eighteen months and even went to Austria with one of Alan's more disreputable buddies, Whaka Kele, to pursue a gold-mining deal into which a number of Perth investors had been persuaded to sink money.[22] Kele told anyone who would listen that he was a Maori chief with a degree from Oxford University, but his real claim to fame was that he was a prize con man who relieved Bond and others of many thousands of dollars. For a time, however, he was one of Bond's closest mates and talked to him on a daily basis.[23]

In June 1994, he and Barnes travelled to Salzburg and stayed at the Kaiserhof Hotel, leaving a huge unpaid bill which showed that Kele had phoned Bond constantly while he was in hospital in Perth. This was shortly after Alan had collapsed in court, claiming to be too sick to face the Manet fraud charges. According to Barnes, Kele spent the rest of the time shooting his mouth off to the hotel manager about how he was looking after Alan Bond's billions for him:

Q: Just on Whaka Kele, you said that he's spouting off to everyone about his control of Bond's millions.

A: Billions. Get the words right.

Q: Okay. Did he elaborate at all on where . . .

A: I was sitting in a room at one stage and he was talking to the hotel manager, of all people, and he was quoting names of companies where it was.

Q: What about locations . . .

A: Oh it was Liechtenstein and Switzerland and the Channel Islands and Bermuda. I don't know. I wasn't paying all that much interest. I was, to be quite sure, bloody embarrassed, because if Bond did have billions away, he didn't want this fool shouting it to somebody he'd never met before.[24]

Of course it was a ridiculous notion that Bond had *billions* of dollars hidden away, and Kele was certainly not a man whose word could be trusted. Given Bond's difficulty in coming up with money for any of the deals he was involved in, there must also be some question whether he even had *millions* of dollars to play with, or whether his and Kele's boasts were simply hot air. But despite the fact that the Tri Kal and D'Jamirze deals fell over for lack of money, Luke Atkins for one is still convinced that Bond had plenty of cash tucked away and believes he simply preferred to let other people risk theirs.

> I'm convinced from documents that I've seen that Bond has money, from people that I've been to see, from trips to Switzerland and New York and people that I've met with. There's no doubt in my mind that there is Bond-labelled money stashed away in Europe.[25]

Neil Cunningham, who lost nigh on $1 million of his own money over St Bees, says he never saw Bond put any of his cash at risk, but he also believes that Alan simply liked it that way. Bond's whole business career, after all, had been built on borrowing other people's money and not on gambling with his own. Cunningham is also sure that Alan had a hidden fortune because, in his words, 'Bond never got excited over anything less than $20 million'.[26]

17

The Enforcer

Michael calmly sat there and said, 'We want the
money back', and I said 'What money?'. He
proceeded to open his briefcase and said, 'This is
what we do to get our money back', and showed
me this handgun sitting inside the bag.

Luke Atkins and Michael Two Thumbs 1994[1]

Neil Cunningham was a fit-looking Scot in his early thirties who had come out to Sydney from Edinburgh at the beginning of the 1980s and made himself a fortune. He had started off selling five-dollar ties in stalls around the CBD, then graduated to a bigger stall at Paddy's Market, and soon afterwards was operating two-dollar bargain stores that clearly generated large amounts of cash. But his big break, which made him more money than he had ever seen in his life, was a property deal in the CBD in 1992. So when he first met Bond in 1993, he was, in his own words, 'ripe for the plucking'.

Cunningham had always admired Alan Bond and regarded him as a role model, because he showed what a poor immigrant might make of himself. And he was worldly enough not to care that the famous entrepreneur had fallen from grace and served time behind bars. So when the two men were introduced to each other by a mutual friend, it was relatively simple for Alan to persuade Neil to jump aboard the St Bees Island deal.

Sadly for Cunningham, however, he did a lot more than come along for the ride, because his new best friend persuaded him to set up a shelf company to own the St Bees project and to fork out enough cash to pay for all the architects' fees, fancy brochures, lawyers, phone bills, helicopters and other myriad expenses that this new company ran up.[2] Bond assured him, he says, that all the finance and development approvals were in place, and mountains of paperwork showed that it was all going to happen. But the promises never came true.

Cunningham claims he was told by Bond that Tri Kal and Gerry Sklar would provide the millions of dollars in finance needed to build the resort, but says that as soon as he set eyes on the Canadian, he knew he had lost his stake. Perhaps with the wisdom of hindsight, he says that Sklar was not what one expected of the head of a major international development company. Or it may well be that Cunningham's bullshit detector worked better than Bond's. In any case, when the project collapsed in early 1995 leaving a string of unpaid bills, Cunningham found himself cursing the celebrated bankrupt entrepreneur and nursing a $1 million loss.

In the meantime, he became entangled in some of the crazier schemes that Bond was pursuing at the time, including at least one involving the D'Jamirze brothers, and he met Alan's long-time lover Diana Bliss.

Diana Bliss frequently told friends and interviewers that she knew nothing about Alan's business deals and stayed right out of them.[3] But in May 1994, when Bond was busy facing interrogation in the Federal Court about his offshore fortune, she was pressed into service as a courier.

On the morning of 10 May, as Alan took his place in the witness box for the second day of the Dallhold examination, Diana walked into Luke Atkins's office at Asia Pacific, just across the harbour in North Sydney. A slight, short blonde-haired woman in her mid-thirties, she was carrying a hatbox with a floral design on it. Introducing herself as Diana Bliss, she closed the door, placed the box on the desk and lifted the lid. Inside, wrapped in newspaper, was a large number of bundles of 100-, fifty-, twenty- and ten-dollar notes. Without hanging around to collect a receipt, she left.

Atkins had been told by Alan Bond to expect a delivery of $130,000, and Diana herself had phoned an hour or so earlier to say that she was at the Sheraton Wentworth Hotel with Neil Cunningham and was planning to bring the money round. But Atkins was still taken aback by it, for even if Asia Pacific's banking pedigree was a bit thin, he was not in the business of handling big boxes of money. So after counting out the cash and finding it $50 short, he hurried nervously to the St George Bank just around the corner, and deposited it in Asia Pacific's account, whence it was transferred on his instructions to Barclays Bank in Singapore.[4]

According to Atkins's sworn statement to police in 1995, the money was to be collected in Singapore and paid as an up-front fee on a loan of US$8.5 million, designed to fund one of Bond's attempted deals. But four weeks later, after countless phone calls, it became clear that something had gone drastically wrong. The loan had not materialised, even though the $130,000 had been paid.

Things then began to get extremely uncomfortable for Luke, because Bond and Neil Cunningham now arrived unannounced at his office and demanded the $130,000 back, with

Bond in particular becoming 'quite agitated'. Atkins told the two men that he could do nothing to help, because he had already transferred the money to Singapore. Soon afterwards, he told his visitors that he wanted nothing more to do with them. And at this point, Bond became even more agitated.

The phone calls to Atkins now began in earnest, from Alan Bond, Alan's son John, and Neil Cunningham, who rang him 'three times a day for two weeks'. As time went by the flood of calls got heavier. Finally, Luke found himself talking on the telephone to a well-known Sydney debt collector and enforcer, Tim Bristow. And soon after that, he found himself being visited by a standover man called Michael Two Thumbs, who apparently had no thumbs, and was obviously looking for a part in an Australian version of *Pulp Fiction*.

> Michael came here in his polyester suit and sat in my office with his long, straggly hair and looked menacingly at people. So much so that the poor young secretary that was sitting at the front desk went to lunch and never came back. And Michael calmly sat there and said, 'We want the money back', and I said, 'What money?'. He proceeded to open his briefcase and said, 'This is what we do to get our money back', and showed me this handgun sitting inside the bag. About ten minutes later Tim Bristow was back on the phone. All I simply did was say, 'Thank you gentlemen, goodbye', slammed the door behind me, walked straight up to North Sydney police and said, 'I've just been threatened'. At three o'clock the next morning my front door was kicked in.[5]

Tim Bristow confirmed to me in 1999 that Michael Two Thumbs was a close associate of his at the time and was doing a lot of work for him. His diaries also confirm that Bristow did a job relating to Bond in mid-1994.[6]

Luke Atkins emerged shaken from his dealings with these hired enforcers, yet otherwise none the worse for wear. But the menacing phone calls and the visit from Michael were not the end of his troubles, for some two months later, on 27 September 1994, he was woken by a loud knocking at the door of his Rose Bay apartment. He donned his pyjamas and opened up to find five members of the Australian Federal Police (AFP) in his hallway, armed with a shotgun and a sledgehammer, and brandishing a search warrant alleging that he had conspired with Alan, Craig, John and Eileen Bond, Diana Bliss, Jim Byrnes and Whaka Kele to defeat the *Bankruptcy Act 1966* by concealing assets from Bond's creditors.

> They asked me who I was and then stood upon the landing, read the document to me and said, 'We're coming in'. And of course this is the time when everyone is going to work, so people are coming up and down the stairway of the flats and I've got five policemen standing there going, you know, 'And by order of the Federal Court'. It was just crazy.[7]

The police went through his flat and removed almost everything that wasn't nailed down, including a plastic garbage bag that contained apple cores, muesli, other bits of stale food, and bits of shredded paper. They also took away a video of the Kingdom of Tonga, produced by Austrade.

> They took all my business cards, all my financial records, manila folders with information about all kinds of unrelated clients. And they actually took all my diaries, my phone records, everything, so I had to go through and try to reconstruct all my clients' details and try to remember who they were, where they lived and try painstakingly to put that together again.[8]

But Luke Atkins was not the only one to be rudely awoken that Tuesday morning, because the police had obtained warrants to search fourteen premises around the country, including Parker & Parker's offices in Perth, and had been given permission by the magistrate to use reasonable force to gain entry or get what they wanted, including breaking open doors and filing cabinets.

At various times that day, the AFP descended on Alan's home in Cottesloe, John and Craig's houses in Peppermint Grove and Whaka Kele's house in Epping. Diana Bliss's unit in Sydney was also turned over, along with offices belonging to the Bond family companies, Jim Byrnes, Neil Cunningham and Whitsunday Island Developments. After a couple of hours at Alan's beachside house the police drove off with some ten tea chests full of documents, while at Parker & Parker's offices in St George's Terrace they grabbed no less than 144 cases of papers that they must have needed a small furniture van to cart away.

The warrants entitled them to seize wills, cash books, cheque books, address books, faxes, telexes, diaries, notes, working papers, computer disks, manuals, software and encryption devices, as long as they belonged or referred to any of thirty-five named individuals or eighty named companies. All members of Alan Bond's family except his younger daughter Jody were on the list, as were Jurg Bollag, John Hatton-Edge, Harry Lodge, Graham Ferguson Lacey and others. The usual raft of exotic companies run by Bollag also featured prominently, as did the Allied Irish Banks, the Zuger Kantonal Bank and a couple of newer names such as the Parliament Bank & Trust Company of Panama, the Ueberseebank of Switzerland and the International Trust Company of Liberia.[9]

The warrants alleged seven offences, of which the two most serious were that Bond had committed perjury during his bankruptcy examination and had conspired to defeat the bankruptcy laws. So it seemed that Bond might not yet have got off scot-free after all. The two major offences carried maximum penalties of five years under the Crimes Act, while the others under the *Bankruptcy Act 1966* carried a maximum penalty of one year. These comprised four counts of failing to disclose information, assets, record books or material particulars, and one of concealing or removing property to the value of $20 or more.

Who had given police the tip-off for the raids or set them on the trail was not revealed, but it was clear that the AFP's criminal investigation was independent of any action Ramsay was taking in his search for Bond's money. And as it would turn out, they had started pursuing Bond long before his Oscar-winning performance in the Federal Court in May 1994.

But whatever the genesis of their action, the possibility of criminal charges was a new threat, and within forty-eight hours Bond's lawyers were in court seeking to have the AFP's seizures declared illegal. This, however, merely stalled the investigation, and before long the AFP were poring over a mass of memos about gold, oil, violins and osmium-187, and trying to make sense of documents that recorded million-dollar deposits in Switzerland and movement of money in and out of Liechtenstein.

Quite possibly, other important evidence had slipped through the police dragnet, for Bond had made great efforts to grab back files that he thought might fall into the wrong hands. For example, the day after his argument over the $130,000 with Luke Atkins, he had turned up at Asia Pacific's North Sydney offices at 8.30am, before Atkins got into work, and told staff he had come to collect all his papers. He had then rifled through the filing system and taken away several manila folders relating to the deals that Atkins and Asia Pacific had been trying to conduct for him. Bollag had called Atkins soon afterwards by phone from Switzerland to ensure that all Tri Kal's documents had been returned.

Over in Perth at around the same time, Greg Barnes's files on Bond and SIDRO Anstalt had also gone missing. Someone had broken into his offices one night and cleaned out every-thing relating to Bond and the Austrian gold deal, yet appar-ently had taken nothing else. Stupidly, they had not destroyed copies of letters and proposals that were stored on the hard disk of Barnes's computer.

Tim Bristow, meanwhile, had also been pressed into action again, though not necessarily by Bond himself. A week before the AFP raids he had been asked to retrieve some documents from an office in central Sydney used by Bond's buddy Whaka Kele. He had broken into the office, only to be arrested by the AFP who had been keeping it under surveillance.

But whether it would have helped the AFP to have any further documents is another matter, because the deals were often described in the most Delphic terms and set up so that it was almost impossible for an outsider to understand them. Even Luke Atkins, who had worked on most of them, was not always sure what had been going on, because Bond and his partners had been so secretive.

> They'd only tell a certain amount of information to a certain number of people. It was almost like assembling the atomic bomb. You know how to do this little bit and you know how to do this little bit, but if anyone tried to piece the story together they'd get the wrong story because they didn't know all the bits.[10]

Atkins's diary contained a meticulous record of phone calls from Bond, Bollag, Bryer and Gerry Sklar during 1993 and 1994, along with details of meetings and tasks he had carried out, plus phone numbers, bank details and the like. But even this was not going to be much help to the police unless they had a guide, and Atkins was in no mood to help. He had tried to talk to someone in the AFP a month or so earlier about Bond and Tri Kal, and now they wanted to wire him up for meetings with Bond, and were suggesting in a heavy-handed way that he ought to cooperate or the taxman might come chasing him.[11] But he chose to leave town instead and go to ground.

Nowadays, Luke Atkins is a hard man to track down. He is not on the electoral roll or in the phone book, and does business via his mobile phone. Unlike Bond's friends, however, who also favour the gypsy life, he rarely answers when you ring, and feeds his phone with pre-paid SIM cards to avoid being given a billing address. Whether that is paranoia or prudence is a matter of opinion.

18

Operation Oxide

The crux of the investigation is whether Bond had or
has assets in Switzerland and Jersey, which he either
failed to disclose to his trustee in bankruptcy or
subsequently lied about when giving evidence on oath.

*Letter of request to Switzerland for help in Bond
investigation, September 1994*

The Australian Federal Police's (AFP's) September 1994
raids were the first sign of any criminal investigation into
Bond for concealing assets from his creditors, but the police
had actually been on his tail for the previous ten months, and
it was remarkable that they hadn't been after him for much
longer.

As it was, it had taken a complaint from the Western Australian Director of Public Prosecutions, John McKechnie, to
get them started. Clearly disturbed that no one was policing
the conduct of Bond's bankruptcy, he had written to Australia's Inspector-General in Bankruptcy, Richard Moss, in
October 1993, enclosing proof that Bollag had held a Swiss
bank account for Bond at the Zuger Kantonal Bank in the late
1980s.[1] Needless to say, this was an account that Bond had
not declared to his creditors.

In the words of a letter from Moss to the AFP the following
month, the Swiss bank documents revealed:

... transactions which occurred during 1987 and 1988 through an identified Swiss bank account in the name of Mr Bollag on behalf of Alan Bond. The transactions concern substantial amounts of money.[2]

The problem with this remarkable evidence was that it had been obtained through the Swiss courts in 1991 in connection with a prosecution of Laurie Connell, and the strict rules of the process stopped the documents being used in any other investigation. Moss had therefore not been able to pass on copies to Ramsay or the AFP, or even let them have a look. But he had at least been able to tell the police what the documents contained and request that they investigate.

In a way, it was poetic justice that Laurie Connell was now causing trouble for Bond, because they had long been partners in crime. And they were undoubtedly two of a kind, in that they were brash, flash and decidedly short on ethics. Connell had made his fortune by the simple device of stealing it from the punters who banked with his Rothwells merchant bank, and had used it to acquire an island in the Philippines, 400 thoroughbred racehorses and six houses around the world. These included an English manor which he had decorated with fine antiques and paintings. His silver collection alone, which he shipped out of Australia in early 1989, was worth some $3 million. His art collection, which included works by Rees, McCubbin, Nolan and Streeton, was worth far more. He had also amassed a collection of family jewels which included a magnificent diamond necklace valued at $1.2 million and a different Cartier watch for every day of the week. The insurance list for this jewellery ran to eleven closely typed pages.

Like Bond, Connell had made damn sure that none of his creditors would ever get their hands on this loot if he went bust, and well before things had begun to fall apart at Rothwells in 1987 he had started shipping it offshore. Even his mansion in Perth had been passed over to a company in the Channel Islands. Connell had not only used trusts in Guernsey and Sark but had also taken Alan's advice and employed the services of Touche Ross in Jersey.

Joe Lieberfreund had followed Laurie's money trail for more than a year, using records from the Allied Irish Banks and Touche Ross in St Helier, and had finally traced several million dollars to Switzerland, which was where he had also stumbled on money belonging to Bond. In November 1991 he had drafted an official letter of request from the Australian government to the Swiss, asking for help in obtaining bank documents and telling them that Connell had looted some $50 million from Rothwells since 1983 to acquire personal assets around the world. Lieberfreund told the Swiss that he and his fellow investigators had tracked down a consignment of antiques worth $700,000 that Connell had shipped in secret from London to Basle in 1989 and, more importantly, had identified three Swiss bank accounts.

One of these, at Ralli Brothers Bankers in Geneva, had received money in August 1987 from one of Connell's Panamanian companies run by Touche Ross, with the reference 'Pinky' attached to the transfer. Another, at Credit Suisse in Geneva, had been sent some cash in July 1989. And, finally, the Zuger Kantonal Bank in Zug had received 'a large amount of money' from a company that kept popping up in Connell's Jersey transactions. As the Australian Attorney General's letter of request to Switzerland put it:

Documents from Touche Ross in Jersey show
Balmoral Securities transferred a large amount of
money on or about 7th December 1987 to account
no: 00 737 999 04, reference: Xavier, at the Zuger
Kantonal Bank ... Inquiries show this company
has multiple bank accounts in US dollars, Australian dollars and sterling, and that it has secretly
handled large amounts of money on Connell's
behalf.[3]

Lieberfreund knew that Balmoral Securities was a clearing
house for funds belonging to Touche Ross Jersey's clients, and
that it handled millions of dollars for Alan Bond and his top
executives as well as Laurie Connell. But even he must have
been delighted by the direct hit that he now scored, because
the documents faxed back to him by the Swiss police, who had
been only too happy to help, revealed that 'Xavier' at the
Zuger Kantonal Bank was an account held by 'Jurg Bollag on
behalf of Alan Bond'.[4]

Only a handful of people in Australia have ever seen the
documents relating to this account, but there is no doubt that
it contained substantial amounts of money until 1988 or 1989.
In the space of eighteen months, around $20 million is said to
have passed through it, with the funds disappearing to
Holland, the USA, the UK and elsewhere.

The trail uncovered by Lieberfreund was a great deal fresher
than the one that Bob Ramsay had been following in Jersey,
which had petered out in 1987. But unfortunately it was still
too old for police to charge Bond with concealing money from
his creditors, because the law required the AFP to show that
he had held assets in the two years prior to his bankruptcy,
and had failed to declare them to Ramsay. And the money in

this 'Xavier' account had vanished at least *three* years before April 1992.[5]

There was also the minor problem that the AFP neither had the actual documents from the Zuger Kantonal Bank nor any details of the bank account they were looking for, and would need to assemble their own dossier of evidence for the Swiss authorities if they wanted to get hold of them. However, the fact that the bank records clearly existed gave them some degree of comfort, for it not only showed that Bond had stashed money in Switzerland but demonstrated that, in principle, one could get proof.

The task of chasing Bond was given initially to a young detective sergeant in Melbourne called Andrew Tuohy, who sat in Bird Cameron's offices for the first three months of 1994, ploughing solemnly through Bob Ramsay's files to see whether there was a reasonable chance of a conviction. By March he had decided that there was enough evidence to make it worth following, and had come up with a game plan of how to proceed.

At this stage, Tuohy constituted the full strength of the AFP's newly christened 'Operation Oxide', but by July 1994 his task force had doubled in size with the addition of a smart twenty-four-year-old called Kelvin Kenney. Both he and Tuohy had degrees in accounting and experience in chasing complex fraud, yet for this they earned less in a year than Bond spent in a week. Ever optimistic, they told their superiors that they would have it all wrapped up within twelve months.

In retrospect, it's hard to see how these two federal agents could have been so sanguine, for most of the assets that Bollag kept warm for Bond were in England, Switzerland or the USA, while the man who controlled this booty was based in Zug. The AFP's budget, in contrast, barely allowed them to travel interstate. They would have to run the operation from an office in Melbourne, only venturing out to interview people when they had set things up in advance and knew that the interview would be productive.

They did not have the power to tap Bond's telephone, which would have been an obvious way to get the evidence they needed, because this was only available for more serious offences. But they were able to get Bond's telephone records, and these showed that Alan and Jurg were keeping in regular contact, with Bond making a dozen calls to Bollag's number in Zug between June 1993 and May 1994 from his house in Cottesloe and another eight calls from the Rockman Regency Hotel in Melbourne.[6]

This obviously helped convince the AFP they were on the right track, but it did not begin to give them the sort of evidence that would bring a conviction. For this they would need a confession from Bollag that he was holding assets on Bond's behalf, or documentary proof of such an arrangement. And both of those were likely to be found only in Switzerland.

What the police and Ramsay both dreamed of, of course, was a piece of paper acknowledging that it was Alan's money that Jurg looked after, which set out Bollag's role as Bond's trustee. And it was perfectly reasonable to expect that something like this would exist, because even in Switzerland, people don't hand over their fortunes to a lawyer without a written contract.[7] But whether the police would be able to get hold of such a document was not clear. Bob Ramsay had made absolutely no progress in getting help from Switzerland, and it was by no means certain that the AFP would do any better, even though Swiss law appeared to give them a decent chance.

The Swiss authorities had long granted their own police powers to breach bank secrecy when investigating major crimes, but had slammed the door firmly in the face of all foreign investigators, until the mid-1980s when the USA had persuaded them that harbouring criminals was bad for their nation's image. By 1994, in theory, it was simple for police to get help in opening the Swiss bankers' vaults. But in practice it was a very different matter, and the system often failed to work smoothly or at all.

To ensure success, it was important for the police to be chasing a high-profile villain from a country that was prepared to apply political pressure to get a result. It helped enormously if drug money was involved or if there was large-scale money laundering. It was far better if at least US$100 million was at stake. And it was guaranteed to go much faster if it was handed to a no-nonsense prosecutor who was tough and experienced in these matters.

Unfortunately, none of these things was true in the case of Bond and Bollag. But Lieberfreund had succeeded with Connell, and in these early stages, at least, everything went like clockwork.

On 16 September 1994, an official letter was sent by the AFP 'To the competent authority of Switzerland' via Australia's Attorney General, requesting the Swiss authorities to obtain documents from various banks, search Bollag's house and offices, and summons Bollag for questioning on oath. It explained that:

> Australian authorities have reason to believe that since 1978 Bond has caused his agents in Jersey and Switzerland to form, through a series of complex business arrangements, various corporate structures located in different parts of the world to act as conduits and repositories for his personal

assets. It is believed that in 1987 control of these assets was transferred to Bollag, a Swiss national.

The crux of the investigation is whether Bond had or has assets in Switzerland and Jersey which he either failed to disclose to his trustee in bankruptcy or subsequently lied about when giving evidence on oath.[8]

The AFP's letter, which ran to twenty-three pages, with another forty pages of supporting documents, went on to provide a summary of the case against Bond, listing his alleged offences and their penalties, and reciting in detail the AFP's evidence that Bond had 'accumulated such assets and misled his trustee'.

It then revealed that the AFP were seeking access to three specific accounts at the Zuger Kantonal Bank in Zug, along with any others that the bank might be operating for Bond. The most important of these was probably an account numbered 00736488-01 and code-named 'Jane', which had received £30,000 on 23 October 1987 from Kirk Holdings in Jersey via the Allied Irish Banks. This, the AFP said, had been accompanied by a note on the banking instructions saying, 'Please ensure that this transfer is paid through London, and make no mention of Kirk Holdings Limited or Jersey'.[9]

More recently, this same 'Jane' account was known to have sent a total of £370,000 from Zug to Dallhold Estates UK between May 1989 and July 1991 to pay the bills at Upp Hall, and to have paid fees for some of the Jersey companies as late as 1992. This was easily close enough to Alan's bankruptcy date for the AFP to bring charges, if the Swiss documents demonstrated the money really did belong to Bond.

A second account, numbered 70084300, in the name of Treuhand Konto Trust, had received SwF300,000 from Kirk Holdings on 20 February 1987, and SwF250,000 in two smaller transactions a few months earlier. And a third account, numbered 20736686, had been sent £500,000 by Kirk Holdings on 14 April 1987 with the reference 'H. Bohler', who was believed to be Hubie Bohler, an account officer at the Zuger Kantonal Bank.

Remarkably, the AFP did not ask the Swiss to obtain records from the Zuger Kantonal Bank for the 'Xavier' account which had been uncovered in 1991 by Connell's pursuers, even though this was the one that had set them on the trail in the first place. Clearly, they had still not stumbled across it in their investigation.[10]

The Australian letter of request had been prepared in secret to deny Bollag and the Swiss banks the chance to destroy files or move money, so Bond had no opportunity as yet to challenge the process. And at this stage the Swiss were only too happy to help. The Swiss Justice Ministry sent the papers to the Public Prosecutor in Zug, Paul Kuhn, who promptly gave the operation the green light. Thus, on 7 December 1994, Swiss police descended on Jurg Bollag's house and offices, and worked their way through his drawers, filing cabinets, cupboards and everything else as they searched for the documents that the AFP had asked for. Exactly what they took away with them is not clear, but they did not leave empty-handed.[11] Bollag had obviously felt so secure in his Swiss home town that he had not bothered to shred his documents.

The Zuger Kantonal Bank had also kept Bollag's records, which they agreed to hand over to the Swiss police without demur. But as soon as the raids were over the trouble began, for Bond and Bollag were prepared to fight every inch of the way in the Swiss and Australian courts to stop the evidence getting back to Australia.

The bank documents and the material seized from Bollag were therefore put under lock and key in Zug until their fate had been decided, which meant that the AFP were neither able to inspect the evidence nor even discover what the Swiss had seized on their behalf. And everyone then prepared for the war of attrition that any action against Bond provoked.

The AFP were fairly sure, however, that it would now be only a matter of time before they got their man. And Bond, according to his friends, was clearly concerned that they might be right.

19

Getting Off

He will have a very rapid comeback once the
bankruptcy is wound up. He'd like to go back and
buy Bond Corp, put a couple of deals into it and
give the shareholders some value. He is a man of
incredible vision.

Jim Byrnes, December 1994[1]

B y the end of 1994, Bond was not only concerned about
the AFP investigation, he was also under increasing pressure from his creditors. In fact, he needed to come to some
arrangement with them even if it cost him several million
dollars, or he would risk remaining a bankrupt into the
twenty-first century.

In the normal course of events, he would have been able to
walk free in April 1995 without paying a cent, but the law
had been changed in 1991 to allow the Federal Court to extend
a bankruptcy by up to five years if it could be shown that a
bankrupt had refused to answer questions or might be concealing assets. And Bob Ramsay had made it clear that he
planned to ask the court to keep the shackles on Bond until
April 2000 for precisely those reasons.

Even more to the point, Alan's trustee had enough
material to be confident of victory, and the Commonwealth

Government had agreed to pay all his legal costs on the grounds that it was against the public interest for Bond to be released. If Alan were allowed to go free, he would be seen to have thumbed his nose at the system, just like that other sick tycoon Christopher Skase had done from the other side of the world. But on top of that, all Ramsay's investigations in Switzerland would cease and there would no longer be any hope of recovering money for his creditors.[2]

In September 1994, four months after Bond's farcical performance at his examination in the Federal Court, Bob Ramsay wrote to the forgetful entrepreneur to tell him that he was 'highly dissatisfied' with his answers and to lay out the evidence in all its damning detail. In his nineteen-page letter he took Bond through the millions of dollars in cash and assets that had swilled around in Kirk Holdings, the Icarus Trust, Engetal, Juno Equities, Lindsey Trading Properties and Bond's London bank accounts, asking him in each case to say what had happened to the money.

Piece by piece, company by company, trust by trust, he set out the evidence that the Jersey empire and all its riches had belonged to Bond. And, finally, he asked him to admit it. Characterising his previous denials as 'inaccurate', and reminding Bond of his legal obligation to answer truthfully, he asked Bond:

> Do you now accept?
> a) That Touche Ross Jersey did act in relation to your personal affairs on the instruction of individuals you authorised to act on your behalf.
> b) That Robert Pearce and Jurg Bollag gave instruction to Touche Ross in relation to your personal affairs.

c) The above mentioned trusts and companies were beneficially controlled and owned by you.[3]

Bond's lawyers, Parker & Parker, wrote back to Ramsay four weeks later to say that Bond was not going to answer these questions because he might incriminate himself—presumably because he might be forced to admit that some of Ramsay's allegations were true, and thus lay himself open to prosecution for concealing his assets from creditors and, even worse, for perjury. Soon afterwards, Ramsay warned Bond that he would ask the Federal Court to compel him to answer the questions whether he liked it or not.

But the prospect of being forced to tell the truth or risk jail for contempt was not the only reason for Alan to contemplate a settlement, because Ramsay was confident that he could get Jurg Bollag into the witness box in Switzerland, and there was no guarantee that Alan's mate would stay silent when the pressure was on. By the end of 1994, the Zug Cantonal Court had already ordered Bondy's banker to take the stand, and Ramsay's Swiss lawyer was sure that the Swiss Federal Court would soon confirm the ruling.[4]

Even worse, the Dallhold liquidator, John Lord, was threatening a huge legal action that could strip the Bond family of a large slice of their fortune. Lord had at last decided to attack a whole series of transactions that had shovelled millions of dollars to Eileen and the children between 1988 and 1991 in the form of jewellery, cars, cash, houses, paintings and forgiven debts. And if all these claims succeeded, the Bonds would not only have to fork out $54 million, including interest, but would also lose their magnificent English country estate at Upp Hall.

To win the jackpot, Lord needed only to persuade a judge

that Dallhold had been insolvent (or more brutally, bust) by November 1988. This would not only allow him to recover any gifts made after that date, but could also expose Eileen, Alan and Craig Bond to huge damages claims and criminal charges for breaching their duties as directors of Dallhold.

As Bond no doubt knew, John Lord had obtained a senior counsel's opinion which said that he had a good chance of winning the $54 million and an even better chance of getting some of that money if he didn't get it all.[5]

Even in the good times, Alan's private company Dallhold had found it hard to pay the interest on its multi-million-dollar borrowings, because the dividends paid to it by Bond Corporation, which formed the bulk of its income, had never been large enough. Typically, it had been forced to sell assets (or revalue them and borrow more) so it could make ends meet. But in late 1988, interest rates doubled, asset prices plummeted and the company suddenly needed twice as much money to pay its massive interest bills—with next to no chance of raising it. Before long, Bond Corporation's share price went into free-fall, the group's bankers got nervous, and Dallhold was pushed to the brink of disaster.

Alan took on an ex-banker to negotiate with the company's lenders—to flatter, promise, massage and play for time. But as the banks began to sniff the strong smell of failure they either scrabbled for better security or tried to get out completely, so it was only a matter of time before Dallhold started missing interest payments and defaulting on its loans. Or in the legal language of insolvency, 'failing to pay its debts as they fell due'.

The evidence suggested that Dallhold was certainly insolvent by May 1989, since this was the month when it defaulted on $70 million worth of loans and a flurry of other things went wrong in the wider Bond business empire.[6] However, there was a fair chance that Lord could prove that the company had been insolvent six months earlier, which would mean that the Bonds would have to hand back their Christmas presents from Alan that year, which included Susanne's $350,000 bracelet, Eileen's $4.3 million worth of diamonds and the Bentley Turbo.

During November 1988, the National Australia Bank had called in a loan of $30 million after Dallhold had missed the interest payment, and an investigative team from the UK company Lonrho had branded Bond's empire 'technically insolvent', with a net worth of *minus* $4,000 million. Thereafter, Dallhold had only stayed afloat by pinching millions of dollars from the unwitting shareholders of two cash-rich companies that Bond had hijacked, and by siphoning off $160 million that it had pledged to its long-suffering bankers.[7]

On this basis, it looked like Dallhold's creditors had a good chance of winning their case, but John Lord knew it would take several years to do so and that they might also lose. He knew, too, that the creditors would be reluctant to risk money if Bond could be persuaded to pay up without a fight. So he resolved to use the legal action as a threat to push Bond into a more generous settlement.

Alan had long been busting to get free and had been talking about a compromise since September 1992, as had his elder son John, who now held the purse strings for the Bond family. So when the two sides met in early November it did not take long to reach an in-principle agreement. By early December, after discussions with Bob Ramsay and the major creditors, a draft proposal was on the table, committing the Bond family to pay $7 million over three years in exchange for Dallhold dropping all legal claims against them. As to where the money would come from, Eileen and John would each contribute $2 million, while the sale of Craig's house in Brisbane would provide another $1.5 million. The final $1.5 million would come from the Bond family at large.[8] The Bonds would also get to keep Upp Hall, the lease of which would be signed over to them by Dallhold Estates UK.

The Bonds' offer would see Dallhold's creditors getting a measly 1.3 cents for every dollar they were owed—or $7 million to wipe out $519 million worth of debts—but in cases like this beggars can't be choosers, and whether this was a good or bad deal depended on one's assessment of the Bond family's wealth. Remarkably, they had been bullied into providing an estimate of their net worth, prepared by the big accounting firm Price Waterhouse, even though Alan had told Ramsay bluntly in mid-November that this was completely out of the question, saying, 'No, can't do that. PW won't do it'.[9]

According to this estimate, the Bonds were worth 'less than $20 million'. But, as John Lord scathingly pointed out, creditors could 'place little reliance' on this figure because the accountants had not been allowed to include any of the assets in the various discretionary trusts, which probably held the vast bulk of the Bond fortune. Nor could they guarantee that they had sighted all of Eileen's and Susanne's jewellery. And finally, the Bonds' booty had been totted up at its book value, which was almost certainly a great deal less than it was worth. So $20 million probably wasn't the half of it.

However, if the balance of the Bond family's money was locked up in discretionary trusts, there would doubtless be huge problems getting hold of it, even if Dallhold won the full $54 million in damages. And on that basis, Lord advised creditors that they should accept. John Bond, he said, had most of the money but was only liable for $2 million of the

$54 million claim, while Eileen's net worth was allegedly less than $5.5 million. If that were so, Dallhold's creditors would be hard-pressed to get more than $7.5 million even if they won.

There was one huge obstacle, however, to accepting Bond's offer, which was that he was making it a condition that his personal creditors also released him from bankruptcy. And here the deal was far less attractive. With no threat of legal action to buy off, Bond had offered only $1.65 million to settle debts of $600 million, which would work out, after expenses, at roughly $1 for every $1,000 that he owed, or one-tenth of a cent in every dollar.[10]

Of course it was natural that Bond would try to escape from bankruptcy, because it was the only way he could get the investigators off Bollag's back, and neither his freedom nor his fortune would be safe until that happened. For precisely the same reason Bob Ramsay was determined that he should not be discharged.

It was therefore a hard decision for creditors to make, since many were owed money by both Bond and Dallhold, and even John Lord wanted to have two bob each way, telling them:

> I would recommend settlement with the family
> members. I do not recommend the settlement in
> the bankrupt estate or the release of Alan Bond
> from claims in Dallhold. However, the settlement
> proposal does not allow creditors to pick and
> choose ... it is all or nothing.[11]

Ramsay's choice was far more straightforward, and in early December he despatched an eighteen-page report to Bond's personal creditors listing a multitude of reasons why they should reject the offer, the key one being his conviction that more money could be found. Although this stopped short of actually telling them to vote 'No', it left them in no doubt that he believed it wrong to let Bond go free while the search for the treasure was still on.

> I have accumulated a great deal of evidence con-
> necting Mr Bond to off-shore entities. I am not
> satisfied with the responses I have received from
> Mr Bond, and my investigations into this complex
> set of overseas trusts and entities and the transfers
> of large amounts of money between them and by
> them is [sic] continuing.[12]

Ramsay warned creditors that Bond's bankruptcy would be annulled if they accepted the paltry amount of money he was offering, and all investigations would cease. The attempt to force Bollag into the witness box would also be abandoned, along with legal action in Switzerland to recover Bond's assets, and Alan would escape giving answers to the questions that he had been trying to dodge since mid-1992.

Attached to the report was a letter from one of Bond's biggest creditors, the merchant bank Tricontinental, declaring the offer to be 'far short of what would be an acceptable amount', and vowing not to back any compromise until investigations by Ramsay and the AFP in Switzerland were complete. Another letter from JN Taylor, which was one of Holmes à Court's old companies, and also a big creditor, expressed similar opposition to the deal.

But in spite of this support, it was obviously going to be a fight to keep Bond in bankruptcy, because many of his personal creditors wanted to accept Dallhold's $7 million payout, and others simply felt sick of the whole process and wanted to throw in the towel.

The Hongkong Bank, for example, were loudly proclaiming that it was a waste of time chasing Bollag in Switzerland, and they were certainly not the only ones who felt that pursuit had become futile. In fact, one had to be a supreme optimist to believe that Ramsay could recover money from Liechtenstein or Switzerland at this late stage even if Bollag did talk. And the record thus far showed that creditors had spent around $3.5 million chasing Bond's assets but had virtually nothing to show for it.[13]

By the time the Dallhold vote came around on 19 December 1994, there was huge interest in Bond's impending escape, and the inevitable media scrum assembled outside the Institute of Chartered Accountants in York Street, Sydney, where the creditors' meeting was being held. The ubiquitous Jim Byrnes was also in evidence, pacing up and down on the pavement, mobile phone to ear, apparently reporting progress or nudging the last of the stragglers over the line, and happy to declare that he and Bond already had it sewn up.

> We have got the money. It is the numbers we are concerned about. We worked all weekend. We bought several of the debts. I don't think we've got anything to worry about.[14]

It was a quiet meeting, as you would expect from a collection of accountants and solicitors, and a quick one. In less than two hours the i's were dotted and the t's crossed, and Bond's $7 million offer was accepted by a large majority. Bond had secured ninety-eight per cent of the votes by value and seventy-eight per cent by number. In other words, all the biggest creditors, including the banks, had come to the party.

After it was over, Bond and Byrnes emerged from the building grinning like two Cheshire cats, displaying thousands of dollars of dental work in the process. Bond, one could see, had gone for the millionaire's package, with teeth so straight and well matched that they looked false. He also seemed to have gone a bit wild with a bottle of red hair dye. Byrnes had invested in a great front row, but appeared to have skimped on the halfbacks. Only the biggest smile could have betrayed the point where the money ran out, but both men were wearing one, for they now only needed to win the vote with Alan's personal creditors two days later and Bond would be out of hock.

When asked whether he was now confident that he would be freed, Bond was suitably cautious, saying: 'It's never there until it's there. There are a lot of technicalities to be ticked off'. But there was no disguising his confidence that he would soon be home and hosed, and before long he had launched into a lecture about the need for Australia to forget the past, look to the future and allow great entrepreneurs like him to go out and 'create a few jobs'.[15]

This was a bit rich for a man who had melted his business empire into a $5 billion black hole, especially when he had left three breweries—Toohey's, Castlemaine and the American company Heileman—making less money, selling less beer, and looking less secure than when he had taken them over. And it was a touch ambitious for a man who had apparently been incapable of running a corner store only twelve months before. Now he obviously had a lot of corner stores in mind.

Before long Jim Byrnes would be telling the world that he had the greatest admiration for his mate and predicting that Bond would rise again, like the man whose birth was about to be celebrated.

He will have a very rapid comeback once the bankruptcy is wound up. He'd like to go back and buy
Bond Corp, put a couple of deals into it and give
the shareholders some value. He is a man of
incredible vision.[16]

Then, as the journalistic throng scribbled in their notebooks
or smiled in disbelief, the two well-heeled bankrupts climbed
into Jim's dark blue Rolls-Royce Corniche, which he had
parked on double yellow lines for a quick getaway, and
chuckled off.

It was clear, however, that the meeting of Alan's personal
creditors two days later would not be such a snack. In fact,
Bond was already convinced that he did not have the numbers
to win and would be struggling to get them unless he had Bob
Ramsay's blessing. So, in typical fashion, he resolved to do
something about both these problems.

An hour or so before the creditors' meeting, the inner
cabinet, or Committee of Inspection, was assembled in Bird
Cameron's boardroom in the Stock Exchange building on
Melbourne's Collins Street to hold its customary cabal.
Suddenly, the doors flew open and Bond burst in, closely
followed by the receptionist whom he had nearly knocked off
his feet in the rush. It was the sort of scene that a playwright
or novelist would die for: angry tycoon confronts his enemies
in their lair, nervous lawyers and accountants shrink in their
seats. Would Ramsay support his proposal, Bond demanded
to know. Well, no, he thought he would not. Would another
million dollars change his mind? Well, yes, he supposed it
might. Exit tycoon whence he came. Accountants and others
exhale.

It was the sort of tactic that Bond was famous for, as was

Murdoch in his younger days and Packer while he still cared about business, and it appeared to have blown the opposition away. An hour or so later, Ramsay was telling the full creditors' meeting that he would now be prepared to back Bond's offer, provided the entrepreneur signed a guarantee that he had disclosed all his assets. This was perhaps like asking a lion to swear that he would not eat meat, but Ramsay and the major creditors were convinced it would make it easier to reopen the bankruptcy if any money was found.

But guarantee or no guarantee, Bond still needed to get one of his biggest creditors, the Arab Banking Corporation, on side if he was to win his freedom. The Bahrain-based bank, which had a crucial 22 per cent of the vote, had accepted a personal guarantee for $133 million from Alan in October 1989 and now stood to be paid a mere $133,000 for releasing him, because it was not going to share in the $7 million pay-out from Dallhold. Not surprisingly, its lawyers had refused to settle for this meagre amount of money.

Needing time to win them around, Bond resolved to ask his creditors for a month's grace. And this he did with typical aplomb. Turning on the full salesman's charm, he promised his unlucky audience an extra $1 million if they were prepared to wait. Soon afterwards, he was wishing them all Happy Christmas and promising to see them at the end of January. Then he was off to run the gauntlet of around fifty TV cameramen and reporters waiting in the lobby downstairs and to tell them that he had absolutely no intention of going to live in Canada or Switzerland. He was confident, he said, that everything was on track. All that was needed was a little bit of patience.

While the great persuader was holding forth in Melbourne, Justice Sheppard was sitting in the Federal Court in Sydney

'This is a Sunday …
please leave … I am
calling the police.'
Jurg Bollag, at home
in Zug, offers a warm
welcome to the author,
July 1993.

Sorry, can't stop. John Hatton-Edge, who ran Bond's Jersey companies, tries to outrun an ABC TV camera crew in July 1993.

In the pink. Bond with Diana Bliss, July 1993, at the first night of *Phantom of the Opera* in Sydney, looking as fit as a fiddle.

Bond and his lawyers in full flight, January 1994.

Losing it. Bond grabs the mike from TV reporter Ros Thomas and hurls it across a Fremantle car park, December 1993. Alan's psychologist had just told a court he was suicidal, depressed and unfit to run a corner store.

Remember me?

So you do
remember me.
A testing moment
for Bond outside the
Federal Court in
Sydney, May 1994.
Bond could not recall
whether or not he
had millions of
dollars hidden
overseas, but he
did remember me.

When the going gets tough, the tough go to hospital. Alan staggers from court in Perth in May 1994, with lawyer Andrew Fraser holding one arm, and psychologist Tim Watson-Munro holding the other. Bond has collapsed on the first day of hearings into whether he is fit to stand trial on the $15 million Manet fraud charges. The court decides he is.

listening to Bond's lawyers argue why Bob Ramsay should be denied access to the documents the police had seized from Bond's home in September. Ramsay had been trying to get his hands on these since mid-November and was convinced that they could have the power to sway creditors. Glancing at the clock, Justice Sheppard mused that it might now be too late to make any difference.[17]

The following day, Sheppard was back in court to pass judgement, which had been given new import by the month's delay, and to deliver a stinging rebuke to the recalcitrant entrepreneur. Bond had argued through his counsel that the documents should remain private because they might incriminate him, which was a strange argument from someone who still maintained that the charges against him were absurd. Sheppard would have none of this, and ordered Bond to tell the police to hand them over.

> Unwilling or uncooperative bankrupts must make available documents against their will or be in contempt of court or in breach of the criminal law. Cooperation can and will be compelled in appropriate cases. If this were not the case bankrupts could make a laughing stock of their obligations . . . Mr Bond is required to do many things he is probably unwilling to do. This is but one of them.[18]

It was a shame that Sheppard had not read Bond the riot act back in May when the entrepreneur was feigning brain damage and memory loss, and a shame that he had not supervised Bond's famous bankruptcy examination himself, for he might have cut through the nonsense. It was now a bit late to get tough.

Sheppard had also been asked to rule on whether Bond should give Ramsay details of the myriad phone calls he had made from the Sheraton Wentworth Hotel during his Federal Court examination in May 1994, when he claimed to have forgotten all about his offshore fortune. And here, too, he decided that Alan must do as he was asked, by revealing who he had called, what he had talked about, and the business or banking transactions that had resulted.

The inevitable appeal by Bond would delay compliance with this order for two weeks, but in early January, Bond would be forced to dredge his dodgy memory for dealings with the D'Jamirze brothers, Whaka Kele, Roger Bryer and others, and to explain why he had spent such a long time talking to someone in a phone box on Zurich's railway station. This, too, offered Ramsay a glimmer of hope that creditors would give him one more chance to get his hands on Bond's Swiss fortune.

20

Free

Mr Bond said I was being a 'fucking vindictive cunt'
and kicked a four-tiered tray off my desk. He said
he would sue me and the newspaper ... and would
ensure I would lose my house in resulting
legal action.

Bond threatening a creditor, January 1995[1]

As Bond gained confidence that he would be released from
bankruptcy, he became more cocksure. Just after the
creditors' meeting on 20 December 1994, he told the *West
Australian* in a rare exclusive interview that he blamed Australia's banks for the collapse of his business empire and Australia's politicians for persecuting him since his demise. It was
the usual yarn that failed tycoons and maverick ex-leaders like
to spin—namely that it was someone else's fault, that ordinary
people still loved him and that his greatest concern was for his
supporters, or in this case, his shareholders.

No doubt some people believed this stuff, and a huge
number certainly still admired him for, as he put it, 'staying
to face the music'. Few realised that he had been given no
choice about staying in Australia since April 1992, in that
(unlike Skase) his passport had been confiscated on his return
from London.

Bond also used his chat with the *West Australian* to repeat his tired old claim that Bollag was just a generous friend and to assure his fans that his health was still improving. 'It just takes time,' said Bond, 'I was quite ill six months ago. I'm much better now, very much better.'[2]

Bond's chances of escaping bankruptcy were also improving rapidly. By the middle of January 1995, the Arab Bank had been whipped into line with a combination of legal action and a $715,000 sweetener, and Jim Byrnes had supposedly found 'up to five' smaller creditors who were willing to sell their vote. If true, this was enough to guarantee Bond victory, and Ramsay would need a miracle to keep his investigations alive.

In late January, Bond's trustee summoned him to Melbourne to answer questions about the documents that the police had seized from his house in Cottesloe. These provided tantalising glimpses of the deals that Alan had been pursuing with Tri Kal and the D'Jamirze brothers. Bond assured him that none had come to fruition, and that he had only been a consultant in any case. But when Ramsay asked about the movement of money into bank accounts in Zurich and about Alan's promise to pay the D'Jamirzes $US3 million, the normally garrulous entrepreneur clammed up.

The police files, however, had strengthened Ramsay's conviction that Bond was hiding money from his creditors and had made him even more determined to prove it. He was already seeking a second Federal Court order to make the AFP hand over material that they had seized from Bond's friends and business partners, which consisted of another eight boxes and twenty Lever Arch files. And he now renewed his efforts to get hold of Joe Lieberfreund's prized Swiss bank documents which had set the police on Bond's trail in the first place.

Ramsay and the AFP had both been told in November 1993

that this evidence could only be used in connection with a prosecution of Laurie Connell, and this was likely to be the answer once more, but Ramsay knew that the documents were dynamite in that they disclosed the existence of a Swiss bank account held by 'Bollag on behalf of Alan Bond' that had contained 'a substantial amount of money' until 1989.[3]

It was obvious, too, that Western Australia's Director of Public Prosecutions, John McKechnie, was busting to hand them over if he possibly could. Even though he initially refused to comply with a notice to surrender them, he turned up to the subsequent private hearing in Perth with the documents in two big boxes on a legal trolley. Afterwards, as his law clerk wheeled the barrow back up St George's Terrace, McKechnie and Joe Lieberfreund walked beside them and allowed the *West Australian*'s photographer to snap the scene for the next day's front page. Lieberfreund was even moved to tell a reporter that they wanted Ramsay to have them, and that they might well cause creditors to change their vote.

> It's extremely frustrating that we can't release them. They are documents which could be relevant and could be crucial. Nobody wants to see justice done more than McKechnie.[4]

This was stirring stuff, but it was soon silenced. Lieberfreund was immediately phoned by Bond's lawyer Steven Paterniti and told that he had better retract or he might find himself being sued. And sure enough, the next issue of the *West Australian* announced that he had made a 'dramatic backflip'. Bond was also quoted on the paper's front page, minimising the importance of the haul.

Quite frankly, any documents could be years and years old. They are untested documents. No one knows whether they're real or factual. And for Lieberfreund to make these sorts of comments is totally unprofessional.[5]

Of course Lieberfreund had obtained the documents himself and knew exactly what they contained. And his profession was to catch people like Bond.

While this was all playing out in Perth, Bob Ramsay and his team had worked through the first set of police documents and written a new forty-two-page report to creditors, with a commentary on the deals they disclosed. The picture was hardly complete, but the millions of dollars flowing into Swiss bank accounts in mid-1994 had convinced him that he should tell creditors to vote 'No' to Bond's offer.

By this time Bond had provided a draft version of the legal warranty Ramsay had demanded, in which he promised that he had disclosed all his assets. But his trustee was no longer interested in his assurances.

In the light of the material I have obtained in the form of the documents seized by the Australian Federal Police, the statements made to me by Mr Lieberfreund and the state of my own investigations to date, I cannot at this stage be satisfied that the warranty made by Mr Bond is correct. I believe on the evidence available to me it is likely that the bankrupt controls assets overseas. I therefore cannot recommend the proposed composition to creditors.[6]

Bond's lawyer Steven Paterniti angrily told the press that there was nothing new in Ramsay's latest analysis: 'All he does is regurgitate all the stuff that everyone already knew before'. Soon afterwards, he sent a ten-page letter to Bond's creditors marked 'Urgent–Confidential'. This letter ridiculed Ramsay's efforts thus far, telling them that the trustee had spent a fortune and made lots of allegations about offshore assets but had not 'proved' Alan owned a single dollar that had not been disclosed.[7]

The choice of the word 'proved' was particularly interesting, given that Paterniti's former partner at Parker & Parker, Harry Lodge, had helped set up Bond's Jersey trust companies in the early 1980s, and that two partners at Touche Ross in Jersey had testified these companies held millions of dollars for Alan Bond. But so was the attack on the value of this Jersey evidence, which Paterniti derided as 'mostly speculative'. This seemed an odd way to describe Hatton-Edge's and Davies's sworn testimony to a Jersey court.

While Paterniti was going in to bat for his client, Bond was busy trying to ensure that he had the numbers for the next, and possibly last, creditors' meeting, which was due to decide his fate on 31 January.

For several days the ebullient entrepreneur had been trying to get hold of Gerry Cavanagh, the credit controller at Western International Travel, who had been away on holiday. Now, with barely twenty-four hours to go until the scheduled vote, Alan marched into his twenty-eighth-floor office and demanded that Cavanagh vote for a settlement.

Cavanagh told Bond that the board of Western International Travel, which belonged to the group that published the *West Australian*, was not prepared to accept a compromise. The original debt had only amounted to $54,000 for first-class travel to the USA, West Indies and the UK, but the amount that Alan was now offering in settlement was more like $100, and this would not even cover the cost of the paperwork.

The refusal provoked an explosion. According to Cavanagh, Bond 'became agitated' and refused to leave the office unless he changed his vote to 'Yes'. In Cavanagh's words, he then 'lost it'.

> Mr Bond said I was being a 'fucking vindictive cunt' and kicked a four-tiered tray off my desk. He said he would sue me and the newspaper, claiming, 'I will make you personally responsible' for not voting for the composition, and [that he] would ensure I would lose my house in resulting legal action.[8]

Cavanagh had been in the business for more than twenty years and had seen debtors blow their stack in the past, but even he was shocked by this aggressive temper tantrum and decided to again ask Bond to leave. When Bond again refused, Cavanagh rang the security guards to have the irate entrepreneur removed. He then walked out of his office, pursued by an angry Bond asking him, 'Why are you doing this to me?'. Some twenty minutes later, perhaps after a visit to his lawyers, a more composed Bond rang to apologise.

In contrast to all this torrid drama, the creditors' meeting next day turned out to be a huge anticlimax. Once again, an army of cameramen and journalists gathered outside the venue, Sydney's Masonic Centre, in anticipation of a result, and once again they trooped away disappointed. This time a technical hitch had arisen over the Dallhold settlement, and over Upp Hall in particular, and after much huddling and whispering in the concrete corridors the vote was adjourned for yet another month.

The new delay gave Ramsay another chance to obtain the AFP documents that he hoped would convince creditors it was worth continuing the chase. And some three weeks later, on Friday 24 February, Justice Ryan told the Federal Court in Melbourne that he would instruct the AFP to hand them over. Within minutes, the police were trucking the eight boxes and twenty Lever Arch files across Melbourne to the office of Victoria's Official Receiver whose job it was to pass them on to Ramsay. For the next four hours, they sat there untouched while everyone held their breath to see if Bond would appeal the judgement. Then, as the clock ticked towards tea-time, Justice Ryan decided that the papers should be surrendered even if Bond did appeal, and the trolleys were duly wheeled down to the loading dock, to Ramsay's waiting van.

Ramsay would have only the weekend to plough through this mountain of material before the final vote. Bond, meanwhile, was confidently telling the press that creditors had already made up their minds, and implying that victory was in the bag.

Late on Monday morning Ramsay held a council of war with his Committee of Inspection, which comprised most of the major creditors, and asked them for yet more time. He told them the documents had thrown up promising leads that he wanted to follow, and that he was now only weeks away from getting Bollag into the witness box in Switzerland and gaining access to Bond's bank accounts. The appeal process in the Swiss Federal Court was almost exhausted, he told them, and he had been assured by his Swiss lawyer that Bollag could not win.

But his pleas found little support. Gavin Rezos from the

Hongkong Bank summed up the mood by saying that they had spent enough on the chase and did not want to throw good money after bad. Ramsay had warned that the Swiss investigations could eat up another $1 million and take another two years to complete, and even though the bulk of the cost would be split between Tricontinental and the Commonwealth Government, no one apart from Lord and Ramsay seemed to have the stomach for the fight. They were tired of Bond and Byrnes and the whole damn shoot. Just as he had hoped, Bond had outlasted them.

With Bond's major creditors determined to settle, it was inevitable that Bond would now be released from bankruptcy, and when it came to the full creditors' meeting Ramsay did little more than go through the motions. He distributed his summary of the police documents which he said showed money transfers involving several million dollars. He stated his belief that Bond had not told him the truth when he denied that any deals had come off. But he did not make a passionate plea for Bond's bankruptcy to be extended.

Before long, Jim Byrnes, as chief escape officer, was proposing the motion to accept Bond's offer. Alan's lawyer Steven Paterniti seconded it, and the creditors voted by a comfortable margin to accept $3.25 million in full payment of Bond's $599 million worth of personal debts. There would be a down payment of $1 million followed by $750,000 a year for the next three years. After expenses, most creditors would receive around $1 for every $600 they were owed, or one-sixth of a cent in every dollar.[9]

The SULA banks had not cast their vote because Tricontinental and the Hongkong Bank had been unable to agree, but all the other major creditors had supported the deal, boosting the 'Yes' vote to eighty-eight per cent by value. Once again, the smaller creditors had been reluctant to let Bond off, so the split on numbers was a far less convincing thirteen to eight. The Australian Taxation Office had voted to keep Bond in bankruptcy, having belatedly assessed him for a whopping $21 million in unpaid income tax.[10] Other, less cunning tax dodgers, no doubt, would have been thrown out of their homes for debts one-thousandth of the size.

Steven Paterniti had anticipated his client's victory and was ready with a cheque for $1 million to cover Bond's first instalment. Bob Ramsay held it up sheepishly for a creditor to photograph. He had worked ridiculously hard over the previous few weeks to keep Bond in bankruptcy and the strain had been getting to him. Now that the battle was over and the adrenalin had drained away, he suddenly looked exhausted and beaten. He would pack up his files, take up his golf clubs and contemplate whether or not to retire. Although frustrated and disappointed, he was also relieved. It had been far harder than anything he had done in his life before.[11]

Bond, for his part, looked like he'd won the America's Cup all over again. After the formalities had been completed he emerged from the meeting with a split-melon smile to tell the media pack that he was happy to be free and to have the stain of bankruptcy expunged. Of course, he said, he would have much preferred for everyone to have got their money back, but it was entirely the fault of the banks that they had not. It was the banks' impatience, he said, that had been the real problem for creditors, because if they hadn't rushed to sell his Greenvale Nickel Project, and if Dallhold's claim against the Queensland Government had succeeded, there would have been, 'Enough money to satisfy all of the creditors in full, and leave a fifty per cent surplus. Everybody could have been paid 100 cents in the dollar'.[12]

This was not only untrue, it was also an absurd argument, in that the same reasoning would have elevated the hapless Warwick Fairfax to the most brilliant dealmaker of the twentieth century. Warwick had lost his family fortune by borrowing $2 billion to buy the Fairfax newspapers, yet seven years after the crash they were worth twice what he had paid for them. It would have also made Christopher Skase a genius, despite his huge personal and corporate collapse. And it would in fact have stopped Bond from buying Greenvale in the first place, because he had snapped it up when the previous owners had gone bust by paying out their bankers at just six cents in the dollar.[13]

As to Alan's other suggestion that the banks who had lent him money had got it all back, this was also wrong, even if you didn't count the interest that had been racking up since 1990. The sad fact was that the collapse of Bond's businesses had caused his creditors and shareholders to lose almost $5 billion. But, like all expert salesmen, he never let the facts get in the way of a good story.[14]

As for the immediate future, Bond told journalists he would continue to work as a consultant. One wit writing to the *Sydney Morning Herald* later suggested he could offer his services to Barings Bank, which had just gone bust after losing $1 billion in derivatives. Another suggested psychiatry, so that he could 'transform pathetic, forgetful, bumbling wrecks into bright, articulate, switched-on all-round good guys, and all with the wave of the creditors' hand'.[15]

Over the next few days, newspapers, radio stations, TV and parliament all reverberated with the public's outrage that Bond had been allowed to go free. Australia's former chief corporate cop, Henry Bosch, described the decision to release Bond as disgraceful.[16] The former chairman of the Australian Stock

FREE

Exchange, Laurie Cox, said it would do nothing but harm to
Australia in the eyes of the world. But as the acting Attorney
General Duncan Kerr pointed out, it had been a commercial
decision by the creditors to let him go. Meanwhile, he assured
everyone that the Australian Federal Police were still investigating Bond for alleged offences against the Bankruptcy Act,
and if assets were discovered criminal charges would certainly
follow.

As the inevitable postmortem dragged on, Ramsay boasted
that it would have been just a matter of time before the documents he was seeking in Switzerland had come into the public
arena. 'I was so damned close. That's what rankles me. I was
six weeks away at most, not from solving the whole mystery,
but from getting inside the Swiss situation.'[17] It was the lament
of the vanquished. He had not laid his hands on a dollar of
Bond's offshore fortune. Nor had he looked like beating Bond
and Bollag.

It was a suitable end to the pantomime that a final altruistic
act by Alan's generous friend had been needed to set Bond
free. Bollag's agreement to write off £400,000 that he was
owed for expenses at Upp Hall had removed the last obstacle
to a settlement.

This magnanimous gesture would allow the Bond family to
live in Bollag's, or should one say Bond's, magnificent country
mansion forevermore. And since the £400,000 Jurg had
forgone was Alan's money anyway, it had cost him nothing.

241

21

Wedded Bliss

> We are certainly going to defend this with great
> vigour. I don't believe the charges should have been
> brought, and if you read the judgement I'm sure you
> can reach the same conclusion.
>
> *Alan Bond outside Perth Magistrates' Court,*
> *3 March 1995*

Bond's celebrations at being discharged from bankruptcy threatened to be short-lived, for he now faced imminent prosecution on two sets of criminal charges that had the capacity to put him behind bars for ten years or more. Four days after his escape from Ramsay's clutches he was due to face a committal hearing in Perth over the alleged $15 million fraud relating to Manet's *La Promenade*. And six weeks before his release he had been hit with a far more serious indictment accusing him of a considerably larger fraud against Bell Resources in 1988–89.

Indeed, the Bell heist was the crime of the century in terms of the amount of money involved. The siphoning off of $1,200 million from Robert Holmes à Court's old flagship to Bond Corporation had reduced a hugely wealthy enterprise to an empty hulk in the space of nine months, and had caused nigh on total loss to its shareholders. It had also directly benefited Alan Bond, in that at least $55 million had been diverted to his private company Dallhold, enabling him to spray millions of dollars in cash and jewels to Eileen and his children when his business empire was on the brink of collapse.

Bell Resources had been one of the stock market's stars in the 1980s but had been savaged by the crash of October 1987. And by the time Bond came on the scene all its assets had been sold and turned into cash. This, however, was why it was attractive to Bond, who desperately needed to lay his hands on the odd couple of billion dollars to keep his empire afloat. By mid-1988 interest rates were rocketing, the share market boom was over and cash flow had slowed to a trickle.

Bond Corporation seized control of the company in August 1988 and rapidly milked it of every last cent, concealing this plunder from the National Companies and Securities Commission (NCSC) until it was too late for shareholders to get their money back. The NCSC, under Henry Bosch, did its best, but possessed neither the funds nor the staff to prosecute the case, and persuaded the government to set up a major inquiry. This job was given in March 1990 to a South Australian QC called John Sulan, who spent almost two years collecting 200,000 documents, examining sixty-five witnesses and identifying what the Australian Securities Commission (ASC) described as 'major breaches of the law'.

In February 1992, the head of the ASC in Western Australia made a confident public statement that it would be only 'a matter of weeks' before prosecutions were launched.[1] But by the time that charges were finally laid in January 1995, it had taken six years, three investigations, 1.2 million documents, and a special waiver from the Attorney General to get Bond in the dock. Even so, at the end of this marathon pursuit, Bond was still rushed into Perth Magistrates' Court on a Saturday

morning to be formally arraigned. It seemed odd after all
this time that the commander of the Bond Task Force, Tim
Phillipps, felt they couldn't wait till Monday.[2]

Bond arrived jauntily at the East Perth court at around
9.25am in a maroon Land Cruiser driven by his skiing buddy
and hotelier friend Geoffrey Ogden, and accompanied by his
lawyer Andrew Fraser who had flown in from Melbourne the
day before. Wearing a grey suit with a white shirt and dark
tie, he stopped briefly to pose for photographers. Holding his
head high, he tried hard to smile, but he looked so uncomfortable that the effect was more like a rictus. He'd been told
only two days earlier that he would be charged for the Bell
fraud and had still not been given the details.

Having dealt with the small crowd of journalists outside, his
first port of call was the lockup, where he was stripped of his
tie and belt, and made to surrender his shoelaces. Next he was
asked to turn out his pockets and hand over his valuables—
his watch, his wallet and whatever credit cards he had left—
while the arresting officer recorded the items one by one in the
property book. As he produced his Ansett Golden Wing frequent flyer card he joked to Tim Phillipps, who had chosen to
bring the charges against Bond in person, that he probably
wouldn't be needing it much in the future. It seemed to Phillipps that he was shocked to be charged and shocked to be
going through this humiliating process, as if no one had told
him it would happen. But he probably thought that he had
escaped scot-free, because more than five years had passed
since the so-called crimes had been committed.[3]

Bond was first up before magistrate Wayne Tarr at
10.00am, and stood pale and silent as the long indictment was
read out to him. There was a Criminal Code charge of conspiracy to defraud, which carried a seven-year sentence, and

three Companies Code charges of failing to act honestly as a
director with intent to defraud shareholders. Finally, there
were three more of misusing his position as a director to gain
an advantage for Bond Corporation. Taken together, if all the
charges were proved, he could face a maximum of thirty-seven
years in jail.

When he emerged from court a couple of hours later, Bond
was tieless, beltless and looking strained, having provided half-
a-million dollars bail to avoid being sent straight to jail. He
now faced the prospect of reporting every Monday to Fremantle police station but, unlike most people in his position,
would be allowed to do it by phone to the Australian Securities
Commission if he was travelling interstate.

While Bond was being driven away by Geoffrey Ogden, who
had been prevailed upon to pledge an additional $250,000
surety in case Bond did a runner, Andrew Fraser told reporters
in aggrieved tones about the new wrongs being heaped upon
his innocent client. 'Once again Mr Bond is being made the
scapegoat,' he said. 'He is not guilty of these charges. We will
defend them to the death.' It was unfair, said Fraser, that the
authorities had brought charges outside the normal five-year
time limit, and unfair that Bond had been singled out to take
the rap when others, who were equally responsible for losing
Bell Resources's money had fled overseas.[4]

Peter Mitchell and Tony Oates had been charged in their
absence with conspiracy to defraud, and with eight and sixteen
charges respectively under the Western Australian Companies
Code. But Oates was in Poland, where he was quite possibly
beyond the reach of extradition proceedings, and Mitchell was
in Colorado, USA, where he had been working for three
years—although he would in fact come back voluntarily to
face the music.[5]

Seven weeks after being charged with what was easily the biggest fraud in Australian history, Bond was back in the same court for yet another appearance on the rather less spectacular Manet fraud charges. The day of reckoning on *La Promenade* was getting closer. Having only been discharged from bankruptcy in Sydney on the last Monday in February, he was required to be back in the dock again in Perth the next Friday to hear Magistrate Ivan Brown commit him for trial. This time, however, he was animated and chirpy outside the court, and keen to tell the press that it was all a big mistake. 'We are certainly going to defend this with great vigour,' he told a knot of journalists. 'I don't believe the charges should have been brought, and if you read the judgement I'm sure you can reach the same conclusion.'[6]

This was putting a favourable gloss on the proceedings, to put it mildly, for the magistrate had clearly reached exactly the opposite conclusion in ruling that there was a case for Bond to answer. But with the irrepressible optimism of a born salesman, Alan had latched on to Ivan Brown's observation that the evidence was circumstantial and that he had admitted nothing, so it might be a tough case for the prosecution to win.

Having faithfully recorded his sales pitch about the charges being in error, a couple of journalists remarked to Bond that he seemed to be far sprightlier than he had been in June 1994, when his lawyers had argued that he was too sick for the Manet committal hearing to proceed. And one even ventured to suggest that it was a bit of a coincidence that he had improved dramatically the instant that the magistrate had ruled him fit to face trial. But Bond was having none of this.

> It's not a little coincidental. If you actually read
> the medical reports at the time, they say that it is

about now that I would start to see a full recovery,
and I'm not fully recovered yet, but I'm much,
much better.[7]

Thanks to the backlog in the Western Australian criminal
justice system, he would now have at least another twelve
months to recuperate before he was forced to face trial. He
would also be guaranteed at least twelve months of freedom
up to that point, whatever the final verdict. And in the meantime, he had an important appointment with his long-time
lover Diana Bliss.

Alan had proposed to Diana several times during their
sixteen-year relationship but she had always turned him
down. No doubt the fact that he had still been married to
Eileen had been a major obstacle, but she might also have
wondered about the wisdom of getting hitched to such an
inveterate womaniser and workaholic. Since the collapse of
his marriage and business empire, however, Alan had been
forced to slow down and stay in Australia, and they had spent
far more time together in far more normal circumstances.
Since mid-1993 they had even lived together for long stretches
in Alan's house in Cottesloe, and by October that year they
were sufficiently reunited for Diana to confess to the *New
Weekly*, 'Obviously I love him, obviously I love and care for
him. I always will'.[8]

At this stage, Diana was still dismissing suggestions of marriage, saying there would only ever be one Mrs Bond, but she
was talking wistfully of whether at thirty-nine she might still
be young enough to have children. And she clearly wasn't
thinking of anyone except Alan as the father.

In October 1994, Alan proposed to her again in a crowded
Japanese restaurant in Melbourne's St Kilda Road and nearly

fell off his stool when she agreed. Till then she had always wanted to hang on to her freedom, so she could be out seven nights a week at the theatre, travel the world and be free to pursue her career as a producer, but it had suddenly hit her that she was tired of being single. She told Jane Cadzow of *Good Weekend* magazine that the revelation had come to her at five o'clock one morning in a cabaret bar in New York, where she was sitting drinking with Australian actor Carmen Duncan and a bunch of gay men, feeling too tired to get a cab. As daylight approached, it dawned on her that she didn't want to be doing the same thing ten years down the line. 'It was the family, it was the family ... that I knew I was missing in my life. And that commitment to a partner. Maybe even getting a dog, that sort of thing.'[9]

She did not want to be single at the age of fifty. She wanted more depth and meaning to her life, she said. And so on Easter Saturday, 15 April 1995, she and Alan tied the knot at the Museum of Contemporary Art on Sydney's Circular Quay.

To avoid the paparazzi, the venue was kept secret from even the eighty-odd guests until an hour beforehand, so that the previous week in Sydney had seen mounting speculation about where this 'wedding of the year' would take place. Most of the smart money had been staked on St Mark's Church in Darling Point or All Saints in Woollahra, but when these drew a blank some journalists staked out the Park Hyatt Hotel and a restaurant called Level 41. This was on the forty-first floor of the building that would have been the Bond Tower had Bond's empire not collapsed in 1990, and occupied the space that had originally been earmarked as Alan's penthouse.

Now, as the hour approached, some fifty members of the Australian and international media were sheltering under the palm trees, clutching soggy notebooks or protecting expensive cameras, and toying with phrases like 'wedded bliss', 'life of bondage' or perhaps 'rain did not dampen their spirits'. It had been conceived as a romantic sunset ceremony but, sadly, a thick autumn drizzle had put paid to that.

First to arrive was the groom, who stepped out of a long white Mercedes limousine looking 'tanned and fat', as the British satirical magazine *Private Eye* liked to put it. Wearing white tie and tails, white gloves, and an expression that John Huxley of the *Sydney Morning Herald* described as his 'trade-mark startled glance at the media', Bond didn't bother to say hello to the journalists or pose for the cameras, but merely grabbed the attention of a security guard and told him to 'get the fuck out front' to exercise a bit of crowd control.[10]

Soon afterwards, when the bride and her entourage arrived in matching black-and-cream vintage Rolls-Royces, the importance of this advice was revealed, because Diana, in an off-the-shoulder magnolia silk dress by Sydney designer Chris-topher Essex, was immediately engulfed in a huge scrum that dislodged her veil, toppled a number of plants and nearly demolished one of the canopies that formed part of the decorations. Fortunately, friends came to her rescue and she was able to proceed into the museum with dignity restored, accompanied by two bridesmaids and four young attendants, to the strains of *Procession* from *The Sound of Music*, played on a baby grand piano.

Behind heavy brass-studded steel doors and shaded windows, the main hall of the MCA had been turned into a chapel, with marble columns, massive Grecian urns, cream roses, candelabra and calico-draped plinths. A simple lectern had been pressed into service as a makeshift altar. Rows of delicate white chairs with gold bows had been set up for the ceremony, while cream couches and cane chairs at the back awaited the reception. Neil Perry of Sydney's famous Rockpool restaurant had organised the catering, while the entertainment had been choreographed by Christopher Essex and the theatrical Miss Bliss.

The scale of it was scarcely on a par with some of Alan's more famous bashes or any of his children's weddings, but the press agreed that it was a pretty spectacular affair and reported solemnly that 'experts suggested' it had cost more than $100,000 to stage.

They also reported enviously that Alan and Diana had earned the money back by selling exclusive picture rights to Britain's *Hello!* magazine, oft-favoured by celebrities for its gushing admiration of wealth, fame and excess. And as the majority of journalists hunkered down outside in the growing gloom, the PR writer hired by *Hello!* set about giving the happy couple a glowing write-up.

For once, though, the hyperbole was possibly justified, because according to several of the guests, Diana and Alan were like love-struck teenagers. Alan was just out of bankruptcy, was outwardly confident of beating his fraud charges and had finally got his long-time love to the altar after many years of trying. Diana, for her part, really did look radiant as they danced together and watched a troupe of Shirley-Temple-look-alikes in pink tutus sing *My Boy Lollipop*.

What had finally made up Alan's mind, he told *Hello!*, was his heart operation two years before.

> I remember the last person I saw before I went into surgery was Di, and her beautiful smiling face was there when I woke up. We have continued to grow from strength to strength, and in a relationship that has had to stand the test of time, through all

the speculation and the hard times, true love has really shined through.[11]

It was a mark of his new wife's love for him that she had chosen to come back to Alan in 1992 just as others were leaving, and she now told the same *Hello!* interviewer it was their troubles that had finally united them.

> When you go through a crisis in your life, you tend to re-evaluate everything ... your friendships, your values, your future ... If anything, this recent period with Alan, with his legal battles and our enforced separation, brought us closer together and made us realise the deep love we had for each other.[12]

As the guest list showed, few of Alan's other friends had showed such loyalty, although his best man Murray Quartermaine was a notable exception, as was Dr John Saunders, the surgeon who had been so worried the previous year about the state of his brain. The fickle ones had simply faded away, as publicity over his criminal charges and bankruptcy mounted. And none of his family had come to celebrate the new liaison either. Out of deference to Eileen, perhaps, Alan's four children had sent a telegram of good wishes but had elected to stay away. Word was that they were horrified by his remarriage. Diana's family and friends, however, had turned out in force, and her mother Phyllis provided one of the highlights by singing *What a Wonderful World* with Di's Aunt Betty and a friend Jo Black. The three women, it was said, were all in their seventies.

In the inevitable search for celebrities, the best the press could come up with was the Sydney model Kate Fischer, who was renowned for her willingness to attend almost any party, but who had yet to shoot to super-stardom by bedding Australia's most eligible bachelor Jamie Packer. In his stead, the ubiquitous Kate had come on the arm of Alan's burly minder, Jim Byrnes, who had no doubt squired her to the scene in one of his or, should one say, his family trust's many Rollers.

Byrnes had been busy all week on Bond's behalf and had earned his keep by helping to squash a story in *New Idea* which had threatened to feature the intimate confessions of a fifty-three-year-old 'masseuse' who claimed to have been Bond's lover. The story was to include a series of explicit and embarrassing letters that Bond had written to the woman from his Wooroloo prison cell in July and August 1992.

Like most of the other women in Alan Bond's life, Cecelie Turner was a blonde, but she was twenty years older than his normal female companions. Quite how she had come to light was not entirely clear, but she had been discovered by a freelance journalist, Jamie Fawcett, who had put her in touch with *New Idea* and perhaps helped her negotiate her $10,000 fee.

Bizarrely, Fawcett had then tipped off Byrnes about the upcoming article (or so Byrnes said in an affidavit to the New South Wales Supreme Court) and Jim had pulled out all the stops to get the item suppressed. His first move was to ring Cecelie herself and ask her what she had confessed to. Then he rang Alan Bond in Perth to tell him the bad news about what she had said. This prompted Bond to say, according to Byrnes's affidavit:

> This is all lies, I've only ever met the woman three or four times in my life and I've never given her anything. It looks as though she or the magazine or both are trying to blackmail me.[13]

One of the three or four meetings that Bond admitted to had clearly been quite recent, for *New Idea* had managed to snatch a couple of pictures of Cecelie and Alan in Sydney in early 1995 to demonstrate that she was telling the truth, and these showed Bond kissing her as he said goodbye to her outside her unit in Woollahra.

Having denied that there was even a scrap of truth in Cecelie's story, Bond beseeched Byrnes to stop the article being published, whereupon Jim rang the author, Pam Lesmond, to warn her that the piece was an invasion of privacy, defamatory and untrue. She suggested that Byrnes speak to her editor because the article had already been written and subbed.

Jim then rang Fiona Wingett, the editor of *New Idea*, whom he knew from 1992, when he had publicly lauded then lamented his marriage to Jackie Love. Wingett no doubt remembered him well, for she had reported being monstered by a 'very large minder' at Jim and Jackie's wedding.[14] Byrnes told the court he offered Wingett a deal—a tasteful exclusive for *New Idea* on the Bond–Bliss wedding, in exchange for them dropping the kiss-and-tell piece about Cecelie and returning Bond's letters—to which Wingett supposedly responded, 'We already have a good story which will appeal to our down-market readers. Our readers prefer trash not romance'.

Whether Fiona Wingett said any such thing is open to conjecture, since editors are rarely so frank about their clientele, but there is no dispute that she turned down the offer and referred him to the magazine's publisher, Susan Duncan, who also told him that they were not prepared to do a deal. Byrnes then warned her that he would see her in court.

The journalists' version of these genteel negotiations, however, suggested that Byrnes had relied on some old-fashioned methods to back up his arguments. In fact he frightened Pam Lesmond so much by threatening to visit her that she complained to the police and then moved out of her house. He was also 'very menacing' to Fiona Wingett, reminding her of his criminal record and telling her that she would have 'a short career in publications' unless she fell into line. Finally, he told Susan Duncan that he had ways of applying pressure that would make her see reason, and warned her to 'be careful'. Lesmond even received a death threat on her answering machine, but from a woman rather than from Jim.[15]

As for his offer of the 'tasteful exclusive', Byrnes omitted to tell the court that he had suggested *New Idea* pay a fee of $50,000. He had also obviously forgotten that the rights had already been promised to *Hello!*.

After Byrnes's persuasion failed to do the trick, Bond and his masseuse, whom he had somehow brought back on side, were forced to break cover, and in early May they rushed into the New South Wales Supreme Court to seek an injunction against *New Idea*, preventing publication of 'details of the private and sexual relationship' that they had allegedly enjoyed. Bond's argument was that he would be defamed by the story, while Cecelie maintained that *New Idea* would be in breach of contract because the journalist had promised to let her see the article before publication.

A full report of these grubby proceedings was naturally carried in the *Daily Telegraph* the following day, along with a big picture of a platinum blonde in a bright white dress, sporting glossy nail varnish, huge earrings and lots of gold. Which, of course, was Cecelie Turner.[16]

The *Telegraph* reported eagerly that the masseuse had sworn an affidavit, laying out in explicit and intimate detail exactly what she had told *New Idea* in the interview. Not surprisingly, however, the newspaper was unable to enlighten readers further, because Bond's lawyers persuaded the judge to suppress it. Alan's letters to Cecelie and his own court affidavit, which presumably set out his version of their relationship, were also included in the suppression order.

Alan and Cecelie's joint summons, however, gave a tantalising insight into what the two plaintiffs feared *New Idea* would say, without saying how they had come to such lurid conclusions. They suggested, for example, that *New Idea* might be planning to allege that Cecelie was not a masseuse but 'a prostitute'; that Alan had written 'lewd and lascivious letters' to her from jail; and that he had proposed that they 'engage in sexual activities of an unusual nature'. It was also suggested that the article would accuse Alan of being 'a person of loose morals' who had 'cheated' on his wife-to-be.[17]

An injunction was duly granted by the court to prevent the article or the letters being published on Monday 10 April, which meant that the scandal would at least not hit the newsstands until after the wedding had taken place. And battle was then joined on the substance of the case. But after all these fanfares, the war ended with a whimper, because when a watered-down version of the article was eventually produced in court it turned out to be worthy of Mills and Boon.

According to *New Idea*, Cecelie and Alan had indeed been lovers for a number of years, enjoying 'mainly a physical relationship', but Cecelie's view of it all had apparently been so romantic that there was not the slightest suggestion of impropriety.[18] The magazine's supposed legion of trash-lovers, who would doubtless have lapped up a few lewd and lascivious letters or some novel sexual manoeuvres, must have been bitterly disappointed.

Jim Byrnes told me afterwards that this whole affair between Bond and Ms Turner had started because Cecelie had written

Alan some 'really erotic' letters while he was in prison and had followed these up with a photo of her from her younger days. Bond, out of curiosity or kindness, had then written back and eventually agreed to meet her.

But Cecelie told the Australian Federal Police a rather different story after the court case was over. Her signed statement to the AFP in June 1995 alleged that Alan had picked her up in a bar in 1981, in much the same way as he had befriended Diana Bliss around that time, and that their encounter had led to what Cecelie described as a close personal friendship and 'physical relationship' over the next fourteen years. Bond, she said, had often visited her in Sydney, and she had occasionally visited him in Perth.[19]

But more interesting than that, Cecelie informed police that Bond had told her in pillow talk down the years about the money he had stashed overseas. In 1991, for example, she had been with him at his favourite hotel, the Sheraton Wentworth in Sydney, while process servers tried to serve him with a bankruptcy notice. According to her statement, Bond had told her that it didn't matter if they did make him bankrupt because he had $50 million invested overseas in companies run by Jurg Bollag.

Much more recently, in 1995, after his bankruptcy had been annulled, Bond had supposedly complained to her that his family and Bollag had forked out $5 million in legal fees to keep his pursuers at bay. Cecelie told the police that she had remarked that Mr Bollag must be a very nice man to help Alan out like this, at which point Bond had allegedly scoffed, 'Well, it's all my money'.

22

Guilty

Any prison sentence is a life sentence in a sense for someone in your position, in that you cannot sink into anonymity, but it will follow you forever.

Justice Kennedy, sentencing Bond on Manet fraud charges, 20 August 1996

Diana had married Alan in the full realisation that his troubles were not over and that a good portion of their life together might in fact be spent apart. And after only nine months of marriage, her worst fears were confirmed, because on 17 January 1996 Bond was sent for trial on the Bell fraud charges with a damning indictment ringing in his ears.

It was possible, said magistrate Ronald Gething in handing down his judgement at the committal hearing, that a jury would find that Bond and his co-accused Peter Mitchell had been 'dishonest', 'deceitful', 'very imprudent' and 'irresponsible' in the way that they had removed $1,200 million from Bell Resources, and that they had shown an 'absolute disregard' for the welfare of Bell's shareholders. It was also arguable that they had engaged in 'an extreme breach of duty'.[1]

According to Gething, the alleged crimes had been committed at a time when Bond Corporation had needed billions of dollars just to stay afloat, yet Bond and Mitchell had not only caused Bell Resources to lend the Bond Group $1,200 million without security and without interest being paid, but had then concealed this fact from the authorities. And lest there be any doubt that Alan himself had been involved, Gething drew attention to the fact that Bond had declared in a TV interview that *all* directors of Bell had taken part in the decision to make the loans.

The committal had originally been expected to run for ten weeks, but was completed in as many days because the prosecution decided to call only a handful of witnesses. One or two of these, however, really packed a punch. For example, David Aspinall, who had been one of Bond's top executives, did what none of Bond's loyal lieutenants had done before— he gave vital evidence against his former master.

Aspinall, however, would have been in the dock alongside Bond himself had he not turned witness for the prosecution at the last minute to save his own bacon. In January 1995, the leader of the Bond Task Force, Tim Phillipps, had rung him and Bond to tell them that they were both about to be charged, and Aspinall's lawyer had quickly rung back to ask if it was too late to do a deal. The next day, on the promise of getting some useful information, Phillipps sat down with Aspinall and his solicitor to see whether the Director of Public Prosecutions (DPP) might be able to grant him an indemnity.

> I still remember the first time Aspinall came in. It was the Saturday morning to start the process off. We spent about six hours talking to him about what he could tell us. We were pushing pretty hard. We said, 'Look this has got to be good, it really has to be the killer punch'.[2]

Aspinall was potentially a crucial witness for the prosecution, because he had been at the heart of the Bell transactions in 1988 and had voiced concerns to Alan Bond in November during a flight on the corporate jet to Chile about how Bell's money was being used. He was also inclined to help, because he and Alan had had a major falling out, and he obviously had no desire to go to prison himself for something that he had only supported reluctantly. But he was in a quandary about how much he should say. And according to Phillipps, he was close to panic.

> He was such a huge man, he was sitting there, sweat just pouring out of him. I was very concerned actually that the stress would be too much for him, that he might have a heart attack.[3]

Phillipps and an Australian Securities Commission lawyer called Greg Weekes questioned the former Bond executive until midnight on the Saturday and started again at six o'clock on Sunday morning. From time to time, one of them walked over to Aspinall's lawyer's office in the former Bond Tower with a draft or a redraft of what he was prepared to say. And finally, very late on the Sunday night, a statement was signed, which was then despatched by secure fax from Perth to the Commonwealth Director of Public Prosecutions, Michael Rozenes, in Canberra. This was then discussed at great length over the phone until Monday afternoon, at which point Rozenes agreed that the information was good enough to grant Aspinall the indemnity he was seeking.

Whether his evidence would in fact make the difference between acquittal and conviction when the case finally came to trial at the end of 1996 was of course open to question, but Gething's remarks at the committal made it pretty clear that it would be extremely useful. Before that happened, however, Bond had to face trial on the Manet charges.

To some people it seemed an odd decision to devote so much effort to chasing Bond over *La Promenade*, for $15 million was pocket money by Bond's standards and pinching the profits on a painting was hardly serious when compared with the Bell fraud, which involved almost a thousand times as much money. It seemed a bit like tackling Al Capone for tax evasion. But as the prosecution allegations unfolded in court in August 1996, it did not seem such a bad choice after all, for Bond had essentially used his private company Dallhold Investments to cheat the public company Bond Corporation and its shareholders. And the evidence showed that documents had then been forged to cover up the offence.

La Promenade was bought by Alan's private company Dallhold in 1983 to hang on the walls of his new office in Perth, and was soon given pride of place in the boardroom. Bond was hugely enthusiastic about this new addition to his burgeoning collection, but unfortunately revealed himself to be no great connoisseur. In 1985, he interviewed a cultured Englishman called David Michael for a job as his special personal assistant, and opened the batting by asking him whether he liked art, to which Michael replied that he loved it.

'What do you think of my Monet, then?' Bond asked proudly, gesturing at his recent acquisition, *La Promenade*.

'It's a Manet,' Michael replied.

'How do you know?' Bond asked, rather put out.

'Well, it's famous,' replied Michael, 'it's called *La Promenade*.'[4]

But if Bond was no expert on Impressionist paintings, he certainly did know that it was best to use other people's money to purchase them, and almost immediately after taking delivery of the Manet he sold it to a finance company and leased it back again, but this time with Bond Corporation's shareholders footing the bill. Over the next five years, the public company shelled out $100,000 a month in lease payments, or $5.6 million, so that Alan and his important visitors would have a masterpiece to look at.

The board of Bond Corporation was quite properly informed at the time by one of the directors, Tony Oates, that their company would have the right to acquire the painting from the finance company when the five-year lease expired. But when the opportunity arose in mid-1988 to buy the Manet for a fraction of its market value, Bond Corporation failed to take its chance to make a multi-million-dollar profit. And it failed because Alan Bond did not tell his fellow directors that the opportunity was there.

Sensing that there was a killing to be made, he decided to slip the money into his own pocket instead. In November 1988, his private company Dallhold bought *La Promenade* for $2.4 million. A year later it sold it at auction in New York for more than $17 million. Thus, the shareholders of Bond Corporation were cheated out of almost $15 million.

Alan had done deals like this before, when he was not in such dire straits. But it is just conceivable that desperation played as big a part as greed in his hijacking of the cash. In November 1987, he had paid a new world-record price of US$54 million for Van Gogh's *Irises* and had immediately had difficulty paying for it. In typical fashion he had persuaded Sotheby's to lend him half the money for his headline-making purchase, while borrowing the rest from a bank, and Sotheby's had refused to give him the painting unless he put up more collateral. In such circumstances, *La Promenade* was the obvious, if not the only, way out, because it was one of the few things in the Bond empire that wasn't already hocked to the hilt. It had therefore been vital for Dallhold to get its hands on the picture.

To satisfy the legal niceties, however, it was necessary to give Bond Corporation the chance to buy the painting so that it could formally reject the offer. In fact, this was a condition imposed by the owners of the leasing company, Macquarie Bank, who were clearly concerned about the propriety of what Alan was doing.[5] But this obviously posed a problem for Alan and his managing director at Dallhold, Michael Cross, because the board of Bond Corporation was hardly likely to turn down a chance to make $15 million for their shareholders. The answer was merely to recommend to the board that Bond Corporation reject the opportunity on the grounds that it was not in the business of collecting art, and to not disclose either the sale price of the painting or its market value. And this was how Bond played it.

The members of the Bond Corporation board had no inkling of any of these shenanigans, but the company secretary Noel Reed was consulted and objected to the transaction, making it clear that he regarded it as dishonest and not in the interest of shareholders. Reed, however, was ignored, and the transaction went ahead, with everything remaining hunky-dory until the auditors, Arthur Andersen, arrived on the scene ten months later.

Even then, there might have been no problems had 1989 been a normal year in the history of the Bond group, but Andersens had just copped a lot of flack over their audit of Bond Corporation's 1988 accounts, in which the company claimed profits of around $150 million that were actually bogus,[6] and they were now determined to let absolutely nothing pass without extra scrutiny.

The auditors duly unearthed the Manet transaction (which was showing up in the accounts as a $4 million dollar loss to Bond Corporation) and objected strongly on the basis that it was uncommercial and quite probably illegal, since Alan Bond had almost certainly breached his duty to Bond Corporation shareholders by not giving the public company the opportunity to buy the painting.

A committee was set up under the chairmanship of John Bond to deal with the problem[7] and a set of working notes was prepared to chart the history of the group's dealings with *La Promenade*. These revealed that it had been decided in 1984 that Bond Corporation would make the lease payments and acquire the painting at the end. The notes were then shown to one of the group's legal advisers, who advised John Bond that his father Alan had broken the law.

An entirely new set of working notes was then prepared, and backdated, in an effort to cover up the crime. These contained a brand new explanation for Bond Corporation's failure to buy the painting, which was that there had always been an agreement between Dallhold and Bond Corporation to share the profits on *La Promenade* between the public and private companies. Alan himself faxed a letter to the Bond Corp board from his schooner *XXXX*, claiming that this agreement had existed, undocumented, ever since the painting was purchased.

But as now became clear at the trial in Perth, there was not one single shred of evidence that Alan's tale was true, apart from the second set of working notes prepared ten months after the event. The only witness to Alan's supposed profit-sharing arrangement was the former managing director at Bond Corporation, Peter Beckwith. And he was dead.

On the other hand, there was ample evidence that Alan's

story was a lie. In the first place, Dallhold had not paid a cent of the profits to Bond Corporation by the time the auditors first raised their objections in September 1989, even though ten months had passed and the financial year had ended. Second, the paperwork from the early 1980s made it quite clear that Bond Corporation and not Dallhold was to buy *La Promenade* at the end of the lease—as the company had a legal right to do. Third, there was compelling evidence that person or persons unknown had altered the working notes to get Alan off the hook, substituting them for an earlier version in which the profit-sharing agreement had not been mentioned.

But the clincher, if any were needed, was that the sudden promise of September 1989 to share the profits had never been redeemed. Several months after the auditors were sent packing, Dallhold handed Bond Corporation a cheque for $4 million in an attempt to show that the $15 million was being divided fairly between the two companies. But this was no more than a sham. The cheque effectively was met with funds from Bond Corporation, so that no real money changed hands. The judge singled this transaction out for special criticism, describing it as 'stunning'.

It was therefore no great surprise on 16 August 1996 when the jury of six men and six women found Bond guilty on all four counts. In the words of the judge, the Crown case had been 'strong ... cleverly investigated, and cleverly presented' and the jury had been astute and diligent in following the complexities of the story.[8] They had deliberated for eleven hours and had been unanimous in pronouncing him guilty.

Alan's wife Diana, who had been sitting in a small side room with his legal team, appeared distraught as the verdicts were announced. Bond, however, cast a glance at one of his defence team, shrugged his shoulders and gave a wry smile. Shortly afterwards he kissed Diana twice and was taken off to the cells. Since it was a Friday, he would have to wait till Monday morning to be sentenced.

Over the weekend, his friends did their best to keep him out of jail by telling the papers that he was too sick to survive another spell behind bars. And come Monday morning his distinguished lawyer, Julian Burnside QC, attempted a similar job, by reminding Justice Antoinette Kennedy that she was sentencing 'not just anybody ... but Alan Bond ... a national hero', whose health was so frail that prison might turn out to be a life sentence. He should be fined, said Burnside, rather than sent to jail, adding dramatically, 'It is not true that the only way to punish Mr Bond is to destroy him.'

Lawyers of course have a duty to do their best for their clients, but it's hard to see how this speech can have been delivered with an entirely straight face. In a world where judges send the poor to jail on a $100 shoplifting conviction, it's a bit rich to expect that someone like Bond should get away with a fine for a $15 million fraud.

Yet, as one listened to Toni Kennedy deliver her sentencing remarks, it seemed that Burnside's pleas might have hit the spot, for she was clearly deeply sympathetic to the fallen entrepreneur. For a start, she felt it necessary to mention the 'vicious, hate-filled ... insatiable' members of the community who wanted to make an example of Bond. Then she urged people to realise that prison was no picnic.

> Time in prison goes a lot slower than time outside ... Having a TV set and turkey for lunch on Christmas Day—features of the prison system dear to the hearts of sections of the media—are no substitute for freedom ... Any prison sentence is a

life sentence in a sense for someone in your position, in that you cannot sink into anonymity, but
it will follow you forever.[9]

After that, she reflected on Bond's heart condition, the stress
he had suffered, the disgrace he had experienced, and the spite-
fulness of some sections of the media. These, she said, meant
that he had already been punished. He had been a wonderful
employer and an inspiring leader, and he was still a loving and
caring father and a man with many fine qualities. His tenacious pursuit of the America's Cup had been admired by all
Australia.

So how had such a wonderful citizen come to be responsible
for a $15 million fraud, one might well have asked? Justice
Kennedy had an answer for that one, too. Putting the best
possible face on things, she said, she could only assume that
Alan's passion for Monets or Manets had got the better of
him, and he had forgotten that Bond Corporation was no
longer his private fiefdom. Though, in fact, it had never been.

At the end of this eulogy, it would have been no great surprise to hear her say that Bond had already suffered enough
and should instantly be set free, for she had said earlier that
there was a limit to the punishment that any man could take.
But Justice Kennedy did no such thing. Emphasising that
Bond's crimes were extremely serious, she said she had no
option but to send him to jail, and duly sentenced him to two
years on the fraud charges and a year on the dishonesty
charges, making three years in total.

Bond looked bemused when the sentence was passed,
perhaps because Justice Kennedy's paean of praise had promised greater leniency, but he could hardly have felt aggrieved,
for he had been facing a theoretical maximum of fourteen

years in jail and a $60,000 fine, and with this sentence he could now expect to be out within twelve months. Diana held his hands and kissed him before he was taken away. Outside the court she told reporters in a short and dignified statement that she and many other Australians were upset that he had been sent to prison, but that she was grateful for Justice Kennedy's comments about his contribution to the community. A few months later she told the ABC's *Australian Story* that the trial had been especially painful and difficult for her. 'Alan and I felt like we were alone against the world because ...'— she paused for a moment, trying to find the words—'... It felt like a conspiracy. It was hard.'[10]

There is a comical, and possibly apocryphal, twist to this tale that has never been reported, which is that *La Promenade* may not have hung on the wall of Bond's boardroom for long after Dallhold filched it from the public company. In late 1988, with the entire Bond Group sinking deeper and deeper into financial difficulty and Sotheby's getting increasingly nervous over the millions it had lent for *Irises*, Alan began to worry that the Manet might be repossessed, so a local printer in Perth was commissioned to make some expensive colour copies. One of these was then coated with lacquer by a restorer to make it look like the genuine article, and swapped for the real thing on Bond's wall. The pukka *La Promenade*, meanwhile, was consigned to the National Australia Bank's vault in St Martin's Tower, where it was assumed to be safe from any bailiffs that might come to call. Finally, it was surrendered to Sotheby's and sold in New York. Remarkably, no one ever noticed the difference.

To serve out his sentence on the Manet conviction, Bond was sent to Karnet Prison Farm in the hills an hour south-east of Perth, where he was pretty much free to do what he liked, apart from go home. There were no bars on the windows, the cells were left unlocked at night, and he was given a hut to himself in which he installed a computer, a stereo and a small TV set along with a few books, files and personal possessions. In a letter to a well-wisher, he said that he was studying French, computing and creative writing, and was feeling better than he had felt for many years.

Indeed, far from looking like he might die in jail, as his lawyers had suggested to the judge, he was now reported to be thriving. Photographs published in Perth's *Sunday Times* showed him sitting cheerfully in the prison grounds with Diana and a couple of friends, the irrepressible Rose Hancock and her husband Willie Porteous. The accompanying story suggested, in a style that Justice Toni Kennedy had so deplored, that for Bond prison was nothing but a picnic:

> Bond looks like he's having the time of his life ... looking younger than his 58 years, [he] does not seem to be feeling any pain from the experience. He certainly doesn't look like he's dying, a prospect given great weight by his lawyers when they pressed for a non-custodial sentence.[11]

Fellow inmates reported that he was not only cheerful but was also bursting with health. He was riding an exercise bike for half an hour every morning, playing tennis two or three times a week and observing a vegetarian diet. As one Karnet prisoner put it: 'He's twenty years older than me and he's fitter than me. He leaves most people for dead, he's that fit'.[12]

Also in the picture was a friend that Alan had made since his arrival, who was probably a useful ally in case he struck trouble with the other prisoners, as he had in his first stint in jail in Wooroloo in 1992.

> The balding, smiling figure in the back row is
> former NSW charter pilot Anthony John Pinkstone
> who, on his own admission, used to work for an
> international syndicate involved in drug smug-
> gling, money laundering and murder ... He and
> Bond are the leading lights in a 'barbecue club'
> which has started up in the prison.[13]

But the lazy days in Karnet would not last forever, because in
December 1996, after serving four months behind bars, the
Bell charges finally came to trial and Bond was faced withthe
prospect of sitting in the dock for several months while the
case was heard. For years he had protested his complete innocence of the misappropriation of any of Bell's $1,200 million
and had branded the charges as a political conspiracy against
him, but having had a few months in jail to contemplate the
matter, he now decided to go quietly. Given the way in which
the magistrate had summed up the evidence at the committal
hearing, where it was suggested that he was almost certain to
be convicted, it was probably a wise decision to do a deal.
Bond's defence would have cost him a fortune in legal fees,
and the six-month trial would have been an ordeal for everyone, including the jury. By agreeing to plead guilty to two
Companies Code charges, he was able to persuade the prosecution to abandon the far more serious charge of conspiracy
to defraud and four other lesser charges. In addition, the DPP
was persuaded to end his attempt to have Bond's sentence for
the Manet fraud increased. Bond was therefore convicted of
two charges of acting dishonestly as a company director with
intent to defraud, each of which carried a maximum sentence
of five years in prison.

A month later, he was back in court for sentencing and three days of mitigation pleas in which friends, doctors and psychiatrists lined up to say how dreadful it would be for him to receive another jail sentence. The climax of this was an address by his counsel Ian Callinan QC, now a High Court judge, who waxed lyrical about what a decent person Alan was and about how his downfall marked the end of a sorry chapter in Australian history. Bond's guilty plea, he said, was 'born out of a strong element of contrition and remorse', and it was absolutely 'unthinkable that he would ever commit offences of this kind again'. Finally, said Callinan, the public humiliation, mockery and contempt that Bond had suffered had already sent a clear signal to others of the dreadful consequences of such crimes—which were presumably that if you stole $1,200 million you could expect some people to tell you this was wrong.

It seemed doubtful, however, that any of this sob stuff had made an impression on the judge, because Justice Murray opened his sentencing remarks the following day by launching into a savage attack on Bond's business ethics, or lack of them. Bell Resources shareholders, he said, had been exposed to 'severe and ultimately disastrous commercial risk' by transactions that were to Bond's 'very great personal advantage and benefit'. Dallhold and Bond Corporation were in a parlous financial state, could not possibly have got hold of the money elsewhere and had little or no prospect of paying it back. The loans, he said, had been 'audacious raids ... made with an intention to defraud ... in virtually complete disregard of (Bond's) duties of honesty and integrity'.[14]

Throughout this verbal assault, Alan sat in the dock unmoved, occasionally sipping from a glass of water. But when Justice Murray moved on to the reasons for treating him leniently he may well have perked up a bit for, like so many other judges who have dealt with Bond, Murray found abundant reason to go easy. Bond, he said, was not far off sixty years old, had benefited the community over the years, had been a good family man, and had inspired great loyalty among his friends and employees. He had also suffered humiliation and a stain on his character, as well as a proposal to strip him of his Order of Australia, which could all be regarded as significant punishment. He had saved court time by pleading guilty and had expressed a desire to make reparation and devote himself to the community. And to cap it all, he had apologised through his counsel Ian Callinan. Murray concluded that this apology 'was not a sham but was genuinely meant', even though Bond had long protested his innocence, attacked the prosecution case and derided the charges as politically motivated.

There would of course be some 'hate-filled members of the public', to coin a phrase, who would suggest that getting your lawyer to say you were sorry might be a small price to pay for pulling off the largest fraud in Australian history, but Justice Murray was clearly impressed, for he now let Bond off with an absurdly light four-year sentence, or less than half the maximum penalty of ten years available to him. If this was all one received for defrauding thousands of shareholders of $1,200 million, it was hard to imagine what one had to do to receive the full punishment.

With luck and a following wind, and time off for good behaviour, Alan Bond would serve less than two years for his crime, or roughly one day for every $2 million, which seemed like one hell of a bargain. Even after serving the seven months that remained of the *La Promenade* sentence he would almost certainly be free before his sixty-first birthday on 22 April

1999, which would mean he would serve only two years and eight months of the seven years that he had been dealt for the two convictions.

Bond must have been thrilled with this outcome, even though it meant being transferred to Western Australia's maximum-security prison at Casuarina, where conditions were a great deal tougher than at Karnet. But the Commonwealth DPP was less than pleased, and immediately appealed against the leniency of the sentence, saying that Australians would be stunned that Bond had got off so lightly. And as news filtered through to the radio talkback shows, it was clear that the DPP had called it right, because there was hardly a caller who was not keen to collect $2 million if the only price was to spend a day behind bars.

Diana Bliss invoked the shock of ordinary Australians by protesting that her husband was to be stripped of his Order of Australia. Alan, she said, was heartbroken because his yachting triumphs had been hugely important to Australia and had no connection at all to his corporate crimes.

> Look, it's just devastating for him at the moment, that they would do it. He won the Order of Australia for a sporting achievement which united the country and all Australians were proud that day.[15]

But while it may have been harsh to take away his medal, there was an argument that it was merely poetic justice, for Bond's America's Cup triumph had made the world's bankers beat a path to his door and, as a consequence, his victory and his crimes had become inextricably linked. If *Australia II* had not won in Newport in 1983, Alan Bond would never have been able to borrow the sort of money that had allowed him to gain control of Bell Resources in the first place. Nor would he have been able to buy *Irises*, the purchase of which was one of the reasons he had been so eager to grab the profits from Manet's *La Promenade*.

It was also in Newport in 1983, to stretch the point a bit further, that Alan had met Jurg Bollag. And if that had never happened, Bollag's Swiss employers, the Dow Banking Corporation, would never have lent money to Dallhold and Alan would not have had yet another posse of police on his tail, chasing him for alleged bankruptcy offences.

But he had met Bollag, and the Australian Federal Police were still struggling to get his banker on the stand, even though Bond's bankruptcy was long since over. In early 1997, two and a half years after the AFP had first sought help from Switzerland, the battle to make Bollag talk was still not over. Bond would have to keep fighting the threat of yet more criminal charges from jail.

23

Zuggered Again

An honest man is someone who doesn't cheat the person who bribes him.

Old Swiss saying

Within hours of the Swiss police raids on Jurg Bollag back in December 1994, Alan Bond had started legal action to prevent the Australian police getting their hands on any of the evidence. The Swiss had seized a pile of documents from Bollag's office that clearly related to Bond and had been promised more by the Zuger Kantonal Bank, who had agreed to surrender everything in their possession. Bollag, meanwhile, had been ordered to face examination by the Zug prosecutor about his relationship with Bond.

The Australian Federal Police (AFP) undoubtedly knew at the time that they were in for a long wait, because Swiss law allowed people being chased by foreign police to challenge their pursuers in the courts. And as John Elliott was busy demonstrating, it was perfectly possible to stall this process for years.

Way back in 1991, Australia's National Crime Authority (NCA) had asked the Swiss to obtain documents from Bank

Cantrade in Zurich relating to an alleged secret $78 million profit made by Elliott and others in the big BHP takeover battle of 1986. The Swiss had granted the application promptly, but Elliott and Bank Cantrade had fought tooth and nail in court to prevent the documents being returned to Australia. And in late 1994, as the AFP began chasing Bond in Switzerland, the NCA had still not got the material.[1]

It was therefore only natural that Bond and Bollag should adopt the same strategy, because even if their chances of winning were slim, there was a good possibility that they could delay matters so long that the AFP's patience would be exhausted.

The saga of Bond's legal challenges is worth recording in some detail, because it reveals how the rich can use the courts to escape justice. As a joint parliamentary committee observed in 1998 in reviewing Elliott's protracted battles with the NCA, the legal system gives those with money far too much scope to wage guerrilla warfare in the courts, in the name of protecting their rights.

> While the system aims to ensure that no accused may be denied a fair trial, at the same time it leaves the way open for well-resourced defendants to defeat the process. People who successfully engage in criminal activity may delay or even avoid the due consequences of their actions.[2]

Or, more bluntly, there is no guarantee in today's world that the rich will ever be brought to trial.

Nor was there any guarantee that the police would ever get Bond. Within hours of the raids on Bollag, his lawyers asked Zug Prosecutor Paul Kuhn for a formal review of the decision to issue search warrants. When this application was turned down they appealed to the Justice Commission of the Zug Superior Court. And when that was rejected in April 1995, Bond appealed to the Swiss Federal Court in Lausanne, who also knocked him back. But this was just the beginning.

Two months later, Bond applied to Kuhn for a new review, on the grounds that his bankruptcy had been annulled, and when this also met with rejection, the legal challenge once more climbed all three rungs of the ladder up to the Swiss Federal Court, which yet again ruled against him.

After these six legal skirmishes, the score stood at Switzerland 6, Bond 0, but the exercise had bought Bond valuable time, for by now the clock had ticked on to January 1996 and the police had been forced to sit on their hands for an entire year. There were plenty more battles to come—when Paul Kuhn ordered that the documents be sent to Australia, Bond was allowed by the Swiss to mount yet another round of legal challenges. These also ascended all the way up to the Swiss Federal Court, which once again ruled against Bond in August 1996, by which time it was Switzerland 9, Bond 0, and another eight months had passed.

During these legal challenges, the vital Swiss documents had been locked in a safe in Zug for twenty months, and the AFP had not been allowed to inspect them. But Bond, bizarrely, had been given access, even though he never tired of telling the world that Bollag's affairs were nothing to do with him.

In May 1994, in the Federal Court in Sydney, Alan had denied on oath to Francis Douglas QC that Bollag was looking after his money.

> Douglas: What I am putting to you is that
> Mr Bollag essentially administers your

> personal affairs overseas. You just give
> instructions to him as to what to do
> with the money over there, and he does
> what you want him to do.

Bond: You know that not to be the case.

Douglas: No, I do not, Mr Bond. In fact I am
           putting to you that that is the truth.

Bond: ... he has no assets of mine.[3]

More recently, in December 1994, after the raids on Bollag's house and offices, Bond had told Mark Drummond of the *West Australian* that it was 'rubbish' that Bollag was holding assets for him and that investigators were on a 'wild goose chase'.[4]

If these vehement denials were true, it was hard to see how documents seized from Bollag could possibly have related to Bond or put him in any danger of prosecution. Yet he had nevertheless decided, after seeing them, to fight as though his fortune and freedom depended on it, so that they would not fall into the AFP's hands.

Bond's determination to keep these documents secret made it pretty obvious that they contained incriminating evidence, and he was forced to admit as much in 1997 when he mounted yet another legal challenge to the Swiss investigation in the Federal Court of Australia. Bond's lawyer Andrew Fraser told the court in these proceedings that interrogation of Bollag and surrender of the documents to the AFP were likely to harm his client because the questions put to Bollag (and his answers) would or might relate to Bond, and because in the case of the raids:

> The material which has been seized will or may be
> used in the prosecution [of Bond] for the proposed

criminal charge of perjury and for offences under
the *Bankruptcy Act 1966.*[5]

No doubt Bond's lawyers would dispute that this constituted
an admission of guilt, and would argue that the material seized
from Bollag would merely have encouraged police to pursue
an unjustified prosecution of their client. But these did not look
like the pleadings of an innocent man.

Nor did the rest of Bond's actions suggest that he was telling
the truth. Alan, after all, was supposedly broke when Bollag
was raided in December 1994, yet he was able to pay his
lawyers hundreds of thousands of dollars to fight the police
chase. And the mere fact that he was so determined to stop
the investigation was powerful evidence that he had plenty to
hide.

Bond had already tried to persuade the Federal Court in
Melbourne to call off the dogs back in 1995, on the grounds
that his bankruptcy had been annulled. But the Australian
courts had given him no more encouragement than the Swiss.
Justice Sandberg ruled in February 1996 that Bond could quite
legitimately be prosecuted, because he had been a bankrupt
when the alleged offences were committed.[6] Bond had, of
course, then appealed to the full bench of the Federal Court,
which had also given him the thumbs-down. This took his
score to Played 11, Lost 11, Won 0.

But even though Bond had lost every battle and spent several
hundreds of thousands of dollars on his defence, he had by no
means lost the war, because he had managed to delay delivery
of the crucial Swiss evidence to the AFP until October 1996,
thus forcing the police to twiddle their thumbs for roughly
800 days. And during this time, the general public had quite
possibly lost interest. Bond, after all, had been sentenced by

mid-1996 to three years in prison for the $15 million Manet fraud and would soon be jailed for another four-year term on the Bell conviction. Many people felt that he had been punished enough.

The documents that were eventually handed over to the Australian police in October 1996 have never officially been made public, but there is no doubt that they showed at least one of Bollag's Swiss bank accounts to have Bond's name written all over it. The Zuger Kantonal Bank had already supplied records of the 'Xavier' account in 1991 to Western Australia's Director of Public Prosecutions, John McKechnie, when asked to help in tracing Laurie Connell's assets, and this material was now also supplied to the AFP agents chasing Bond.

But far more importantly, the AFP learned that a second account at the Zuger Kantonal Bank, code-named 'Jane', had been held by Bollag as trustee for Alan Bond. The records showed that at least $20 million had flowed through this account in the early 1990s, with money arriving in large chunks and then departing to various destinations around the globe. Crucially, this 'Jane' account had also coughed up hundreds of thousands of pounds to pay the bills at Upp Hall until July 1991 and had paid fees for some of Touche Ross's Jersey companies in 1992, which meant that the trail was fresh enough for police to bring charges against Bond for perjury and for concealing his assets.

Unfortunately, by late 1996, the millions the account contained had long since vanished. The bulk of the money had probably been moved to Liechtenstein, where the Private Trust Bank in Vaduz was thought by police to have a couple of million dollars of Alan Bond's money. But it was hardly worth bothering to give chase, because Liechtenstein was such a tough nut to crack. And once again Bond and Bollag had been given far too much warning that investigators would come knocking.

Even if they couldn't recover the money, however, the evidence in Zug looked strong enough to mount a prosecution against Bond, particularly if the AFP could use the material to persuade Bollag to tell all. Getting Bondy's banker onto the stand was therefore the crucial next step.

The Zug prosecutor, Paul Kuhn, duly sent a summons to Bollag at the end of January 1997, telling him to present himself for questioning in early April. Meanwhile, back in Australia, Andrew Tuohy and Kelvin Kenney studied the Swiss documents, drew up a list of 7,000 questions, packed their bags for Europe, and tried not to get too excited about the prospect of getting their man at last. The Australian press also booked their tickets to Zug, in the hope of witnessing the kill, even though the examination would be conducted in Swiss German, behind closed doors.

At this stage, the AFP were optimistic that Bollag would talk, and privately confided to journalists that he had little choice but to do so. Bollag, they said, risked three months in jail for contempt of court if he refused to answer their questions, and was unlikely to want to do time for Bond. Word from the Bond camp indicated that they were also concerned he would crack.

Consequently, when Bollag walked into Kuhn's office in Zug on 7 April, accompanied by a bevy of Swiss and Australian lawyers, there was an air of expectation that he would at last come clean about all the houses, horses and paintings that he had provided for the Bond family. But before the examination could even get under way, one of Bollag's lawyers stood up to spoil the party. His client, he said, could not be forced to answer questions, because the Australian police had not yet brought charges against Bond and were merely investigating his alleged concealment of assets. Bond's Swiss lawyer then leapt to his feet to make a similar statement and, with Bollag's lips firmly sealed, the hearing was adjourned for the prosecution to regroup. The waiting press stood by puzzled as the phalanx of lawyers and policemen trooped out into the cold morning air after less than an hour.

A flurry of faxes was then exchanged between Zug and Canberra, in which the Australian Attorney General's Department assured the Swiss that the law was quite clear and the interrogation must continue. But when the hearing resumed the next day, Bollag once again declared that he planned to stay silent, in defiance of a fresh directive from Kuhn that he answer all questions. And at this point Tuohy and Kenney had little choice but to pack their bags and catch a cab to the airport.

Shortly after they got back to Melbourne, Andrew Tuohy obviously decided that he had had enough of the whole business. In May 1997, after thirteen years in the AFP and more than three years chasing Bond, he left the police force to investigate fraud for a firm of accountants in the private sector, who would pay him twice as much money and give him cases where he had a far better chance of success. No doubt it would be a huge relief to operate outside the criminal justice system for once, where he would not need to prove the bleeding obvious beyond reasonable doubt.

Back in Switzerland, the examination of Bollag was now adjourned till June 1997 so that the Swiss courts could decide whether or not he could be compelled to answer questions, and before long they had given Bond and his banker another defeat to add to their score. But by the time the courts had made their decision Paul Kuhn had become bogged down in other cases in Zug, so the hearing had to be put off until November 1997, which was another five months away.

In the meantime, Bond and Bollag had opened up a second front of legal action in the Federal Court of Australia, running the same argument as in Switzerland, that Bond hadn't been charged and that his alleged offences weren't serious anyway. This, however, was comprehensively demolished in October by Justice Ron Merkel, who clearly felt it was time to take a stick to Bond in the interests of justice. Having scotched each one of Bond's arguments, he told the court that he would have thrown out Bond's application in any case because it was disgraceful that he hadn't raised these issues in his previous attempt to kill the investigation in 1995. Bond and Bollag's delay in bringing the proceedings, he said, was 'unexplained, inordinate, inexcusable and unreasonable', adding:

> It is harmful to the administration of justice for applicants to challenge the criminal investigation process in a manner that both fragments and dislocates it ... It is a serious misuse and abuse of the litigation process to contest proceedings in this manner ...

> Whilst the applicants have an undoubted right to challenge the use of coercive power in relation to them, they do not have the right to do so as and when they choose, by electing, reserving and preserving their points so they can be raised if and when it suits them or their litigation strategy. Yet that appears to be precisely what Bond and Bollag have done in the present case in order to delay the investigation into their dealings.[7]

Merkel's stinging condemnation meant that Bond still hadn't won a trick in thirteen legal battles in Switzerland and Australia. And it looked as though his luck might now run out on this number. In fact defeat appeared to be even more likely when Bollag's examination resumed on 3 November because Bond's banker surprised everyone, including his own lawyer, by telling the prosecutor that he was now prepared to take the stand. But just as victory for Bond's pursuers looked certain, the prize was once again snatched away. On the second day of the examination Bollag began to parry questions by claiming privilege against self-incrimination, or as the Americans would put it, by taking the Fifth Amendment.

The AFP had anticipated this problem and granted Bollag indemnity from prosecution so that he could not be charged with any crime—which they believed would make it impossible for him to incriminate himself. But they had not done enough homework on the arcane provisions of Swiss law, for Article 29, paragraph 2 of the Zug Criminal Procedure Code allowed a very broad definition of what self-incrimination might mean. According to Bond's Swiss lawyers, Bollag could decline to answer any question if he could convince the court that it would impugn him or make him personally responsible. Valid grounds for refusal, they said, might include the risk that it would expose him to civil action, jeopardise his reputation and social position, reveal defects in his character, force him to admit previous lies, expose him to disgrace or shame, force him to admit taking part in disreputable business such as money laundering, or even expose him to financial loss.

On this reading of the law, Bollag would be able to duck almost any question about his dealings with Bond, because typically he would either have to admit lying to the tax authorities about his income and wealth or confess he had lied to everyone else when he had denied it was Bond's money he was looking after. But whether Bond's lawyers were right or not about what Zug's laws allowed him to claim, the AFP were almost certainly wasting their time, because arguments about Bollag's right to stay silent would now trigger another round of legal challenges and postpone the examination again.

Worse still, as the current session disintegrated into farce, Bond and Bollag began yet another legal action in the Swiss courts to challenge release of the transcripts. Since Bollag had been examined in Swiss German and the AFP had not been allowed to tape the proceedings, Kelvin Kenney had only the vaguest idea of what Bondy's banker actually said. And he would now have to wait an age to find out.

In the end, it took nine months until the transcripts were eventually released by the Swiss, after yet more legal defeats for Bond, and only then did the full scale of the catastrophe become clear. Bollag had spent the best part of three days either refusing to answer questions or claiming that he couldn't remember.

By this stage almost four years had passed since the Swiss had been asked for help in tracking down Bond's assets in September 1994, and almost five years since the AFP's investigation had begun in November 1993, and it looked like taking another two years to get to the final showdown—or anticlimax. If Kuhn eventually decreed that Bollag had to answer questions, his decision was likely to be fought in the courts for six months or more. Then there would be a delay while a new examination was scheduled and then, if Bollag kept mum again, there would be another round of legal actions to challenge any punishment.

And in the meantime, even though nine months had elapsed since Bollag's examination, Kuhn had not even begun the process of deciding whether Bollag's reasons for claiming privilege should be accepted. In fact, he did not appear even to have received the written statement of reasons that Bollag was required by law to give.

To cap it all, the AFP now learnt for the first time that Bollag was most unlikely to face jail if he did defy the Zug prosecutor by staying silent. Prison, it seemed, was a punishment reserved for the most serious cases—such as drug trafficking or murder—while refusing to give evidence in a bankruptcy case was likely to be met with a fine of a few thousand dollars.

So in October 1998, faced with little chance of success, the AFP finally threw in the towel. Bond had lost every legal battle of the campaign but had still won the war. Soon afterwards, the AFP's assistant commissioner Nigel Hadgkiss told a bankruptcy conference in Melbourne:

> It became abundantly clear that Bollag was not a cooperative witness and would use any means available to him to thwart the investigation ... It was clear that if we decided to pursue this matter and sought Bollag's further examination in Switzerland he would be claiming privilege ... and would seek to challenge any decision through the Swiss courts.[8]

The AFP had spent $750,000 of taxpayers' money on the pursuit, while Tuohy and Kenney had devoted seven years between them to chasing Bond, yet they had still not managed to get their man. So what had gone wrong?

One view is that it was problematic having Paul Kuhn lead the fight. Kuhn was by all accounts an honest, diligent, dutiful prosecutor but he was also a small-town lawyer battling a team of international heavyweights. He was also wrestling with a criminal justice system in Zug that was understaffed and overworked. He had therefore not had the time, energy or experience to pursue Bond with sufficient vigour.

But neither were the Australian authorities blameless. Even though Kuhn barely spoke English, the AFP and Commonwealth Director of Public Prosecutions (DPP) did not take a translator to Switzerland. Nor did they hire a Swiss lawyer to represent them in court and guide them through the system. So the Australians found themselves playing away from home in a language they couldn't speak, with rules that they didn't fully understand. And this hardly gave them the best chance of success.

But on a broader, strategic scale, Bond's pursuers also failed to appreciate what was necessary to win a case like this. Swiss lawyers say that the Australian authorities should have got far tougher with Bollag and should have put far more pressure on him to talk. Had the Americans been running the case, they say, investigators would have played hardball. Bollag would have been arrested the minute he stepped outside the country and extradition proceedings would have been used to induce him to talk.

As an example of how investigations in Switzerland can succeed, Swiss lawyers point to the case of Benazir Bhutto and her husband Ali Zardari, who were convicted of corruption and sentenced to five years in jail in Pakistan in 1998. During the investigation, the Pakistani Government uncovered evidence that the Bhuttos' Geneva lawyer, Jens Schlegelmilch, had hidden more than $100 million in offshore companies that he controlled. Faced with his refusal to talk, they persuaded the Swiss to threaten Schlegelmilch with money-laundering charges, whereupon he agreed to give evidence.[9]

The Bhuttos, of course, were higher profile than Alan Bond, and several other factors made it an easier case to win. There were suggestions that drug money was involved, large sums were at stake, and new anti-money-laundering laws had come into force. But the Pakistanis also played tougher than the Australians by using their ambassador to put pressure on the Swiss Government to achieve a result. No one in the Bond investigation had imparted such a sense of urgency to the Swiss authorities or put the screws on Bollag. Australia's police and politicians had either not believed it to be necessary or had felt it to be improper.

It was also a puzzle why the AFP didn't attempt to bring charges against Bond in Australia without the Swiss banker's evidence. To the ordinary person it was surely obvious that all the houses, horses and paintings belonged to Bond or his family. Plus, there was the testimony of Touche Ross in Jersey that they were dealing with Alan's affairs and that the millions of dollars in Kirk Holdings belonged to Bond. Then there were the letters of instruction to Touche Ross that Alan himself had signed in 1982 and 1987. And more recently there were documents from the Zuger Kantonal Bank showing that the 'Jane' account had been held for Bond by Bollag and had paid bills for Upp Hall and the Jersey companies as late as 1992.

It seemed hard to believe that there was no prospect of a jury finding that Bond had possessed considerable offshore wealth at a time when he was denying on oath that this had ever been so. It also seemed hard to believe that no jury would conclude that he had concealed millions of dollars worth of assets from his creditors. Yet neither the AFP nor the Commonwealth DPP felt that it was worth mounting the case. Agent Kenney told the *Australian Financial Review*:

> The likelihood of achieving a prosecution is not
> high. The fate of the investigation rested on the
> evidence of Bollag and without that we never had
> a case. He was the linchpin.[10]

By the end of 1998, of course, Bond was already serving time
in jail for serious offences and paying his debt to society, so
one could argue that he had been punished enough. But there
were other compelling reasons not to let Bond get away with
it. His ridiculous claims that he couldn't remember having
money offshore, his absurd story about a philanthropic Swiss
banker buying him baubles, and his public protestations that
he was brain-damaged, were such a flagrant insult to the
system of justice that they should never have been allowed to
go unchallenged. As it was, his escape sent a strong message
to Australians: if you have enough nerve and enough money,
like Alan Bond and Christopher Skase, you can get away with
anything.

As for Jurg Bollag, who would now never have to tell the
truth to investigators, he had served his master well. There's
an old Swiss saying that an honest man is someone who
doesn't cheat the person who bribes him, and Bollag had lived
up to it. He had not run off with Bond's money. Nor had he
betrayed him to the authorities, despite the pressure to do so.

One had to say that Alan Bond had chosen his servant
wisely.

24

Cook's Tour

It was at all times Alan Bond's intention that the
artworks would be acquired for Craig Bond ... or
such entity as Alan Bond determined.

Allegation in Supreme Court of South Australia[1]

The end of the Australian Federal Police (AFP) investigation
is by no means the end of this story, because Alan Bond
was still the target of a huge legal action that might cost him and
his son Craig several million dollars and quite possibly result in
criminal charges for fraud being brought against them both.

The statement of claim in this case, which began amid great
secrecy in the Supreme Court of South Australia in 1996,
charged that Alan and Craig Bond had 'knowingly instigated,
directed and participated in a sham transaction ... intended
to disguise a dishonest and fraudulent scheme'.[2] And there was
a mass of evidence to back up the charge.

The 'dishonest and fraudulent scheme' bore remarkable
similarity to Alan's conduct over Manet's *La Promenade*, for
which he was jailed in 1996, in that it involved the disposal
of thirteen paintings by Bond Corporation in January 1990
for $5 million less than their market value. Ostensibly, the

artworks were sold at arm's length to an art gallery in Fremantle. But according to the statement of claim filed by the liquidator of Bond Corporation Holdings, they were handed over to Craig and Alan Bond for a small fraction of their real value.

Meanwhile, Bond Corp's managing director Peter Beckwith allegedly got a handsome kickback for allowing it to proceed. According to the statement of claim:

> The sum of $250,000 was paid by Alan Bond ...
> for the benefit of Peter Beckwith as consideration
> for the participation of Peter Beckwith in the
> fraudulent and dishonest scheme.[3]

By far the best known of the thirteen disputed paintings was John Webber's *Portrait of Captain Cook*, which has graced the front of many an Australian history book. A great favourite of Bond's, it had held pride of place in Dallhold's boardroom throughout the 1980s, when he posed beside it for posterity and told the world that he had much in common with the great explorer. Both he and Cook, he suggested, were bluff, daring buccaneers whose fellow countrymen had failed to recognise their true value.

Shortly after he was made bankrupt in 1992, Bond was asked by Bob Ramsay if he knew what had become of the painting which at that stage had vanished into thin air. He wrote back to say that it had been sold by Bond Corporation and that he had played no part in the sale, implying that he had no idea where it had gone. But if the Bond Corp liquidator is to be believed, Bond knew perfectly well where the Captain Cook portrait was hidden and how it had come to be there, because his old friend Jurg Bollag and his art dealer Angela Nevill had been looking after the painting and at least six other missing artworks since January 1990. And according to Nevill's sworn testimony, both were acting on Bond's behalf.

January 1990, when the paintings went missing, marked the beginning of the end for Bond and his business empire, for it was the moment that his house of cards really began to collapse around him. Dallhold had been defaulting on its loans for months, Bond Corporation had announced the biggest loss in Australian corporate history, and Bond Brewing had just been placed in the hands of the receivers.

Meanwhile, Bond's most valuable art treasures were fast disappearing out the door. *Irises*, the famous Van Gogh painting that he had bought only two years earlier for a world-record US$54 million, had been confiscated by the Swiss banks who had helped finance it, and Manet's *La Promenade*, which Alan had snitched from Bond Corporation in the hope of saving his Van Gogh, had been despatched to auction in New York to pay the bills.

As the bailiffs banged on the gates of his empire, Bond had clearly decided to salvage what he could from his art collection before it fell into the hands of his creditors. According to the Bond Corp liquidator's statement of claim, Alan and his managing director Peter Beckwith arranged for the Captain Cook and six other valuable Bond Corp artworks to be shipped out of the country under cover of a pretended sale to a local racing identity, George Way. Or, as the statement of claim put it:

> Alan Bond orally informed George Way ... that he wanted to acquire the SECL [Bond Corp] artworks and transport them to England ... that he required the assistance of George Way ... that he would pay Way a fee of $50,000 plus expenses ... that the paintings would then be Alan Bond's.[4]

Bond allegedly told Way that he would lend him the money to buy the paintings (which were being sold by Bond Corp at one-sixth of their true market value) and prepare the sale documents. All Way would have to do was provide blank sheets of his gallery's notepaper, sign the finished papers and then collect his fee. The ownership of the paintings would then pass to the Bonds.

George Way, who was a friend of Eileen Bond, was a well-known scoundrel on the Perth racing scene who had enjoyed a long and colourful career as a racehorse trainer until 1987, when he had been banned from the world's racetracks for twenty years after two of his winners tested positive to the go-faster drug etorphine—commonly known as elephant juice. To the surprise of many, he had then opened an art gallery in Fremantle to sell paintings to his millionaire mates like Laurie Connell, which he found was an easier way to make a living.

In fact, George knew a fair bit about art, and he also knew a good business deal when he saw one. So he allegedly agreed to let Bond use his High Street Gallery as a front for the 'purchase' of these valuable Bond Corp paintings, in exchange for an easy $50,000. But it is clear that he never took delivery of the pictures. Nor did they go anywhere near Fremantle. Nor did he ever own them. As Way must have known perfectly well, the paintings were being acquired by the Bonds. The 'sale' to Way was merely a sham and a way for Bond to get hold of the artworks at a knockdown price.

On 4 January, the curator of Bond's private art collection, Diana de Bussy, arranged for the *Portrait of Captain Cook* and the six other most valuable paintings to be crated up and collected from the Bond Tower by Grace Brothers Fine Art. She had been told that they were headed offshore and had outlined the arrangements in a memo to George Way and Alan

Bond. The shipping invoice stated that they were being sent overseas for exhibition and promotion but, as de Bussy feared, they were not meant to come back.[5]

Two days later, on 6 January 1990, the paintings were driven out to the airport and loaded onto a British Airways Boeing 747 bound for London. The next morning they arrived at Heathrow Airport and were trucked off to a fine-art storage warehouse, James Bourlet & Sons. A week after that, they were delivered to Bond's art dealer Angela Nevill in Kensington. Jurg Bollag had phoned to tell her that they were coming and to say that he had authority to sell them.

The diminutive Lady Nevill was hardly the most charming woman in the art world or the most popular. Several of those who dealt with her described her as haughty and tough as nails. But she was both well connected and as blue-blooded as they come. The Nevill family title dated from the fifteenth century, and one of her noble ancestors had sat in judgement on Mary Queen of Scots. More recently, her brother, the Marquess of Abergavenny, had served as a page of honour to the Queen and her uncle had been Her Majesty's representative at Ascot races. Unkind critics in England whispered that Bond had chosen her because he coveted a knighthood. But no one suggested that Nevill didn't deserve his custom. She was an excellent judge of pictures, and utterly discreet.

Nevill had been dealing in art for Bond since the late 1970s and had assembled an amazing collection with his money. She had also made a small fortune for herself by charging 10 per cent commission plus expenses on everything she bought for him. And now she was about to make even more money by helping him dispose of it again. Within six weeks of the Bond Corporation paintings arriving in London, she managed to find a potential buyer for one of the most valuable works, a French Impressionist portrait of Dora Hugo by Paul-Cesar Helleu. Back in Perth, Alan Bond allegedly told his managing director at Dallhold to accept the offer.[6]

George Way, who supposedly owned the painting, was kept completely out of the loop. Three weeks later, when the sale was completed in London, it was not even Way's company that sold it. The contract was signed by Angela Nevill and Jurg Bollag, with his new Isle of Man company Firstmark, which had been set up six months earlier, acting as the vendor. Nevill was asked on oath by the liquidator's lawyers in 1996 what role Bollag and Firstmark played in the sale. She replied, 'At all times I clearly understood that George Bollag and Firstmark were acting on behalf of Alan Bond and the Bond family'.[7] Soon afterwards, she amplified the role of Firstmark by saying, 'I understood ... Firstmark to be an entity related to Alan Bond or the Bond family'.[8]

On Bollag's instructions, £230,000 from the sale of the Dora Hugo portrait was telexed back to George Way in Perth to be passed on to Bond Corporation. Angela Nevill took her 10 per cent commission and the London lawyers took their fees. Bollag then ordered the lawyers to pay whatever money was left from the sale to the 'Jane' account at the Zuger Kantonal Bank in Zug. Or in other words, to Alan Bond's offshore money box.[9]

Over the next three years, Bollag and Nevill sold a further five of the thirteen artworks and collected another $621,000, allegedly for Bond. Some of this was despatched to Bollag's JF Consulting in Zug, some was paid into the client account of Bollag's London lawyers, and roughly half, or $306,000, was paid into an account at the Private Trust Bank in Vaduz, Liechtenstein, held in the name of SIDRO Anstalt—or in other words, to Alan Bond again.[10]

But getting rid of the Captain Cook portrait was a far tougher proposition for Nevill and Bollag, because it was so well known and because the obvious market was in Australia, where the bankrupt Bond was still being chased by Ramsay's investigators. It would take enormous nerve to sell it there and it would ultimately cause enormous problems because it would bring the issue of the missing artworks squarely into the public eye.

By June 1993, when the Bond camp had plucked up enough courage to offer the Captain Cook painting for sale, the mysterious disappearance of the Webber portrait from the Bond Tower in 1990 had become a big story back home. So when the then managing director of Sotheby's Australia, Robert Bleakley, phoned the director of the National Gallery of Australia, Betty Churcher, from New York to tell her that he could obtain the painting for the gallery, there was great excitement, which soon leaked into the press.

Bleakley told Churcher that the asking price was $3 million. But within three weeks he was offering to cut it to $1.6 million on the basis that the Captain Cook's mystery owner was keen for the painting to return to its rightful home.[11] Betty Churcher may well have had suspicions that it was being sold by Bond, because there had been reports in the newspapers about the suspicious sale to Way, and these would have been amplified by a report from the gallery's curator of Australian art, Mary Eagle, identifying the vendor as 'a private collector believed to be Alan Bond'. But she nevertheless signed the purchase proposal and added her own handwritten note to say that she 'strongly recommended' the gallery buy the painting.[12] Perhaps Churcher should have realised as soon as she was approached by Bleakley that the Cook painting was more trouble than it was worth, but she believed strongly that it belonged in Australia. Her response to the doubts raised by a cynical press was that it was okay to buy the painting because Sotheby's was acting for the vendor.[13]

The National Gallery's council, however, was far from convinced that the purchase was safe. The price had been halved with suspicious speed, which suggested the seller was desperate, and gossip indicated that Bond was still the owner. So while it was agreed to press ahead with the acquisition, it was only on condition that Sotheby's produce evidence of the provenance—or origin—of the work.

Provenance is very important in the art world, and when paintings disappear in mysterious circumstances one needs a cracking good story to get them back onto the market. But Bleakley had one. Having assured the gallery that he was definitely not acting for Bond and that his principal had 'no current connection' with the bankrupt art collector, he said:

> It may be of assistance to you and your board to understand the way in which I became aware of the painting's availability on the market. By sheer coincidence, I was advised through a contact in the film world in New York that his wife, who is an Englishwoman, wanted to talk to me about a painting that could possibly be of interest to Australia. I knew that she was from a wealthy English family and that her father was prominent in international business affairs. You can imagine my astonishment when I learned that the painting was the Webber portrait of Captain Cook.[14]

One can imagine the auctioneer's astonishment, indeed, when it also turned out (by another sheer coincidence) that Lady Nevill was the mystery vendor's agent.

But Bleakley's account of the meeting in New York was far more astonishing for what it did not reveal. As he admitted on oath in 1996 when examined about these matters, he was given the name of this wealthy English businessman, yet never bothered to contact him to confirm the story or ask about the painting. Nor did he talk to the man's daughter, the Englishwoman. Instead, he went straight to Bond's art dealer Angela Nevill to ask whether she was involved in the sale—which she was. Even then, he did not ask Nevill to verify what he had been told about the vendor—for whom she was acting. As Bleakley also admitted on oath, he had known since May 1992 that the *Portrait of Captain Cook* was one of several Bond paintings that had been sold to George Way for a great deal less than their real value, because he had read about it in the *West Australian* newspaper. And he agreed that the circumstances of this supposed sale had made him suspicious.

> Q: What you learn as you read this is that pretty soon after the Bond corporate collapse apparently a significant aspect of the Bond art collection was sold at what appeared to be an extraordinarily low price?
>
> A: Yes.
>
> Q: And obviously that would raise a question mark in your mind about the genuineness of the transaction. You don't know, but it's a question mark?
>
> A: Yes ...
>
> Q: Obviously you lodged in the back of your mind just a question mark, 'This is something, if I'm going to be dealing with these works of art, the lawyers will have to have a look at?'.

A: Yes.

Q: You looked at this yourself and thought 'This
looks like a sham price', didn't you?

A I did.[15]

Even more to the point, Bleakley knew that Angela Nevill had
received several of the Bond paintings because he had actually
sold two of them for her in 1992 and split the 10 per cent
commission.

According to Nevill's sworn evidence in August 1996, she
made it clear to Bleakley that the two artworks he was
selling on her behalf formed part of the Alan Bond collection. She also made it clear that the vendor was still 'associated with the Bond family'. And Bleakley admitted as much
to the liquidator's lawyers in 1996. When asked on oath
who was the vendor of one of these two lesser paintings,
he replied:

A: I believe it was a Bond entity of some sort ... I
mean, I knew that it was formerly in the Bond
collection.

Q: You knew that it was one of the paintings that
was the subject of the George Way transaction,
didn't you?

A: Yes, I did.[16]

But if Bleakley had any concerns that the *Portrait of Captain
Cook* might also be being sold by someone connected to Bond,
he did not tell the National Gallery. Instead, he assured them
and everyone else that the valuable painting had nothing to do
with the bankrupt entrepreneur, telling Terry Ingram of the
Financial Review in July 1993, 'We have been assiduous in

this instance, as you can imagine. I am convinced that the work does not belong to Alan Bond'.[17]

In fact, Bleakley had still not asked Angela Nevill who owned the famous painting, and had still made no attempt to confirm his New York story about the 'wealthy English businessman'. But he had obtained a letter from Angela Nevill assuring him that the Captain Cook was not being sold 'by Alan Bond or any company affiliated with him', and he would argue on oath in 1996 that it was perfectly reasonable to rely on this assurance.

He did not tell the press that he was selling the painting on behalf of Bond's art dealer and sharing her commission.[18] The National Gallery, however, soon found out about Lady Nevill's involvement for themselves. In early August 1993, the gallery's Assistant Director, Collections, Michael Lloyd, hopped on a plane to Switzerland to inspect the painting, only to be met by Nevill and escorted to a huge bonded warehouse at Zurich Airport called the Zuricher Freilager.

The fact that the painting was under lock and key there, so close to Jurg Bollag's home town, may well have rung more alarm bells for the prospective purchasers—not least because the Freilager was as secure as a Swiss bank and as safe from prying eyes.[19]

Be that as it may, in one of the strongrooms a Swiss restorer scraped away at the surface of the painting under Lady Nevill's watchful eye and pronounced it to be in pristine condition, while Michael Lloyd took a colour slide to show to the folks back home. This left only one remaining problem, which was how the hell the great explorer's portrait had got there and who was selling it if Bond was not.

This was certainly what was exercising the mind of Lionel Bowen, chairman of the National Gallery's council, who felt it was extremely unwise to buy the painting on trust when Bond was being so publicly investigated in Australia for all manner of alleged crimes, including concealing assets from his creditors. 'It had been in Perth and ended up in Europe, and we wanted to know how it had got there.'[20] A lawyer in the Australian Government Solicitor's office, Peter Lundy, was therefore commissioned to trace the history of the painting since its disappearance in 1990.

It did not take Lundy long to determine that the *Portrait of Captain Cook* had vanished in January 1990 after being sold to George Way for a fraction of its real value. Nor was it hard to discover that the Bond Corp liquidators believed they had a claim over the painting. And he soon learnt that the Australian Securities Commission had been asked to investigate the 1990 'sale' to Way for suspected breaches of the law.

Lundy obtained legal advice from a Perth QC, Eric Heenan, that it would be unsafe for the National Gallery to buy it, but Churcher and Lloyd were so keen to get the painting for Australia that they demanded a second opinion. Next, Lundy consulted one of the world's experts, a Paris-based lawyer called Van Kirk Reeves who advised New York's Guggenheim Museum, and came back with the same verdict. But even this did not suffice. So his third stop was London in January 1994, where he discussed the matter with Angela Nevill, face to face.

Of course, Nevill knew full well that the painting belonged to Bond, because it had been in and out of her sight for the previous four years, and because she had discussed it regularly with Alan and his acolytes. It had been delivered to her in January 1990 only a week after being shipped from Australia and she had then arranged storage. Two months later, she had met Michael Cross, Alan's managing director at Dallhold, to discuss plans for selling it. And two months after that, in early May, she had met Alan himself in London and agreed to send a photograph of the Captain Cook portrait to a potential purchaser. Thereafter, she had taken instructions from Jurg Bollag, whom she knew to be Bond's agent, over the attempted sale of the painting to the National Gallery.

Nevill told Lundy none of this. Instead, she assured him that the painting had passed through a couple of 'European collections' since its sale to Way, and offered to enter a contract with the National Gallery in which her firm, Nevill Keating Pictures, would act as the vendor. She refused, however, to give guarantees that her gallery was the rightful owner or to pay compensation should the painting be repossessed. Lundy thought her 'pretty evasive' and reported back to the National Gallery that the proffered contract was 'legally worthless'.[21]

Yet even now, after three rebuffs, Churcher and Lloyd were not prepared to give up, and for the next several months letters and contracts were batted back and forth by Nevill, the gallery and Sotheby's, in an attempt to frame guarantees that would be acceptable to both sides. Eventually, all was in vain. Nevill's inability to demonstrate that Bond was not selling the Captain Cook made the gallery realise it was absolutely essential to be told who was. And Nevill could hardly do that. If she had told the National Gallery about the painting's travels since its 'sale' to George Way, they would almost certainly have run a mile. And had she explained to them that the latest official 'owner' (come 1994) was an untraceable offshore company called Transit Trading Ltd, run by Alan Bond's notorious Swiss banker friend Jurg Bollag, they would doubtless have run further still. She would also have had the Bond Corp liquidator and Bond's trustee in bankruptcy banging on her door and demanding the painting be handed over.

So, after almost eighteen months of negotiations, both sides had reached a stalemate, and at the end of 1994 Churcher, Lloyd and the National Gallery were forced to conclude that they could not safely buy the picture, however much they wanted to.

But that did not mean that the doughty Captain's voyages had come to an end.

25

Gotcha

Q: So you might have had something to do with it?
A: I don't recall. I didn't say I might or I might not.
   I just said I don't recall.

*Craig Bond, asked about money transferred from
Jersey*[1]

On 28 February 1995, the day after Alan's release from
bankruptcy, an advertisement for offshore companies
caught Craig Bond's eye in the in-flight magazine *American
Way*, perhaps as he relaxed in his business-class seat. Soon
afterwards, he was on the phone to Universal Corporate
Services in Texas to buy a shelf company in the Bahamas for
US$1,000, having made it perfectly clear to the sales manager
that he needed one where the owner's identity could be kept
secret.

A week later, Craig phoned Universal again from Upp Hall
to say that his new Bahamian company, SHC International,
needed a bank account. He was advised to open one at Standard Chartered in Jersey and was sent the requisite forms.[2]
Shortly afterwards, $215,320 was wired to his new account
from Nevill Keating Pictures in London. According to the
Bond Corp liquidator's statement of claim in the South

Australian Supreme Court action, this cash had come from the sale of the missing Bond Corp artworks.[3]

But Craig's secret new Bahamian company was not just set up to be a money box. It was also to take over as owner of the *Portrait of Captain Cook*. Bollag, it seems, was being edged out of the Bonds' financial affairs now that Alan was no longer a bankrupt.

According to the liquidator's statement of claim, Alan's other son, John, was allegedly involved in negotiating this reshuffle.

> On or about 8 or 9 March 1995, John Bond met Bollag in Singapore at which time John Bond and Bollag discussed and arranged the cessation of the involvement by Bollag and entities associated with him, including Firstmark ... in the affairs of the Bond interests including holding assets on their behalf. In the course of this meeting, John Bond and Bollag agreed that Captain Cook would be put in the name of an entity directly controlled by Craig Bond.[4]

John Bond filed a defence in the Supreme Court of South Australia, where the Bond Corp liquidator is based, in which he had accepted that this meeting with Bollag took place, but denied that the Captain Cook portrait or the above matters were discussed. He also denied any involvement with the disputed artworks.[5]

By this stage the Captain Cook had been moved from the Zuricher Freilager to a warehouse near London's Heathrow Airport in anticipation of its delivery to the National Gallery, but in April 1995 it was moved again to Christie's fine-art storage facility on the south bank of the Thames in Nine Elms. And for some extraordinary reason Craig Bond now went along to Christie's in person to make all the arrangements for storage and insurance. Having gone to great lengths to establish a dummy company in the Caribbean to disguise the painting's real owner, he identified himself to Christie's as Craig Bond and told the firm he could be contacted by telephone at Upp Hall. And in case this hadn't left a clear enough trail for investigators to follow, he then paid a £730 bill with a cheque from his private account at Barclays Bank in Buntingford, a small town close to the Bonds' English country mansion.[6]

With ownership and custody of the Captain Cook portrait in Craig's safe hands, the famous explorer stayed quietly at anchor for the next nine months. But in early 1996 Robert Bleakley found an Australian private collector who was interested in buying the painting if the problems of title could be sorted out—the collector being the famous TV game-show millionaire, Reg Grundy. Nevill and Craig consequently flew to Perth in March 1996 to ask an old school mate of Craig's called Lee Christensen, who worked for the law firm Phillips Fox, whether there would still be legal problems selling the painting now that Alan's bankruptcy was over.

And then all hell broke loose.

Half a world away in London, on 19 March 1996, the offices of Nevill Keating Pictures were raided by the UK's Serious Fraud Office, who were helping Australian police investigate allegations that Bond was concealing assets from his creditors. The raiding party of eight or nine officers banged on the door at 6.30am to be welcomed by Lady Nevill's husband Billy Keating in his pyjamas, reeking of drink and happy to chat. Her ladyship, in contrast, was taut, angry and uncooperative. Nevill's reluctance to help, however, did not stop her visitors taking away storage receipts, records and invoices for several of the missing Bond Corporation artworks, including the *Portrait of Captain Cook*.

According to Nevill's evidence on oath five months later, the police had barely left her office when the telephone rang. It was Jurg Bollag, whom she had not heard from in some time. 'He simply said that I was "on my own" and to do what I had to do. He then wished me luck and said goodbye.'[7]

Hard on the heels of the police raiding party came lawyers for the Bond Corp liquidator, who soon obtained a secret UK court order to stop the Captain Cook being moved from Christie's without his consent. Meanwhile, back in Australia, Craig was hit with a summons to appear before the Supreme Court of South Australia, where the liquidator, Richard England, had started secret legal proceedings a few months earlier.[8]

It was not entirely coincidence that the police and England had pounced on the paintings at exactly the same moment, for both had realised that the other was about to do so and had fought fiercely about who should go in first. But it was remarkable that the liquidator had managed to keep his investigations secret from the Bonds. This had only been possible because the court had imposed a blackout on the proceedings, after being told by the liquidator that there was little prospect of getting the artworks back if Bond got wind of what was happening. As one of England's lawyers explained to the court:

> ... there is a real and substantial risk that ... deliberate steps will be taken to stultify the liquidator's investigations and to put assets beyond or further beyond reach ... Further, I am concerned that ... steps may be taken to manufacture or concoct evidence.[9]

The various secrecy orders surrounding the case would not all be lifted until late 2000, and only then would it become entirely clear how much evidence had been gathered. But by using the same sort of powers as Ramsay had employed so effectively to get into Bond's Jersey companies in 1993, England's sleuths had persuaded courts in the USA, England, the Bahamas, Jersey and the Isle of Man to crack open companies and bank accounts all over the world. They had also compelled fifty witnesses to give evidence on oath and had eventually coerced the extremely reluctant Lady Nevill to tell them everything she knew. It was a testimony to what the legal system can achieve when it's allowed to operate as our law-makers intended.

But when poor Craig Bond stumbled onto the stand in Adelaide's Supreme Court on 29 March 1996 to be examined about the fate of the disputed $6 million worth of artworks, he had no clue that anyone had even been on his trail. And he clearly hadn't the faintest idea what was about to hit him.

Back in 1990, the thirteen Bond Corp paintings had been partly paid for with a cheque from a Craig Bond company, and it was this silly mistake that had first raised suspicions: if George Way had been buying them, it seemed odd that Craig was footing the bill. So it was this that Craig was asked about first.

His explanation was that Way had phoned him out of the blue to ask whether he would lend him some money, and had then faxed him a list of the paintings. Craig told the court that he had not thought to ask what the paintings were worth, yet had agreed to lend Way the best part of $1 million.

It soon became clear, however, that this money had never been lent, and that Way had agreed to hand the paintings over to Craig on receipt of his $50,000 fee. Craig was then asked whether he knew what had happened to the artworks after this. Prefacing his answer with the word 'Privilege' to ensure that his evidence could not be used in any criminal proceeding, he replied, 'I have no knowledge of the paintings and no knowledge of what happened to the paintings after they were sold to Mr Way'.[10]

As he stood on the stand and uttered this denial, Craig had no idea of what his interrogators knew, and even less notion of what they would soon discover. But within three months they would find out that he had delivered the *Portrait of Captain Cook* in person to Christie's in April 1995 and then paid bills for storage from his UK bank account. A year later, on re-examination, they would therefore be able to make him admit that this claim to ignorance was a lie.

> Q: Let us not be in any doubt about this. At the
>   time that you were examined on 29 March
>   1996 you knew well of the whereabouts of the
>   Captain Cook painting.
> A: I'm not denying that.[11]

Craig was also asked in this first examination whether he had received the paintings. And again, he lied on oath, as he would do throughout his examination: 'Privilege. No I never received the paintings'.

By the time his re-examination came round in April 1997, however, he had added some extra words in biro to make the transcript read as follows: 'Privilege. I never received the paintings *from Mr Way of High Street Galleries*'.

When asked on oath why he had made this change, Craig said it was because he had had time to reflect and correct his answer. He then got himself into terrible trouble trying to explain what he meant by this.

Q: In modifying the answer as you have, you appear to have drawn a distinction between never receiving the paintings from anybody and never receiving the paintings from Mr Way of High Street Gallery?

A: That's correct.

Q: Is that the distinction you intended to draw?

A: Yes, that's true, that's correct.

Q: Why did you intend to draw that distinction?

A: Well, because it's the factually correct answer.

Q: Do you mean to imply that you had in fact received the paintings from someone other than Mr Way?

A: No, not entirely. No.

Q: Not entirely?

A: No.

Q: To some extent you meant that?

A: Perhaps.[12]

Craig explained on reflection in his first examination in 1996 that he might have inadvertently had something to do with the *Portrait of Captain Cook*. He told the court that he had been asked by Angela Nevill in 1995 to take two paintings to a high-security storage warehouse in London, and it occurred to him that one of these might have been the Captain Cook.

Indeed, on further reflection, he recalled that it was the Captain Cook. Angela Nevill had asked him to take charge of it (even though he didn't own it) and deliver it to Christie's to have it stored on behalf of a company whose name he could not remember. She had done this, he said (implausibly), because she had heard that he might have a claim against this company and might like to negotiate a settlement with them.

Craig told the court that Angela Nevill had then given him
the name and telephone number of a company in the Bahamas.
He had rung this number and spoken to a woman who ran
the company. And she had asked him to sell the Captain Cook
for her.

The trouble with this ludicrous story was that when the
liquidator's lawyers soon interviewed the woman in the
Bahamas and asked her whether the tale was true, she told
them that it was a pack of lies.

In August 1996, five months after Craig's first uncomfortable session in the witness box, Mark Hoffmann flew to
Nassau on behalf of the Bond liquidator to examine Nancy
Lake, the sole director of SHC International. A Canadian
accountant who had lived in the Bahamas for eighteen years,
Lake ran the local office of Universal Corporate Services,
acting as a director (and generally the only director) of the 150
international corporations that UCS had set up for clients.

Bahamian secrecy laws were supposed to make it almost
impossible for investigators to unmask the real owners of such
companies (which was why people like Craig wanted to use
them) but Mark Hoffmann had obtained an order from the
Bahamas Supreme Court compelling Lake to surrender her
files and submit to examination, on the basis that SHC was
possibly involved in fraud.

Lake told Hoffmann on oath that she had made no decisions
for the company and had simply done what she was told by
Craig Bond. She said that it was owned by Craig and had been
set up in March 1995 with two bearer shares. Crucially, she also
told Hoffmann that SHC owned the *Portrait of Captain Cook*.[13]

According to Lake, Craig's Bahamian company really acted
as a postbox. She had a standing instruction to send mail to
Craig at Upp Hall by express post as soon as it arrived; had

no authority to sign cheques or deal with the company's Jersey bank account; and merely forwarded bank statements, unopened, when they arrived by post.

Lake had never met Craig in the flesh but had talked to him over the phone several times. He had also sent her letters telling her what to write to Nevill Keating Pictures on SHC notepaper. She was able to produce one such letter stating that SHC was the owner of the *Portrait of Captain Cook* and instructing Nevill to place it on the market. Another letter from SHC instructed Christie's Fine Art to store the Captain Cook and a 'naval portrait'.[14] She then produced a handwritten letter from Craig telling her to keep only those documents that were necessary for her administration—an instruction that she had clearly ignored.

Armed with Lake's testimony, a stack of documents and more information from other inquiries, the lawyers resumed their examination of Craig in Australia in April 1997. Under pressure, Craig's memory began to improve slightly. He recalled that SHC was the Bahamas company. But he was sure that he had had no dealings with it.

The lawyers then produced a document showing that SHC had telexed $51,031.24 to one of Craig's companies, Hullmes Pty Ltd, at Bank West in Northbridge on 18 January 1996. The lawyers asked him why they had paid him this money. Craig could not recall. And why had SHC also telexed $51,188.03 to another of his companies, Tambar? Craig couldn't recall that either. Nor could he help with any information about SHC.

> A: What do you mean, what do I know about
>   it? ... I know that it's a company registered in
>   the Bahamas I believe, that it apparently owns

some art work and really very little other than
that.

Q: Likewise, is it your evidence that you had
nothing to do with the transfer of funds into
the Tambar and Hullmes accounts from SHC
International Inc.?

A: Privilege. I don't recall.

Q: So you might have had something to do with it?

A: Privilege. I don't recall. I didn't say I might or I
might not. I just said I don't recall.

Q: Is it conceivable that you did have something
to do with it?

A: I don't recall.

Q: You mean you don't recall whether it's conceivable or not?

A: Privilege. I do not recall.[15]

As the evidence began to pile up, Craig's memory improved
more markedly. He now remembered that SHC had an
account at the Standard Chartered Bank in St Helier, Jersey,
and what's more, that he could sign cheques on it. So he was
asked whether he knew how much money was in the account
or where it had come from. He said he had no idea. Did he
set it up, he was asked? No, he didn't believe he did.

Then came the crunch. His examiner, Dick Whitington QC,
produced documents from Standard Chartered, signed by
Craig, which showed that he had opened the account on behalf
of SHC on 7 March 1995 and that he had nominated himself
as the only person who could sign cheques and the only person
from whom the bank could take instructions.

Craig was then forced to admit that he had indeed opened
the Jersey account.

Next, Whitington produced a handwritten letter from Craig to Standard Chartered instructing the bank to transfer the two amounts of $51,000-odd to Tambar and Hullmes—the very amounts that he had just been asked about. By this stage, Whitington had already asked who owned SHC, to which Craig had replied:

A: Privilege. I have no idea who the owner is.
Q: No idea at all?
A: Privilege. No idea whatsoever.
Q: Have you ever had any beneficial interest in SHC International Inc.?
A: Privilege. None whatsoever.

Now he asked again.

Q: You say that neither you nor any person, company, trust or entity associated with you had any beneficial interest in SHC International at the time?
A: Privilege. That is correct.
Q: You are quite certain about that?
A: Privilege. Yes, I am.
Q: I suggest to you that's false.
A: Privilege. That's not correct.[16]

Armed with this denial, which appeared to put Craig at risk of prosecution for perjury, Whitington then produced a series of instructions from Craig to Standard Chartered. One was to pay money from SHC's account to Upp Hall Leisure and Entertainment, another to pay a car company in Perth. He then produced bank documents to show that Craig had instructed

Standard Chartered to close SHC's account in June 1996 and send the balance of £29,547 to Craig's personal account at Barclays Bank in Buntingford.[17]

As if this was not enough, Whitington then recited testimony from Paul Pettit, the owner of Universal Corporate Services, that Craig had instructed him to set up SHC. Once again, Craig could not remember Mr Pettit or the phone call. But once again, the lawyer had all the evidence he needed to jog his memory.

In the first place, there was a cheque for US$490 drawn on an account at the Overton Bank & Trust in Fort Worth that Craig had signed, which had been received by Universal in payment for setting up SHC. Then there were the phone records from Upp Hall which showed fax and phone calls made to Universal Corporate Services in March 1995 when the company was being set up.

Craig was now reminded that if he failed to answer questions truthfully he would be committing an offence. He told the court he was aware of this. He was then taken through all his denials again.

Did he remember Paul Pettit? No, he did not.

Did he have any beneficial interest in SHC? No, he did not.

Did he have anything to do with directing the affairs of the company? No, he did not.

Did he have anything to do with setting it up? No, he did not. Did he procure Nancy Lake to act as director of SHC? No, he did not.

Had Craig had any idea what the liquidator's lawyers were going to produce next, he might have been more careful with his blank denials, which once again laid him open to charges of perjury. And had he been warned by Master Bowen Pain, who was presiding over the examination, that he was in

serious danger of being jailed for contempt, he might also have
been more careful. But he had no idea and he wasn't warned.
So he was drawn further into the trap.

Whitington now produced Craig's own handwritten letter
to Nancy Lake in the Bahamas on 21 March 1995, which
referred to Paul Pettit, whom he had supposedly never heard
of, to SHC, which he had denied having dealt with, and of
course to Nancy Lake, whose name he claimed to have forgotten. And contrary to Craig's denials on oath, this letter
demonstrated that he had indeed called all the shots. Not only
was he ordering Lake to forward all mail to him by express
post and to send him Universal's bills, he was also instructing
her to destroy all copies of his correspondence, which she had
clearly not done. All in all, it was a devastating document.

> Q: You didn't expect the liquidator at today's
>   examination to have a letter such as this, did
>   you?
> A: I didn't know what the liquidator might have.[18]

Craig was then shown a further handwritten letter he had sent
Lake in March 1995, instructing her to contact Angela Nevill
with regard to selling the Captain Cook. In English that was
little better than his famous father's he had written:

> Dear Nancy,
>
> I would like to send a letter to Lady Angela Neville
> [sic] of Neville-Keating [sic] Pictures ... the letter
> should be from SHC INTERNATIONAL INC and
> singed [sic] by you as DIRECTOR. Following is
> the required draft.[19]

Craig was now forced to agree that this showed he had in fact directed Nancy Lake in the affairs of SHC International, which he had specifically denied moments earlier. Once again, he had been caught lying on oath.

Having dealt with SHC, Whitington moved on to the aftermath of the raid by the UK Serious Fraud Office. After the paintings had been frozen by court order in May 1996, Craig had employed a firm of Irish solicitors to help him get the Captain Cook back. They had written to Christie's in December 1996 to say that they would turn up at the warehouse and demand the painting's return.

Whitington now produced records of calls made from Craig's mobile phone showing calls to these Dublin lawyers, calls to SHC in the Bahamas and a call from Australia to Standard Chartered in Jersey. Craig, however, simply disputed that he had made them, either saying that he could not recall, or suggesting that they had been made by someone else using his phone. At this point, Whitington either lost his patience or decided that it was time to get tough. Turning to the judge, he said:

> We think Mr Bond at this stage should be given a warning. Frankly, we think the implications for him are very serious. We think the time has come for him to acknowledge that the game is up, to stop this charade which in our view he has been conducting since Monday in persisting in saying that he can't recall things which patently he may be able to recall. The time has come for him to appreciate he can either acknowledge his participation in these events and handle it as best he can or can press on with this charade and in our

submission put himself in contempt of court but at risk of serious criminal prosecution from the authorities for a whole host of offences.

We think with great respect the time has come where Mr Bond should be given a warning as to his conduct and answers in the witness box.[20]

Reading through the transcript it is hard not to sympathise with Whitington's point of view. There is no question that the law lays down a duty to answer questions in such an examination fully and truthfully, and there is no question that Bond had done quite enough to risk charges of perjury or contempt, yet Master Bowen Pain chose to decline the opportunity to read the riot act. Instead of warning the witness to shape up or be shipped out, he directed his words to Whitington, telling him, 'A decision as to whether he is given a warning is my decision. I will make that as and when I deem appropriate'.

Craig was extremely lucky to have escaped punishment for contempt much earlier, because he had led the court on a ridiculous dance for a year in his efforts to avoid being examined. After his first appearance in March 1996 he had simply failed to turn up on three separate occasions—in August and September 1996 and then again in February 1997. His last failure had been the most blatant. The liquidator's lawyers had sent him a Perth–Adelaide air ticket, so he could have no excuse for non-attendance, and warned him that he faced a penalty of $10,000 or two years in jail if he did not show up. Regardless, he had stayed away, sending a doctor's note from England to say that he was unfit to travel because he had a respiratory infection. Unfortunately for Craig, however, Malaysian Airlines's computer showed that he had left Perth on 13 February after receiving the summons, with no apparent intention of returning to Australia until 28 February, which was nine days after he was due to appear.[21]

On that occasion, Master Bowen Pain had referred the matter to his superior, Justice Debelle, who had indeed summonsed Craig for contempt. Craig had then decided to give in, paying $120,000 in costs to the liquidator's lawyers and agreeing to turn up. The matter had then been dropped, so it had cost him money but not his freedom.

In the intervening period, Craig had also been trying his damnedest to persuade courts in the UK and Australia to have the examination halted, fighting three unsuccessful legal actions on this point. He had also taken legal action to have transcripts of his examination destroyed. And finally, he had asked the court for copies of all the material that the liquidator had collected, including transcripts of interviews, so that he would know what they had discovered. But the liquidator's lawyers had argued successfully that everything should remain secret if they were to be given a chance of success.

Once the liquidator's lawyers had finished grilling Craig, their next key target was Alan Bond. But he was clearly just as desperate to avoid questions about the artworks as his son, and so another protracted legal battle began.

The initial order to examine Alan on oath was issued by the South Australian Supreme Court on 24 April 1997, but for convenience sake it was decided to fly to Western Australia to interview him in prison. In late May, Dick Whitington and Master Bowen Pain therefore made the trip from Adelaide to Karnet Prison Farm south-east of Perth, where the superintendent's office had been set aside for them to hold the hearing. Meanwhile, Bond's lawyers, Andrew Harris and Tony Howard QC, flew in from Melbourne.

As they sat in the superintendent's office, they could see Bond walking round the yard outside, sporting Oakley sunglasses and jungle greens. But getting him inside to answer questions proved to be difficult. Having been given a month's notice of the hearing and having waited for everyone to make the long trek to Karnet, Bond's QC Tony Howard now raised a crucial technical objection: the court had no power to take oaths outside South Australia or to bring Bond up from his cell. The liquidator's lawyers suggested that the superintendent might order Bond to appear under section 22 of the *Prisons Act (WA) 1981*, and that a Western Australian judge could certainly do this. But after a long telephone conference, Justice Heenan of the Western Australian Supreme Court decided that he could not make an order without hearing submissions over the next ten days. So the court packed its bags, and the lawyers trooped off home again.

Back in Adelaide, Master Bowen Pain soon decided it was crazy to return to Perth if it was going to cause all this argument, and ordered Bond to appear for examination in South Australia instead. But this didn't go ahead on 1 July as planned, because Bond's lawyers instituted fresh legal action to strike out the examination as an abuse of process. They lost this argument at the first attempt, then appealed to the South Australian Supreme Court and lost again. They then appealed to the full bench of the Supreme Court and lost for a third time in October 1997.[22] Next, they sought special leave to appeal to the High Court and applied for a stay of the examination while this was heard. And when the application for a stay was turned down, they applied for another. Finally, after losing at the fifth attempt, Bond and his lawyers were forced to give in. It was the old familiar pattern of legal trench warfare, in which one could lose all battles yet still hope to win the war by outlasting the enemy. This time, however, their opponents were not going to give up.

On 23 November 1997, Alan Bond was therefore escorted onto a plane from Perth to Adelaide, sandwiched between a couple of Western Australian prison officers. On his arrival, all the other passengers were made to wait as he was whisked off in an unmarked station wagon to spend a few nights in South Australia's Yatala prison. The following day he was brought up from the cells into the criminal court building to face his interrogator.

It had taken a huge effort to get him this far but, as so often in the Bond story, the examination now threatened to be an almost total waste of time. By an extraordinary coincidence, Alan's old amnesia had suddenly reasserted itself. And before long he was humbly asking the court for forbearance.

> Perhaps it should be put on the transcript that in the last ten years I've had a number of medical problems which resulted in four strokes, and I have had open heart surgery and only eighteen months ago I had a blood clot and I've been quite seriously ill and I have had quite a bout of depression and I have lost a lot of memory. I would like them to understand, going back, dates long ago, I have grave difficulty with remembering things.[23]

This picture of frailty was in stark contrast to the portrait Alan had painted to journalist Paul Spike in November 1994 or the evidence that had been given in the Manet fraud trial in June 1994 of his robust state of health. But Bond's court-induced memory problems proved useful yet again, because he was now able to claim that he could not recall even the most basic information.

Two bankrupts in a Roller. Jim Byrnes and Alan Bond can't stop grinning after Dallhold's creditors vote to do a deal, December 1994.

Secret documents are paraded through Perth by Western Australia's Director of Public Prosecutions, John McKechnie (left) and his investigator, Joe Lieberfreund, January 1995. The Supreme Court refused to let Bond's trustee in bankruptcy see them, even though they disclosed a Swiss bank account held 'by Bollag on behalf of Bond'.

Have we got the numbers? Bond and Byrnes look anxious during a break in the creditors' meeting, January 1995. Soon afterwards, the crucial vote on Bond's settlement offer was postponed.

Who's won? Bond's trustee in bankruptcy, Bob Ramsay, holds up the $1 million cheque while Alan Bond signs the papers that will release him from bankruptcy.

Free. A beaming Bond finds release from bankruptcy is a cure for all ills.

Get your roubles here. Prince Vladimir D'Jamirze (centre), at home with his brothers, February 1995.

Wedded bliss. Alan and Diana seal it with a kiss, April 1995.

Happy together. Honeymooning on the Gold Coast.

Fit to face trial? Bond running to court for the committal hearing of the Bell fraud charges.

Defiant. Bond at the $15 million Manet fraud trial, August 1996. Found guilty on two charges of fraud and deception, he was sentenced to three years in jail.

Guilty. Bond is driven to prison in a police van after pleading guilty to two charges of defrauding Bell Resources, December 1996. He was sentenced to four years in jail.

Prison picnic. Alan, Diana and friends at Karnet Prison, 1996.
Rose Porteous and her husband Willie are on the right.

Two of a kind. Alan poses by Webber's
famous *Portrait of Captain Cook* in 1988.
Cook's countrymen didn't value him either,
said Bond. The missing portrait was
discovered by police in London in 1996.

It must run in the family.
Craig Bond forgot all about his
involvement with the voyages
of the Captain Cook until
confronted with the evidence.

Angela Nevill, Bond's art dealer, who tried to sell the *Portrait of Captain Cook* to the National Gallery of Australia in 1993.

Robert Bleakley, former Managing Director of Sotheby's, negotiated with the National Gallery of Australia to sell the *Portrait of Captain Cook* on Nevill's behalf.

Technical knockout. Bond walked free from Karnet prison in March 2000 after the High Court freed him on a legal technicality.

Where next? All set to bounce back, March 2000.

He could not, for example, remember that his artworks had formed the Alan Bond Collection. Nor could he recall that he had been executive chairman of Bond Corporation Holdings. He had also forgotten which office he had occupied in the Bond Tower, which year he had resigned as a director of Bond Corporation Holdings and which year his managing director, Peter Beckwith, had died.

His desire to assist his interrogators also failed to impress. At one point Master Bowen Pain was moved to observe that Bond was not trying to answer the questions or listen to his questioner.[24]

But for all that, some crucial points were conceded to the liquidator. Bond's diary showed that he had met George Way at 11.00am on 2 January 1990, half an hour after meeting Peter Beckwith, and he admitted that he had discussed the purchase of the paintings with both of them. There was also evidence that he had discussed the sale of the pictures to Way on 19 December 1989 with Beckwith and Michael Cross, his managing director at Dallhold. So it was clear that he knew about the transaction.

Thereafter, he had met Jurg Bollag twice in London in March 1990, three times in May 1990 and three times in June 1990, sometimes with Cross and sometimes with Nevill.[25] He even accepted that he had discussed the *Portrait of Captain Cook* on at least one of these occasions, but came up with a truly wonderful explanation of why he had done so.

According to Bond's sworn evidence, Jurg Bollag had rung him in March 1990 to say that he (Bollag) had acquired some paintings from George Way, including the Captain Cook. He had then sought Alan's advice on selling them. It was a truly fantastic story, a real gem, which prompted Dick Whitington to ask him sarcastically:

Q: Did you say 'Good Heavens, what are you doing with my Captain Cook painting?' or something like that?

A: Privilege. It was never my Captain Cook painting.

Q: When he told you that, were you surprised?

A: Privilege. It's so long ago I can't remember.[26]

Perhaps it was in fairyland that Bond had mislaid his precious memory capsule. For if he really thought anyone would swallow this, he'd obviously started living there himself. But he had always lived a charmed life—as events had a habit of demonstrating.

26

Free Again

Alan Bond sits with one hand on the Bible,
looking me straight in the eye as he swears:
'I have no hidden money overseas. I have no
hidden money *anywhere*'.

Australian Women's Weekly, *April 2000*[1]

I n March 2000, Alan Bond was let out of jail after spending
less than three-and-a-half years behind bars. His release
after 1,298 days meant that he had spent roughly one day in
prison for every 1 million dollars Bell's unlucky shareholders
had lost through his fraud. He had set many records in his
time. But this one probably beat them all.

Only days beforehand, a young aboriginal man had been
sentenced to a year in prison in the Northern Territory for
stealing $23 worth of cordial and biscuits. Had the same
formula been applied to Bond, he would have been forced to
wait another 50 million years for his release. As the former
chairman of the National Crime Authority, John Broome, told
ABC Radio, the comparison made Bond's lenient treatment
quite obscene.

Typically, a legal technicality had freed him more than a
year before he was due to complete his jail term. In 1997, his

sentence for the Bell fraud had been increased from four to seven years after an appeal by the Commonwealth DPP. Now an appeal to the High Court by Bond had ruled that the Commonwealth DPP had acted beyond his powers. In its infinite wisdom, the law allowed the Commonwealth to investigate and prosecute Bond, but would not permit it to appeal against his sentence.

There was no argument from the High Court that Bond's increased punishment had been too severe, nor any suggestion that his guilt had in any way been diminished by his release. As the judges admitted, almost sheepishly, it was a technicality, pure and simple—the sort that vigilant lawyers are paid to exploit. Of course, had Bond been given a proper penalty in the first place, they would never have had the chance to exploit it. And had he been a run-of-the-mill criminal, without access to a virtually unlimited supply of funds, his lawyers might never have found the loophole.

News of the High Court reprieve for Bond was expected at the opening of judicial business in Canberra, which came at the ungodly hour of 7.15am in Perth, where the clocks were three hours behind. So a big crowd of journalists had trekked to Karnet Prison Farm shortly after sunrise. As arrangements were made for Bond's release, they were forced to wait outside the jail all day in the 37-degree heat.

The reporters had been told that Bond would be picked up by his wife Diana, so they had been scanning the roadway all morning for the approach of a big BMW or Mercedes. They then spotted her arriving in a modest Mitsubishi Magna with plastic fake mag wheels and watched her drive into the prison to wait with Alan while his release papers came through from Perth.

Late in the afternoon, as these vital documents rolled off

the fax, the storm clouds that had been threatening all day suddenly broke into a huge flash of lightning that scored a direct hit on one of the prison buildings, cutting the power supply and injuring around a dozen inmates. Perhaps the gods were displeased. Shortly afterwards, at around 5.00pm, as Bond took his first tentative steps to freedom, ambulances arrived to ferry the casualties to hospital. By this time the crowd of forty-odd journalists and photographers had dwindled to only about half that number, but there were still enough to constitute a decent scrum. They had been told by the prison authorities exactly where Diana would park the car and which side Alan would be on. There was to be a statement but no questions.

Bond walked out in a dark brass-buttoned blazer, white shirt and purple tie, with an uncertain smile on his face, his hair completely white. When asked politely what the future held for him, he responded that he wanted to spend some time with his wife, who had supported him loyally, and with his children. Prison had been an ordeal, he said, he could not pretend otherwise. He was relieved to be free at last, and he would not be rushing back into business.

The following day, he was bailed up in his house in Cottesloe, apparently refusing all interviews. Meanwhile, behind the two-metre-high walls, he and Diana were telling their story to *The Australian Women's Weekly*, who had paid $50,000 to secure the exclusive. This was considerably less than rumour had suggested, and the *Women's Weekly* had been assured that the money would be paid to charity.[2] The magazine's editor would remind readers that Bond was 'among the most infamous of Australia's corporate criminals' and a man who had 'tragically changed the lives of thousands of ordinary Australians'. But otherwise, the *Women's Weekly* would make no apology for allowing Australia's biggest corporate fraud to tell his side of the story.

Prison had clearly been no picnic for Bond. Despite the fact that he was no risk to anyone, he had spent more than half his sentence in the maximum-security jail at Casuarina, where he had twice been attacked. In the first incident, a fellow inmate had wrapped a steel telephone cord round his neck and tried to strangle him, leaving him bruised and cut for days. The prisoner had become impatient while waiting for Bond to finish talking on the phone to Diana. On the second occasion, Alan had been picked on in the canteen, where an inmate had threatened to throw food in his face. Both times, an unofficial bodyguard had come to his aid. The *Women's Weekly* said press reports had identified Bond's minder as a man serving an eight-year sentence for payroll robbery, and Alan claimed he had taught him to read in exchange for protection.

Earlier in his prison career, Bond had reportedly been looked after by a powerful drug dealer called Tony Pinkstone. Those who knew Tony told a story of how his car had been stolen and he had put word out to friends that he would like it back. The car had duly turned up outside his house the following morning.

Bond told the *Women's Weekly* he had spent a fair bit of time in jail teaching fellow inmates about business and giving courses on business ethics, which seemed a frightening prospect. He had also learnt how to use a computer and penned a couple of rather thin chapters of his autobiography, telling tired old tales of meeting Princess Margaret at Windsor and lending her a fiver for the collection plate. But he had spent the bulk of his time studying art and painting. He had even stayed on at Casuarina for a few extra weeks to finish his diploma in fine art, because he could not complete the study at Karnet. By March 2000 he had somehow become one of the highest-priced living artists in Australia, which is a remarkable comment on our fascination with celebrity.

Bond's first great sales success, a portrait of West Coast Eagles footy star Peter Matera, can still be seen on the walls of Perth's oldest bordello, Langtree's, if you're brave enough to visit. And the Perth madam who bought it for $25,000 at a charity auction in 1998 has since been offered $50,000 to sell it. But there are plenty of other Bond paintings on public view, even though Alan has been careful not to depress prices by flooding the market. There is even a copy of his famous US$54 million Van Gogh, *Irises*, which Alan painted and gave away for cancer research.

Sadly, Alan is no Van Gogh himself. Unkind critics suggest that he paints by numbers, and one of his pictures of wading birds, which sold for $3,800, is a straight copy of *Beach Buddies* from a book called *How to draw and paint water colours*. But this has not stopped him having huge success.

The National Portrait Gallery in Canberra, which opened in the old parliament house in March 1999, has works by most of the best artists in Australia, from the early nineteenth century to the present day. There is a wonderful Whiteley that won the Archibald prize in 1978, several memorable paintings by Pugh, and a smattering of Nolans, Boyds and Dobells, along with the odd Tom Roberts and a solitary Picasso. And slap bang in the middle of them, there also hangs a Bond, being a self-portrait of Alan.

Surprisingly, it is neither heroic nor flattering, for it makes him look quizzical, like a lawyer, or one of those wading birds that cocks its head to listen for its lunch. It shows Bond grey-haired and wrinkled, in wire-rimmed glasses, with one eye askew, and it is almost cartoon-like—a cross between Roy

Lichtenstein and a pavement artist. When the gallery commissioned it in January 1999 they said they had no intention of buying it. But clearly they decided that it was good enough to show, given the artist's undoubted notoriety. In this context, its caption could be less brutal. Although it starts by celebrating Alan's America's Cup triumph, it continues bluntly, 'Bond's reputation as one of Australia's business leaders plummeted in the 1980s, and he is currently serving a seven-year sentence for the misuse of corporate funds'.

After Alan's release, of course, the description will have to change.

Despite the soft stories about his painting, and gentle treatment by the *Australian Women's Weekly*, surprisingly few people spoke up for Bond in the aftermath of his release. The callers on Perth's talkback radio stacked up four to one against him, and the papers also reflected little public sympathy. Not only was it felt that he had got off lightly, but it was widely reported that he still had a vast amount of money to fall back on. 'Bond free to spend $70 million' was how Sydney's *Daily Telegraph* trumpeted his release, adding in the text,

> 'Bond does not leave prison a poor man, estimates putting his family wealth at $70 million, with possibly another $50 million offshore'.[3]

Others sounded off in harmony, with the *Sydney Morning Herald* headlining its front-page story 'One day in jail for every stolen million'.[4] The *Women's Weekly* article had attempted to meet the problem head-on by getting Bond to deny the rumours. They had even taken advantage of his newfound Christianity to ask if he would swear on the Bible, and he volunteered to get one and do just that.

> Alan Bond sits with one hand on the Bible, looking me straight in the eye as he swears: 'I have no hidden money overseas. I have no hidden money *anywhere*'.[5]

But before the *Women's Weekly* had even gone on sale, this oath was already beginning to look distinctly suspect, because the missing *Portrait of Captain Cook* had turned up again in dramatic circumstances. The lifting of a confidentiality order had revealed that the $6 million painting was sitting in Christie's high-security warehouse in south London, where Craig Bond had left it in April 1995.

The Cook portrait had been there under lock and key since May 1996, thanks to a secret UK court order that had secured it for Bond Corp's liquidators.[6] Alongside it was an array of 1,400 watercolours, maps and drawings called the Freycinet Collection that almost certainly belonged to Alan Bond himself. This famous assortment of artworks, produced on a voyage to Australia in the early 1800s by the French navigator and cartographer Louis Freycinet, had been bought by Bond in the mid-1980s through his Jersey company Kirk Holdings and valued shortly afterwards at $4 million. Yet they had not been declared to Alan's trustee in bankruptcy, and had clearly been hidden from his creditors, notwithstanding Bond's biblical promise to *Women's Weekly* readers.[7]

Another painting of historical importance to Australia, which had vanished from Bond Corporation as Alan's empire collapsed around him, was in the Christie's warehouse, subject to the same UK court order. *Portrait of Matthew Flinders*, by the French artist Antoine Toussaint de Chazal, had been bought by Alan Bond in 1987 for $492,000, again through Kirk Holdings. It had hung in the Bond Tower until

December 1989, when it was crated up and flown to Switzerland.

The Flinders portrait was loaded onto one of the Bond corporate jets, bolstered with cushions and strapped to the cabin floor, along with another of Alan's paintings, *Natives in the Eucalypt Forest* by the colonial artist John Glover, which had cost Bond £425,000 in December 1984. According to eyewitnesses, the plane was met on the tarmac at Zurich Airport by Jurg Bollag and an unidentified woman, who supervised the loading of the artworks into a van.

The Swiss banker had written to Bond just before the shipment to claim that he owned both paintings and had merely been lending them to Alan to hang on his walls. He even provided evidence that they had belonged to his Isle of Man company, Firstmark, since 1987. But since the company had not been set up until two years later, this was extremely hard to believe. And Angela Nevill certainly disputed it.

In 1996, Nevill testified on oath that she had bought both the Glover and the Flinders portrait for Alan Bond. She said that Alan had given her instructions to buy the paintings and that she would have rung Dallhold or Bond to ask who was paying for them. She said that she had always regarded Kirk Holdings as belonging to Alan Bond or his family, and she was absolutely adamant that she had not bought these or any other artworks for Bollag, adding:

> George Bollag was not a collector of artworks, nor did he seem to have any great appreciation for them. He was more interested in them as saleable assets.[8]

But the discovery of the missing paintings was by no means

Bond's biggest problem. A few days before his interview with the *Women's Weekly* hit the newsstands, the *Sydney Morning Herald* reported dramatic evidence of a huge money-laundering transaction, in which US$3.2 million (A$4.3 million) of Alan Bond's offshore fortune had been washed back to Australia from Liechtenstein.[9]

According to affidavits filed in the South Australian Supreme Court by lawyers for the Bond Corp liquidator, Richard England, the US$3.2 million was wired to the ANZ Bank in Brisbane on 28 February 1995 from a bank in Fort Worth, Texas, only one day after Alan's release from bankruptcy—and only one day after he had signed a warranty to creditors that he had no hidden assets.[10]

The money had started out from a company called SIDRO Anstalt in the Liechtenstein capital of Vaduz, and had then bounced through a network of offshore companies and bank accounts in Jersey, the British Virgin Islands and the United States, all of which had been set up by Craig Bond or on his instructions. SIDRO, which was run by Jurg Bollag, was well known to Bond's bankruptcy trustee, Bob Ramsay, and to the Australian Federal Police, who had identified it as one of the key resting places for Alan's offshore fortune.[11] On arrival in Australia, the money was paid to two Bond family companies, which used some of it to finance a land deal and pay Alan's legal fees, and distributed some to members of the Bond family.

This was easily the biggest parcel of money that Bond had repatriated but it was not the only one. Back in 1996, England's lawyers had obtained bank documents from Standard Chartered in Jersey which showed that US$600,000 (roughly A$800,000) had moved through an account belonging to Craig Bond's company SHC in November 1995, coming in from Liechtenstein and going out again to Texas, on Craig's instructions.[12] However, at that stage Richard England's lawyers had been unable to track the funds back to Australia.

The speed and size of this transfer had prompted Standard Chartered to report it immediately to the Jersey authorities as a suspected money-laundering transaction. But typically, Craig had denied knowing anything about the money or where it had come from when examined on oath in April 1997:

> Q: I suggest that you well knew at the time you facilitated this transaction that the US$600,000 was the proceeds of the sale of some of these paintings, the sale having been procured by Mr Bollag in conjunction with Lady Angela Nevill?
>
> A: Privilege. I do not know anything whatsoever to do with that $600,000.
>
> Q: I suggest you also participated in procuring those sales?
>
> A: I emphatically deny it.[13]

It was not until three years later that one of the liquidator's lawyers, Jason Karas, found the proof they needed. In August 1999, he flew secretly to Fort Worth in Texas to examine one of Craig Bond's old Australian friends, Peter Philpott, to whose company and bank account the US$600,000 had been sent. After obtaining a court order compelling Philpott to hand over all documents relating to the Bonds and to answer questions on oath, Karas was able to plot the progress of the US$600,000 all the way from Liechtenstein to the Bonds in Perth. And at that point the earlier transfer of US$3.2 million was also discovered.

Philpott told Karas on oath that he had been asked by Craig

Bond in January 1995 to set up a company, named Stoneham, in the British Virgin Islands and open a bank account. Shortly afterwards, he received a telephone call from Alan Bond's favourite Swiss banker, Jurg Bollag, telling him that US$3.2 million would be sent to Stoneham's account at Barclays Bank in Tortola, the capital of the British Virgin Islands. Philpott was instructed to pass it on to the account of another company called Dampier, which he had set up for Craig Bond in Texas, and thence wire the money to Australia.[14]

According to Jason Karas's affidavit, filed in the South Australian Supreme Court in February 2001, the sequence of transactions went like this:

> On about 1 February 1995, Stoneham entered into an investment advisory services agreement with SIDRO ... in respect of monies to be paid into the account opened by Stoneham. The existence of this agreement was to remain confidential ...
>
> On 8 February 1995, Stoneham received in its Barclays account the sum of US$3,244,445.25 from Swiss Bank Corporation in New York.
>
> On 27 February 1995, Barclays debited the account of Stoneham with the sum of US$3,200,095 and transferred the same to Dampier at its account at the Overton Bank & Trust, Fort Worth, Texas ...
>
> On the following day, 28 February 1995, Dampier transferred US$3.182 million to the ... ANZ Bank in Queensland.[15]

According to the affidavit, the $US3.2 million (which had now been exchanged into A$4.3 million) was then credited to the trust account of a solicitor working for the Bonds, who distributed the money on John Bond's instructions. Roughly $2.1 million went to a Bond family company called Carindale Land Corporation, to purchase development land in Brisbane, and another $2.1 million was paid by cheque to another Bond family company in Perth called Hastings Finance.[16]

Hastings, according to Karas, acted as the Bond family's banker, collecting and distributing substantial amounts of money to family members, and arranging for the payment of Alan's legal bills. Since 1995 it had received $5.3 million in profit from the Brisbane land development, on which, according to the sworn evidence of the Bonds' accountant, Delores Caboche, it had paid no tax. Hastings had also made huge loans to Bond family trusts that had simply been written off. In the space of just two years, 1996 to 1998, these had amounted to a remarkable $17 million.[17]

It had not been easy for the liquidator's lawyers to discover this information. In his affidavit, Karas complained bitterly that the Bonds had tried their level best to cover it up.

> Complicated steps have been taken by or with the knowledge of at least Craig Bond, John Bond and Delores Caboche to disguise the source of funds obtained by Carindale ...
>
> Each ... [has] given at best grossly misleading evidence on oath in the course of their respective examinations as to the position of Carindale and its interaction with Dampier Inc and SHC and have provided deliberately masked documentation so as to frustrate the liquidator's inquiries.[18]

In May 2000, the liquidator's lawyers asked the South

Australian Supreme Court to freeze all of Carindale's assets, which included almost $5 million worth of development land. The court was also asked to order Craig and John Bond to give full disclosure of all assets held by them at March 1996 or acquired since that date, on the basis that Karas believed there to be:

> A real and severe risk that the defendants will continue to take steps to dissipate assets available to them, and in particular the assets of Carindale, so as to frustrate the ability of the plaintiffs to recover any judgement sum that may be ordered in their favour.[19]

While Justice Debelle deliberated about whether to take this draconian step, other developments in the art fraud case were coming thick and fast. In the most dramatic, on 7 June 2000, the judge decided that the *Portrait of Captain Cook* was indeed the property of Bond Corp's creditors. Soon afterwards, news came that the painting had been sold to the National Portrait Gallery in Canberra for $5.3 million and was being put on a plane back to Australia. Hard on the heels of this major victory, the Supreme Court of South Australia also granted the liquidator possession of the *Portrait of Matthew Flinders*. And this, too, was soon on its way down under, to the Art Gallery of South Australia, which had snapped it up for $780,000.[20]

Then, in September 2000, Justice Debelle delivered what appeared to be a killer blow to the Bonds' hopes of defending the case. First, he agreed to freeze the assets of Carindale and its Brisbane land venture on the basis that the liquidator's $13 million artwork fraud claim appeared to have a good chance of success. Second, he ruled that the allegations of money laundering were proven, to the extent that Carindale had indeed received US$3.2 million from offshore in what the judge described as 'a payment to Bond interests, arranged by Bollag'.[21]

Not surprisingly, the setback dealt a severe blow to Bond's confidence that he would win the case, and before long he was telling the press that he was keen to reach a compromise. But the liquidator's lawyers were now so flush with success that they were not prepared to accept anything less than payment in full.

To the informed observer, the liquidator's case appeared to be a lay-down misère. And when the matter finally came to a hearing in March 2001 it took only two days of witness evidence for the Bonds to throw in their hand and to agree to pay the $12 million that Richard England was still seeking.[22]

As the *Australian Financial Review's* Mark Drummond pointed out, in breaking the news of the capitulation: 'Alan Bond has never been one to pay a dollar for something when a few cents would suffice, especially where his creditors are concerned'. But on this occasion he had been made to cough up every last cent.

'We literally eyeballed them and said anything less than a full recovery is inadequate,' England cheerfully explained. 'We were determined to get full tote odds, because we regarded it as an open and shut case.'[23]

According to England, the Bonds had been trying to settle the claim since 1997, but had been offering only a third of what they were now forced to pay. England told the *Financial Review* that his refusal to accept a compromise had been met 'almost with disbelief'.

Naturally, the Bonds made no admission as to liability or

guilt, but it was hard to argue that the allegations of fraud, money laundering and an offshore fortune belonging to Alan were anything but bang on target.

As to why the Bonds had finally run up the white flag, one could only speculate, but the surrender followed fresh evidence that Alan, Craig and John Bond had been involved in repatriating another $1.1 million from Texas in December 1995.

On top of that, the Supreme Court had been told to expect testimony from a London real estate agent who claimed to have shown Alan and Diana Bliss round 13 Evelyn Gardens, Chelsea, in May 1987, and negotiated the sale with Alan. This, remember, was supposed to be Bollag's apartment, so Diana Bliss would be open to accusations that she had perjured herself by swearing on oath that Alan knew absolutely nothing about it.[24]

Apart from these new revelations, there was the unwelcome prospect of Alan's art dealer, Angela Nevill, telling how she had sold the missing paintings for Bond; of Craig's Texan friend, Peter Philpott, confessing how he had moved Alan's money back to Australia on Bollag's instructions; and of Nancy Lake dishing the dirt on Craig and his secret Bahamian company. The danger of all this coming out in public was that it could persuade the Australian Federal Police to start chasing Bond again.

When they abandoned Operation Oxide in 1998, the AFP had assured everyone that they were only putting the Bond investigation on ice until new evidence emerged. Two years later, they had vowed to examine all the material gathered by England's investigators. And two months after that, the Minister for Justice, Amanda Vanstone, had pledged that the AFP would seriously consider whether the pursuit of Bond should be resumed.[25] If details of Bond's art fraud and offshore money transfers were splashed across the front page of every newspaper in Australia, it would be almost impossible for the AFP to do nothing—which is what they clearly wanted to do.

Once Alan had agreed to pay $12 million to settle the case, there was little or no chance that the AFP would come looking for him again. The two agents who ran Operation Oxide had left the force and found jobs with big accounting firms; budgets were tighter than ever; and drugs rather than corporate crime had become the AFP's major target. Most of all, no one wanted another long, bruising fight that they might well lose. There would still be problems getting Bollag to testify; it would be almost impossible to get documents out of Liechtenstein; and it might still be hard to prove perjury or concealment of assets beyond reasonable doubt.

But Kelvin Kenney, who had chased Bond for four years before recommending in 1998 that Operation Oxide be shut down, thought it was at least worth a try. 'It would be great,' said Kenney, 'if it could be proven that this money was Alan Bond's or for his benefit. It would be great to see the investigation reopened and justice done.'[26]

Sadly, everyone knew it would never happen.

27

In Exile

Alan has paid a hell of a price. London is his new
home. He is trying to keep his head down and
I would encourage him to do so.

Bond's friend, Robert Quinn, September 2000[1]

In August 2000, fifty years after he arrived on Australian
soil as a ten-pound Pom, Alan Bond returned to England
with the intention of making London his home. He is now
living with Diana Bliss in a $3 million penthouse opposite
Kensington Palace and doing what he knows best—making
money in property.

The apartment is in a five-storey mansion block that was
bought for $10 million in early 2000 by a British Virgin Islands
company called Bonaparte Investments. In April 2001 it was
being offered for sale as five separate units for a total of
$12.7 million. And you win no prizes for guessing who was
behind it. According to an investigation by Melbourne's
Sunday Herald Sun:

> A real estate agent involved in the potential sale of
> the Kensington building confirmed this week that
> Alan Bond was directly involved.[2]

But property dealing is not Alan's sole money-making venture. In mid-2000 he bought the UK rights to an Australian money-lending business called ChequEXchange, which he plans to operate in Britain under the name 'Money Centre'. If all goes to plan, Alan Bond, the world-class debtor, will soon be on the other end of the credit equation, with Money Centres popping up all over Britain, offering short-term loans—average £250—to people who can't get money elsewhere.

The building housing Bond's new corporate headquarters, which he shares with top-drawer names like Christian Dior and Moet & Chandon, is in swish Belgravia Crescent, roughly halfway between Buckingham Palace and Harrods. Money Centre's chairman is an old friend called Robert Quinn, who kicked the tin so generously in 1991 by wiring $200,000 from a Swiss bank account to pay Alan's legal fees.

Quinn told London's *Sunday Telegraph* late last year that Alan's new mini-bank business was owned by a Bond family trust.[3] And he assured readers, in the time-honoured formula, that the ex-bankrupt entrepreneur was merely acting as a consultant, helping them find suitable sites for their new mini-bank branches. According to Quinn, the rates of interest will be high—for which read exorbitant.

Back in Australia, where ChequEXchange first set up its shingle in 1999, 'payday lending' has been one of the fastest-growing and most controversial industries. By mid-2000, there were 80 outlets operating under three rival brand names, with projections that the number would grow to 400 within a year. However, the business had attracted violent criticism from the people whose job it is to protect Australian consumers. In the words of the New South Wales Fair Trading Minister, John Watkins, to state parliament, payday lenders were 'nothing but loan sharks playing on people desperate for cash'. Or to quote the verdict of his Queensland counterpart, Judy Spence: 'They're manipulative, exploitative and unfortunately preying on the vulnerable and weak in our society'.

It seemed apt that Bond, who liked to present himself as the battler's friend, should be making his comeback in such a controversial business.

A report by the Queensland Fair Trading Department in August 2000 noted the example of one couple who had borrowed $50 for two weeks in July 1999 and then rolled it over several times, to find that within ten months their debt had blown out to $980. By then, they were paying fees of $196 a fortnight just to stop the debt getting bigger, and were in a trap from which they could not escape.[4]

According to the Queensland report, the three main players in the industry, of which ChequEXchange was the biggest, were effectively charging interest rates of between 235 per cent and 1,300 per cent per annum. At the top end of the scale, this was seventy times more expensive than the average credit card, and thirty times higher than the maximum rate of interest permitted by Australia's consumer credit laws.

Whether Bond's venture in the UK will adopt similar practices remains to be seen. By mid-2001, he had still not opened his first branch and his plans were on hold. Having paid a deposit of $250,000 to secure the UK rights, he had refused to pay the balance that he owed on the $1.05 million deal. Finally, in June, he settled for a fraction of the $800,000 still owing, and ChequExchange confirmed that his Money Centres would go ahead without them.

28

Facing the Music

Let us ensure our legislative processes are ever
vigilant against the likes of Bond and Skase so ...
the Australian people will have faith in the ability
and priority of government to bring those to justice
who would otherwise seek to damage our reputation
as an honest and fair country.

Senator Murray, 1997[1]

I t is often said by Bond's supporters that he at least stayed
to face the music, unlike Christopher Skase. But it is not
clear that he stuck around willingly to take his punishment.
When he was made bankrupt in April 1992, both his Australian and British passports were confiscated by his trustee in
bankruptcy, Bob Ramsay, so he had little choice but to stay
put. Even if he had left Australia illegally, he would not have
lasted long offshore. Thus the biggest difference between Bond
and Skase may simply have been that Skase had a passport,
while he did not.

It is also often said that Bond's $1,200 million fraud on Bell
Resources was a victimless crime. But the company's many
shareholders who lost their savings would hardly agree. And
it was certainly a crime that benefited Bond and his family. At
least $55 million of the money taken from Bell ended up in
Bond's private company, Dallhold Investments, whose bank

accounts were used by Bond to fund his own lavish spending.

But even if Alan is a notch up from Skase, which seems unlikely, considering the scale of his crimes, the real scandal of the Bond story is that he managed to hang on to a very large, very public fortune and make a very big fool of the Australian judicial system in the process.

One cannot be sure exactly how much Bond and his family got away with from the $5 billion wreckage of Alan's businesses, but even if they had only escaped with Upp Hall in the UK, it would be scandal enough. From 1991 to 1995, Bond swore black and blue that this $12.5 million English country mansion belonged to Jurg Bollag, yet as soon as his bankruptcy was annulled, the charade was abandoned. In the year 2000, it is the Bonds, not the Bollags, who are lords of the manor, and it is the Bonds who are again the legal owners.[2]

And of course Upp Hall was not the only valuable asset the Bond family walked away with. They also hung on to a huge amount of wealth—probably amounting to several tens of millions of dollars, in jewellery, property and family trusts—which came from Alan Bond's now-collapsed business empire.

Looking at Bond's bankruptcy and at other cases involving rich, well-advised businessmen, it is clear that trusts have the capacity to make a mockery of Australia's bankruptcy laws. Bond's trustee in bankruptcy, Bob Ramsay, initially believed that it was perfectly reasonable for people to shelter assets from their creditors by parking them in trusts. But by the time he finished with Bond he wasn't so sure. In March 1995, a couple of weeks after Bond's release from bankruptcy, a frustrated and disappointed Ramsay gave an interview to *Business Review Weekly*, in which he said, 'A trust is only a device to put assets at arm's length ... there is a moral case for reconsidering the status of those assets'. Or in other words, maybe we should change the law in Australia to stop creditors being dudded in this way.[3]

Attacking the status of trusts would undoubtedly create storms of protest from the legal profession and their well-heeled clients, but it is worth noting that most European countries, whose legal systems are not based on English law, refuse to accept that trusts are anything more than a device for cheating creditors. These Civil Code countries treat the apparent owner of an asset as the real owner and ignore trusts that have been erected to keep creditors at bay. Surely it should be possible, even in our common-law system, for Australia to do the same.[4]

In the meantime, we are forced to tinker at the margin, by catching money on the way into trusts or on the way out again. One of the so-called 'Skase amendments' to the bankruptcy laws in 1991 attempted to stop rich bankrupts *receiving* vast amounts of money from trusts or 'friends' and living the high life, while their creditors got nothing. This provision, which came into effect just after Bond was bankrupted, required bankrupts to pay half their 'income' above $24,000 to their creditors. But in Bond's case it failed, because the law was badly drafted, and the Federal Court ruled that he did not have to pay.[5]

On the other side of the equation, we could do more to prevent assets being placed in trust, or given away to family and friends as bankruptcy approaches. The law in this area has been changed constantly since the 1980s but has not really been toughened. Today, a trustee in bankruptcy can claw back all transfers of property (or gifts) made below market value in the two years before bankruptcy.[6] But if the Hawke Government had accepted the proposals of the Law Reform Commission back in 1988, trustees would have been allowed to go back *four* years in certain circumstances. The Bond family would then have had to prove that the $26 million they received from Alan between April 1988 and April 1992 had *not* been given to them with the intention of denying money to Bond's creditors.

In 1995, another attempt to make the law bite harder was abandoned in the face of determined opposition from the legal and accounting professions. This would have altered the definition of insolvency from the present one, where you are broke if you cannot pay your debts 'as and when they fall due', to a situation where you would be judged to be broke if your liabilities (including personal guarantees) exceeded your assets. The relevance of this is that a trustee can overturn transactions up to five years prior to the bankruptcy if it can be shown that the debtor was insolvent when money was given away. The new test, which is used in the USA, would have been far simpler and far harsher, and would have caught far more people attempting to cheat their creditors. It would also have trapped Bond, and allowed Bob Ramsay to recover some of the millions Bond gave to family and friends as his empire collapsed.

But the drawback, as far as accountants and solicitors were concerned, was that this new definition of insolvency would also have snared a large number of accountants and solicitors, who signed over assets to their families or to trusts in the early 1990s to protect themselves from professional negligence actions stemming from the corporate collapses of the 1980s. So the change was never made.

Even more blatant than Bond's use of trusts, however, was the way in which he stashed millions of dollars overseas. It was obvious to anyone familiar with the case that the money was there. Yet the tyranny of distance and the difficulty of getting overseas cooperation made it impossible for investigators to get their hands on the money or to bring criminal charges against Bond for concealing it.

The key problem for those chasing Bond was that the millions were either hidden in Switzerland or controlled by a man who lived there. And this posed insuperable difficulties both for the police and Bond's bankruptcy trustee. Shortly after Bond's discharge from bankruptcy in 1995, Ramsay stated confidently that he would have got his hands on Alan's fortune if he had only had a few more weeks. But nowadays he accepts that he would never have succeeded.[7] Had the money still been in Jersey, as it was in the 1980s, it might well have been a different story, because the Jersey courts are keener to help foreign investigators.

But the money was not in Jersey because it had been moved. And herein lies the rub. In these days of electronic transfers, you can move money twice round the world in twenty-four hours, yet it takes investigators months, if not years, to get the foreign court orders they need to find the funds. And as soon as investigators get close, the money can be moved again. Meanwhile, those who have hidden the assets can use the courts to stall their pursuers for years.

As Bob Ramsay so eloquently describes it, it is like giving the criminals a 100-mile start in a 101-mile race.[8]

Once money gets offshore, it is difficult and expensive to trace. And lack of funds in bankruptcy or liquidation means there often aren't enough resources to chase the money far enough. More to the point, it is not worth creditors funding the search unless there are many millions of dollars hidden overseas. There's no point in risking $2 million to get back half that amount.

John Broome, the former chairman of the National Crime

Authority, says that it is incredibly easy to get money out of Australia even with the reporting requirements that now cover large cash transactions or international money movements. 'Give me $10 million in Australia and a week to spread it around the world, and I could have it hidden in places that no investigator would ever discover it,' he says. Where, I ask? He reels off the Philippines, Singapore, Japan, Eastern Europe, even London. And how? 'Buying shares in one place, selling in another, sending the money through a couple of banks, and a couple of companies. It's not a problem to do it. It's a nightmare to unravel. The best the investigators will get is evidence of a crime. Their chance of getting hold of the cash is just about zero. The ones you catch, they either make a stupid mistake, or you get lucky. And if you get the sort of advice that's available to people like Bond and Skase, you'll never get them.'[9]

Broome's answer is to lock up a few advisers. On top of that, it would be worth taking away the protection of legal professional privilege in bankruptcy cases, as they do in the UK, so that expert advice on how to hide assets would be exposed to public view if the client became bankrupt. This might cause lawyers and accountants to think twice about advocating or defending dishonesty in the way that some clearly do. A third line of attack, which was introduced in the USA in 1997, could require lawyers to certify that they have made reasonable inquiry into the accuracy of what their bankrupt clients tell the court. This would have been particularly useful in the search for Bond's fortune.[10]

Australia's top corporate cop from the 1980s, Henry Bosch, shares the view that lawyers rather than the law are at the root of the problem. Amid all the editorials calling for the law to be changed in 1995, following Bond's discharge from bankruptcy, the *Sydney Morning Herald* focused on Bosch's disgust at 'how far respectable and apparently honest lawyers will go in representing the interests of clients who they must know are behaving unethically and perhaps illegally'.[11]

Senator Murray from Western Australia clearly agreed that lawyers and the legal system were to blame for Bond's escape. On 19 November 1997, in the Senate, he gave his home-town hero a blast under protection of parliamentary privilege.

> Like many Australians I have been frustrated by the failed pursuit of the Alan Bond millions.
>
> I am advised that documents recovered by the AFP have revealed a number of significant transactions involving millions of dollars spirited into and out of the country by Mr Bond during his bankruptcy, none of which has ever been disclosed to his trustee.
>
> The AFP investigation is now four years old and has not yet delivered any charges. Thousands of hours of investigative work and many millions of dollars have been spent investigating Bond. It seems Mr Bond has had available to him these missing millions and has consequently been able to mount a sufficiently funded legal challenge to every possible threat of prosecution. Why any lawyer would be prepared to profit from such missing millions is beyond understanding. Federal Justice Ron Merkel, in dismissing a recent application by Bond and his banker Jurg Bollag, said it was an audacious and serious misuse and abuse of the litigation process.[12]

Murray went on to tell the Senate about the enormous number of other legal actions that Bond had taken, either to avoid giving evidence or to challenge his sentence.

> Such an abuse of our legal system is a sad indictment upon our legal system which allows wealthy individuals to mount a number of successive appeals not available to ordinary Australian citizens. This is especially unpalatable when the wealth has been acquired, as has been proved beyond reasonable doubt in the Bond case, from corporate victims.
>
> Let us ensure our legislative processes are ever vigilant against the likes of Bond and Skase so, as we move towards the next century, the Australian people will have faith in the ability and priority of government to bring those to justice who would otherwise seek to damage our reputation as an honest and fair country.

In some ways, of course, Bond was special. He was richer, smarter and more determined than most corporate criminals. And he was also more persuasive. But in another way he exemplified our inability to deal with complex white-collar crime. In the 1980s, he made a monkey out of the corporations laws and tax laws; in the 1990s, he made a fool of the bankruptcy laws and the legal system.

The lesson of Bond is an old one—that there's one law for the rich and one law for the poor. Or maybe no law for the rich. If you have enough nerve and enough money and your lawyers are smart enough, you have an exceptionally good chance of beating any investigation. You deny everything; you fight every legal point; you exhaust your pursuers by delaying and delaying and delaying.

But the legal system and the judges who run it must share the blame for this. It is simply not acceptable for people like Bond to be allowed to paralyse the courts for years on end, without ever winning a trick, and without ever paying a penalty. It is one thing to ensure people's rights to a fair trial, it is another to allow highly paid lawyers to bring the judicial process to a grinding halt. Judges need to be tougher on those who appear before them. They need to run their courts properly.

In this context, perhaps the biggest insult to the legal system and the Australian people was the way in which Bond managed to avoid answering questions about his offshore assets in the Federal Court in May 1994 by claiming that he had suffered severe brain damage.

The convenient illness is nowadays the last refuge of the scoundrel, whether it be Skase with his emphysema, Suharto with his stroke or Pinochet with his senility. But rarely has an affliction been so obviously concocted as it was with Bond's amnesia. The courts in this country had the opportunity on several occasions to rule that he was fit to answer questions on oath, as the law demands, and to punish him for not doing so. But the courts failed woefully on almost every occasion. Bond's loss of memory became a national joke, much loved by cartoonists and columnists. Yet it was Bond who had the last laugh.

Here, again, one must highlight the role of Bond's lawyers and medical experts, who assisted him in his pantomime. It is perhaps worth noting that Alan's chief criminal lawyer, Andrew Fraser, who acted for Bond while he was claiming brain damage, now faces charges in Victoria of trafficking in cocaine. It is perhaps also worth noting that Tim Watson-Munro, the psychiatrist who made the statement about Bond's inability to run a corner store, pleaded guilty in late 1999 to possession of the drug and to having a $2,000-a-week cocaine habit, or should one say, addiction.[13]

But Bond was not the only one who got away with a fortune. His managing director at Bond Corporation Holdings, Peter Beckwith, also had trusts in Jersey and almost certainly took advantage of Bollag's services to hide money overseas. And he was just as successful in hanging on to it—or his widow was, after he died of a brain tumour in 1990.

Beckwith's trustee in bankruptcy, Garry Trevor, told creditors in December 1997 that he had identified a string of foreign properties that he believed belonged to Beckwith. These included an English manor house sold for $1.8 million, a villa in France, a condominium in Colorado and a house in Chelsea. Together, these would have been worth a minimum of $5 million, yet Beckwith's creditors were advised that it would be too hard and too expensive to go chasing them.[14]

Beckwith's house in Jutland Parade, Dalkeith, which he signed over to his wife before his death, sold for $8.5 million in 1997, but his creditors had to take lengthy legal action even to get a share of that. They ended up settling for $2.68 million, most of which was eaten up in legal costs, and in the end Beckwith's creditors received a paltry $850,000 for the $32.9 million they were owed—or just 3.6 cents in the dollar.

So it wasn't just Bob Ramsay who was unsuccessful in cracking the pot of gold. Nor was it just Alan Bond who got away with it. There were plenty of other smaller fry in the 1980s and 1990s that police simply didn't bother to chase because they weren't a national priority or a national disgrace. Their losses and their fortunes were mere tens of millions.

Indeed, possibly the most remarkable aspect of Bond's conviction for the Bell fraud was that the police and the Australian Securities Commission did finally get their man. It took them seven years, three investigations, a team of twenty investigators and 1.2 million documents to pin him for the biggest fraud in Australian history. But the police who chased Bond's bankruptcy offences (which carry far more modest penalties) did not have the budget or the political commitment.

Perhaps it's not surprising that the people who led the various Bond investigations in the 1990s have now left the police and gone to private pastures. The pay is better there, the burden of proof is lighter, and it is arguably easier to ensure that justice is done.

It would be nice to think that in the future this might change and the system might do better. But I for one won't hold my breath.

Endnotes

1: Oh Lucky Man

1. Montague CJ in *Dive v Manningham 1551*, quoted in Dennis Rose, *Lewis's Australian Bankruptcy Law*, 10th Edition, Law Book Company, Sydney, 1994, p 8.

2: Bankrupt ... Not Broke

1. Alan Bond was specifically excluded as a beneficiary of the Alpha Trust, formerly the Alan Bond Family Trust No 1, on 4 July 1991, one day before Dallhold went bust. This was done to make doubly sure that the trust's assets were kept away from Alan's creditors.
2. The *Independent*, 27 January 1990, 'Down-Under, but not yet out', Teresa Poole.
3. It was impossible to know how much the family trusts had borrowed against their gross assets. In 1993, *Business Review Weekly* was able to find around $10 million worth of loans. There may have been more, which would have

reduced the Bonds' net worth below $70 million. It is worth noting that in 1994 the Bond family told Bond's trustee in bankruptcy, Bob Ramsay, that their net worth was 'less than $20 million' even without taking any of the assets in the family trusts into account.

4. Most of the onshore trusts set up for Bond and his family in the 1980s had some element of discretion but also specified members of the Bond family as beneficiaries. At least one of the offshore trusts for Bond was a true discretionary trust: it did not specify a beneficiary, but a separate letter of wishes made it clear that the settlement was 'intended for Alan Bond and his family'. (See Icarus Trust, p 99)

5. In 1999 the federal government announced changes to the tax laws designed to make the use of trusts far less attractive. In theory, these should also make trusts less attractive for those who want to put their assets beyond the reach of creditors. It remains to be seen whether they will have that effect and whether other devices will be found to do the same job.

6. Alan Bond's bankrupt estate, statement of affairs, April 1992. NB 1071 of 1992.

3: Never Say Die

1. *West Australian*, 27 September 1991, p 1, 'Perth grand prix: Alan Bond overtaken by writ', David Humphries.

2. Interview with author, March 1999.

3. *ibid*.

4. Channel 7 News, Perth, 26 September 1991, reporter Howard Gratton.

5. Rogers J, 23 September 1991 in NSW Supreme Court, 50191, 50431, 50489 of 1991.

6. *Sydney Morning Herald*, 12 March 1992, Eric Ellis, 'Battling Bond in Chelsea hideaway'.

4: *Divorce*

1. Susan Mitchell, *Public Lives, Private Passions*, Simon & Schuster, Sydney, 1994, p 51.
2. Mitchell, *ibid*, p 61.
3. *New Weekly*, 21 October 1993, p 24, 'I love him ... I always will', Suzanne Monks.
4. *Woman's Day*, 15 June 1992, p 6, 'Bondy's blonde tells all', John-Michael Howson.
5. *Woman's Day, ibid*.
6. David Michael, unpublished manuscript, 1992.
7. Michael, *ibid*.

5: *Friends*

1. Bond's was the second biggest personal bankruptcy the world had ever seen. The record belonged to Robert Maxwell's son Kevin, who filed for debts of £406 million in the UK in September 1992.
2. *Business Review Weekly*, 13 March 1995, 'How Bond beat bankruptcy', Philip Rennie.
3. Bond argued each time that he needed to be in Europe to sell the Greenvale nickel mine and to take up consultancy jobs that could earn money for his creditors. But there was more than a whiff about the offers he was getting, in that they came via exotic tax havens from Bond's old friends. The Bermuda-based Van Diemen's Company, for example, wanted Alan to act as a consultant to its cattle, sheep and tree-farming business in Tasmania, but needed him to travel to London to meet the directors, whose leading light was an old mate of Alan's called Graham Ferguson Lacey. Another would-be employer was linked to an American stockbroker friend, Robert Quinn. His company, Heyside (UK), was an off-the-shelf affair that had been activated the

day before Bond went bankrupt and had as its registered office a basement suite in the north of England that it shared with several hundred others. A third proposal came from a company called Expo Development, which was owned by the Romulus Trust and the Remus Trust, and was based in the British Virgin Islands. Its managing director was Jurg Bollag, who would play a central part in the Bond story over the next three years. Bollag wanted Bond to travel to the USA to advise on a diamond-mining project.

4. *Daily Telegraph Magazine*, London, January 1995, p 28, 'The name's Bond ... Alan Bond', Paul Spike.

5. Report from Dennis Tannenbaum in Bond's bankruptcy proceedings, NB1071 of 1992, filed in Australian Federal Court, February 1994.

6. Spike, *ibid*.

7. Bond was released because one alleged liar had fingered another. A Perth builder called Max Healy, charged with perverting the course of justice, accused Alan's mate Laurie Connell of lying in court to get Bond convicted, and of boasting of this fact in a discussion about giving false evidence to get Connell off race-fixing charges. With doubt cast upon the original verdict, the conviction was quashed. In November 1992, after facing the charge for a second time, Bond was acquitted.

8. Tony Weatherald interview with freelance journalist and investigator, Jamie Fawcett, 1996.

9. Mitchell, *ibid*.

10. Weatherald interview with Jamie Fawcett.

11. Bond's legal team produced no witnesses in Perth, so there was no apparent justification for the switch of venue. Justice Hill described the move as 'totally unwarranted' and awarded costs against Bond.

12. The *Bankruptcy Amendment Act 1991* received Royal Assent on 17 January 1992 and came into force on 1 July 1992. It contained significant and wide-ranging changes to the *Bankruptcy Act 1966*. The key amendments are to be found in sections 23, 24, 25, 26, 27. The act gave bankruptcy trustees greater power to investigate a bankrupt's affairs offshore, to limit his or her overseas travel, to object to a bankrupt being discharged from bankruptcy, and to recover assets that had been disposed of in an attempt to defeat creditors. It also set new limits on income that a bankrupt could retain, requiring that 50 per cent of income above a certain limit (initially set at $24,000) be shared among creditors. See Annual Report of the Insolvency and Trustee Service, Australia, 1991–92 and 1993–94 for details and evaluation of the changes.

6: Bondy's Banker

1. *Armand Leone (plaintiff) v Susanne Bond Leone (defendant)*, Superior Court of New Jersey, Chancery Division, Family Part, Bergen County. Docket NO: FM-20312–88.
2. Bollag's old boss Ed Merszei told me in 1993 that Jurg was 'definitely in the business of asset management' with 'a lot of high-net-worth clients'.
3. Certified statement of Susanne Bond Leone in *Leone v Leone*.
4. Reply certification of Armand Leone, p 2, 23 May 1988, *Leone v Leone*.
5. Armand Leone, *ibid*.
6. Certified statement of Alan Bond, p 2, 30 May 1988, *Leone v Leone*.
7. Simon Farrell, examination under section 77C, *Bankruptcy Act 1966*, 10 March 1993, pp 41–43.

8. Alan Bond, examination under section 81 of *Bankruptcy Act 1966*, Federal Court, 3 May 1994, p 52.

9. The SULA acronym came from the Syndicated US$ Loan Agreement put together for Bond in January 1990 by Hong-kong Bank, Tricontinental and Bank of New Zealand.

10. Dallhold's records confirm that Bollag's Isle of Man company Metal Traders was also paid $1 million a year in fees to act as consultant on the project. The true own-ership of this company was hidden. Its shareholders were the Langtry Trust Company and Langtry Consultants, based on the island of Jersey, another offshore tax haven.

11. *West Australian*, 27 December 1994, p 1, Mark Drum-mond, 'Bond debunks Bollag "myth"'.

12. The letter to Lacey was produced as an exhibit in Bond's bankruptcy examination in the Federal Court in May 1994.

13. Richardson to author, June 1993.

14. *Australian Financial Review*, 12 March 1995, p 1, 'What a hide: Bond's secret stash', Peter Hartcher.

7: Lord of the Manor

1. Interview with freelance journalist and investigator Jamie Fawcett, 1996, parts of which were published in *The Aus-tralian*, 11 October 1997, p 19, 'The go-between'.

2. *The Upp Hall Estate*—brochure by William H Brown, Grantham, Lincs, UK.

3. *Dallhold Estates (UK) Pty Ltd v Susanne Bond*, Bishop's Stortford County Court, case no: 920219; defence and counterclaim.

4. The documents were alluded to in Australia's Request for Mutual Assistance in Criminal Matters to Switzerland (Exhibit ARF2 in VG446 of 1997), which was drafted by

the Australian Federal Police. The letter said: 'This decision [to sell Upp Hall to Dallhold] was made in order
to avoid consolidation disclosure problems in Bond Corporation's accounts arising out of the fact that Susanne
Bond, the daughter of Bond (who was a director of Bond
Corporation Holdings Limited), was living on the property on a non-commercial basis'. The letter of request
went on to say that Dallhold's London lawyers, Fresh-
fields, sought tax advice from Price Waterhouse about
the tax implications, and were told that it was important
that Dallhold's rental payments to Lindsey should be 'at
a commercial open market level'. This was only relevant
if Lindsey and Dallhold were related parties, which led
police to conclude in this letter that Lindsey was really
a front for Bond.

5. *Armand Leone (plaintiff) v Susanne Bond Leone (defen-
   dant)*, Superior Court of New Jersey, Chancery Division,
   Family Part, Bergen County. Docket no: FM-20312–88.
   Certified statement of Susanne Bond Leone.

6. The three teams were chasing money for Bond Corporation Holdings Ltd, Dallhold Investments Ltd and Bond's
   bankrupt estate. Often they did not know what the others
   were doing. Sometimes they felt they weren't entitled to
   share information; sometimes they felt it wasn't in their
   interest to do so; sometimes they just didn't realise it was
   important. Almost always, they were struggling with an
   unimaginable mass of detail that made it a near super-
   human task to keep track of what they had discovered.

7. On 25 February 1992, Justice Chadwick ruled in the High
   Court of Justice in the UK, Chancery Division, that the-
   creditors of Dallhold Estates (UK) Pty Ltd would best be
   served by keeping the company alive. This was because, in

his opinion, Dallhold Estates was likely to win unencumbered possession of the valuable leasehold of Upp Hall. In relation to Susanne's lifetime tenancy he said: 'In the circumstances that that interest appears to be based upon no documentary title at all and to be based upon gratuitous promises said to have been made to her by those formerly in control of Dallhold Estates—promises which it is difficult to see that they could properly make consistently with their duties as fiduciaries—I am bound to take the view that the administrator would be likely to succeed'.

8. *Dallhold Estates (UK) Pty Ltd v Susanne Bond*, Bishop's Stortford County Court, case no: 920219; defence and counterclaim.

9. Interview with freelance journalist and investigator Jamie Fawcett, published in *The Australian*, 11 October 1997, p 19, 'The go-between'.

10. John Bond attempted to explain this generous rate of interest to Bob Ramsay by suggesting that Lindsey was to share in profits on the resale of the farmland, but neither Bollag nor Lindsey Trading Properties had a right to demand that the properties be sold. And farm prices were falling at the time.

11. The estimate is from a confidential Dallhold report to creditors in December 1994, filed in the Federal Court.

8: Millions Offshore

1. Bond always called Bollag 'George'.

2. Even if one can get a court order and make the accountants or lawyers talk, there may still be insuperable problems. For example, they may not know whether the person they're dealing with is the owner or the front man. And they may simply be taking instructions from the trustee of a discretionary trust, in which case there would have to be a whole

new legal battle to get hold of the money. Indeed, it seems perfectly possible that those chasing Bond's fortune could have gone round the world and found just that. Any assets held by Bollag would almost certainly have been in a trust of some sort. In theory, they could have been as safe from creditors, even if the trust was unmasked, as the Bond family home and other Australian assets had been in the trusts Bond had set up in Australia in the 1970s.

3. A comprehensive Financial Tracing Report was prepared for the 1990–92 Royal Commission into WA Incorporated (*Royal Commission into Commercial Activities of Government and Other Matters*) to show how money had been sent offshore by players in the WA Inc saga. Several versions of this were completed, drawing on work by Lieberfreund and further investigation by a Western Australian lawyer, Andy Palmer. The full report, which is believed to run to more than 400 pages, has never been published, but segments of it were obtained by a journalist in early 1993.

4. Details of these companies are contained in leaked segments of the Financial Tracing Report. The report reveals that two dozen companies paid fees into the bank account of a Touche Ross service company called Balmoral Securities. Estimates of how much money was channelled through these companies depend on whether the fees were 0.25 per cent, 0.50 per cent or 1.00 per cent. The investigators concluded that the middle figure was most likely, putting the money flow at $50 million.

5. Plaistowe to author, June 1993.

9: Jersey

1. Federal Court, 3 May 1994, section 81 examination of Alan Bond, p 41.

2. Bond repeated this denial about offshore advisers in his bankruptcy examination in the Federal Court on 3 May 1994, p 14.
3. Royal Court of Jersey, *Re: Alan Bond, a bankrupt*. Transcript of evidence, John Geoffrey Davies, 3 November 1993, p 74.
4. *ibid*, p 83.
5. *ibid*, p 10.
6. *ibid*, p 10.
7. *ibid*, p 41.
8. Royal Court of Jersey, *Re: Alan Bond, a bankrupt*. Transcript of evidence, John Hatton-Edge, 4 November 1993, p 148.
9. A favourite link in the money chain was the little-known First Interstate International Bank of California, which had an office at 885 Third Avenue, New York.
10. Even the simplest of transfers from, say, London to Sydney in US dollars can go via two banks in New York and one in Melbourne and look incredibly complicated, because smaller banks often use big international banks as gathering points in preference to sending the money directly.
11. Broome to author, September 1999.
12. To take an example, a transaction in Bond Corporation Holdings Ltd that no one bothered to examine involved the payment of some $10 million for an option over a Mexican insurance deal that was written off almost as soon as the money was spent. It might well have been entirely legitimate, or it might have been a neat way of getting money into the international banking system. It simply illustrates the principle that one could not follow all the trails.
13. Alan Bond never repaid Dallhold this $4.5 million.

14. Around $600,000 had gone to buy horses Puntero and Nicky du Marais for Susanne to ride, and around $4 million had been spent on paintings from Bond's London art dealer, Nevill Keating Pictures. The odd $600,000 had also been sent off to Sydney to Rivkin James Capel to buy shares for Bond, and the odd $100,000 had been spent on diamonds from Graff & Co in New York.

15. Bond bankruptcy examination, Federal Court, 4 May 1994, p 100. Bond had four accounts at London's Arbuthnot Latham Bank, at least three of which he had failed to declare to Bob Ramsay.

16. Diana Bliss, section 77C examination, 24 June 1994, transcript, p 45.

17. Debbie Shaw, a client manager at Touche Ross, had taken a phone call at the end of May 1987 in which Bollag had asked that Kirk send a £50,000 deposit on Evelyn Gardens to a firm of London solicitors. She had then instructed the Allied Irish Banks in St Helier to send the money from Kirk's account.

    Details of the loans and non-repayment are disclosed in records from Touche Ross which were exhibits in Alan Bond's examination in the Federal Court in May 1994. For what it's worth, Juno also received the balance of Kirk's account at the Allied Irish Banks when it was closed in December 1992. And while the amount was only £51.87, it was the principle that counted.

18. Bond bankruptcy examination, Federal Court, 4 May 1994, p 85.

19. *ibid*, p 144.

20. The neighbours certainly believed the house belonged to Bond. In March 1992, several told journalist Eric Ellis that they saw Alan there frequently. One said it was 'common

knowledge' that Bond owned it. Yet the woman who answered the door at number 14 told Ellis, 'Mr Bond wants you to know that this is not his house and that he is a guest and is staying here only for a day'. *Sydney Morning Herald*, 12 March 1992, 'Battling Bond in Chelsea hideaway', Eric Ellis.

21. Exhibit in Bond bankruptcy examination, Federal Court, 3–5 May 1994.

10: *Trouble With Harry*

1. Henry Souttar Lodge, section 77C examination, 14 July 1993, p 62.

2. Royal Court of Jersey, *Re: Alan Bond, a bankrupt*. Transcript of evidence, John Geoffrey Davies p 9, p 57.

3. Lodge, *ibid*, pp 61–2, 68.

4. *ibid*, p 71. These various trusts either owned assets used by the Bond family, or were trustees of companies that owned such assets. Pianola owned a valuable property in London's ultra-swish Belgrave Mews, worth £1.5 million, bought in the early 1980s. The Icarus Trust owned a house in Chelsea's Selwood Place, bought in 1982 through Engetal Properties. Juniper Trust eventually owned Kirk Holdings, the key Jersey-based company that had at least $50 million pass through its bank accounts in the mid-1980s.

5. The letter was an exhibit at Bond's bankruptcy examination, Federal Court, 3–5 May 1994.

6. Lodge, *ibid*, p 57.

7. Lodge, *ibid*, p 59.

8. *The Australian*, 4 March 1995, Paul Barry, 'Bond's money trail'. *The Australian*, 14 March 1995, letter from Harry Lodge:

Paul Barry's article, Bond's Money Trail (*The Weekend Australian Review*, 4–5/3) would have readers believe that I have assisted Mr Alan Bond to conceal from his creditors assets which allegedly are now held on his behalf by a Mr Bollag, a knowledge either conveyed or imputed to my former firm, Parker & Parker, from which I retired in June 1989 at the age of 65.

The article also seems to suggest that I failed to give a frank account of my involvement with entities administered in Jersey when examined by Mr Bond's trustee in bankruptcy. I reject and strongly resent those allegations.

Some 16 years ago during the period June 1979–July 1980 while I was managing the London office of my old firm I received instructions to arrange for the establishment of a number of offshore trusts and companies in the Channel Islands for various clients. Those trusts and companies were established with total propriety and in accordance with Jersey Law by chartered accountants Touche Ross and Jersey solicitors. The company Pianola and the Juniper Trust referred to in the article were established at this time.

Later, and sometime after I left the London office and before October 1984, it appears the Icarus trust and associated companies were established by Touche Ross in Jersey but apart from at some time signing a consent to act as a person from whom the trustee could seek instructions I was not involved in the formation of these entities.

Mr Barry refers to a meeting in Jersey on October 26, 1984. At that time I was on holiday in London with my wife. I travelled to Jersey in my private capacity and at my own expense for the purpose of renewing acquaintance with the Touche Ross senior partner, Geoffrey Davies, whom I had previously met in 1979/80. Mr Davies took the opportunity to inform me of various matters concerning mutual clients. I made some rough notes of our conversation. Intended as a reference should I need one in the future, I had no occasion to refer to those notes again. They formed part of a Parker & Parker file delivered by that firm to Ramsay some eight years later, on his appointment as trustee in 1992.

I was not at any time after the establishments of these entities, involved with the administration of any of them and while I had been placed on lists of persons whom the trustees of the trusts could consult or seek instructions I was never at any time consulted or asked to give instructions. I have no knowledge whatsoever of any undisclosed Bond assets.

I held several powers of attorney from Alan Bond, the first executed in 1969 and the last in 1983.

From time to time I signed documents in exercise of that power when requested by Bond executives, on occasions when Bond was not personally available in Western Australia. I did not exercise the power at any time when I was out of WA.

It concerns me greatly that quite a wrong impression may have been created by the author of the article by merging on the one hand my involvement in 1979/80 in the establishment of trusts or companies which may now be associated with Bollag with on the other hand, their subsequent administration over the intervening years, and the alleged location of undisclosed assets within them.

H.S. Lodge
Nedlands, WA

9. Filed in Federal Court, Bond bankruptcy, NB 1071 of 1992. The initials at the top of the page, HSL, indicate that the bill applies to work done by Harry Lodge or one of his juniors.

10. Filed in Federal Court, Bond bankruptcy, NB 1071 of 1992.

11. Filed in Federal Court, Bond bankruptcy, NB 1071 of 1992.

12. Filed in Federal Court, Bond bankruptcy, NB 1071 of 1992.

11: *Zuggered*

1. Exhibit in Bond's bankruptcy examination, May 1994.

2. Selwood Place was messy anyway because the accountants at Touche Ross believed that Engetal Properties, the company that owned it, had been transferred to Bollag in

1991 and that some consideration had been paid. It would therefore have been especially hard for Ramsay to prove that Bond's creditors were entitled to the proceeds.

3. The Jersey and UK banking documents for Kirk Holdings and Arbuthnot Latham show transfers to at least three numbered Swiss accounts. Other significant transfers were made to accounts at the Zuger Kantonal Bank held in the name of Juno Equities and Crasujo.

4. Bankers and fiduciaries were not obliged to report suspect transactions until April 1998. The money-laundering laws introduced in the early 1990s merely allowed them to.

5. This record would not have merely identified a discretionary trust in Liechtenstein or the British Virgin Islands, because the Swiss know far too much about hiding people's money to swallow the line that personal fortunes are managed by trustees who can give the money away to any Tom, Dick or Harry. The record would have had to disclose the real beneficiary.

   In Liechtenstein it is still possible to open a numbered account without telling the bank who owns the money, so they can't give your secrets away even if they want to. The same is true in Austria, much to the anger of the rest of Europe. The banking system there still has hundreds of millions of dollars in anonymous, numbered bank accounts, which can be opened by anyone who has been resident in the country for more than three months. The banks will even allow you to deposit cash in a suitcase, which you can then withdraw in the currency of your choice almost anywhere in the world, by quoting an account number and your PIN.

6. Only one man claims with any credibility to have broken through the Swiss banks' defences, and that's a Swiss

investigator called Reiner Jacobi, who helped uncover the missing Marcos fortune. He apparently was leaked the information by an insider.

The Swiss firm of investigators who contacted me offering to get documents and account details relating to Bond did not come back boasting of their success.

12: Lucky Jim

1. *Who's Who in Business in Australia 1992*, Information Australia, Melbourne.
2. *Sydney Morning Herald*, 24 December 1994. 'The Bankrupt's friend is always on a Roll-er', Ian Verrender.
3. In December 1997, a Sydney court was told how Terry and Colleen Halls of Bowral withdrew $55,000 'back pay' from their Retravision shop and banked it in their children's accounts. They said they were acting only on the advice of Jim Byrnes, who had motored down to the Southern Highlands from Sydney in his Bentley to talk to them. Byrnes was not called to give evidence. The Retravision business collapsed within weeks, the Halls's two children were bankrupted, and the couple were convicted of fraud. *Sunday Telegraph*, 4 January 1998, 'Fraud couple relied on ex-Bond adviser', Warren Owens.
4. Affidavit of Melanie Baxter, 13 April 1992, Federal Court of Australia, NSW district, bankruptcy, P2951 of 1991. *Re: James Warren Byrnes, debtor, ex parte NZI Securities Australia Ltd, creditor*.
5. Cole J, 18 March 1992, NSW Supreme Court Commercial Division, 50335 of 1991.
6. Robert Canning swore an affidavit on 30 July 1991 (which was filed in the Federal Court on 15 August 1991) that Byrnes had 'occasioned a violent physical assault' upon him

when he tried to serve a bankruptcy notice on Byrnes on 17 July 1991 (B2092 of 1991). Canning was a mild-mannered guy, 170 centimetres tall and no body builder. Jim Byrnes was a head taller. Byrnes allegedly grabbed Canning by the tie and shook him backwards and forwards, shouting, 'Don't come into my office . . . get out of my office'. Byrnes then sent him flying across the room where he fell over a couple of chairs. After that, Byrnes allegedly kicked him, grabbed him and propelled him backwards through the doorway. Canning went straight to North Sydney police station to report the incident, with tie askew, lip bleeding and various bruises, but declined to press charges.

7. Byrnes to author, 1999.
8. *Daily Telegraph Mirror*, 11 April 1992, 'Page 13'.
9. *Sunday Telegraph*, 13 September 1992, Janise Beaumont, 'Now jitter-bug Jackie's really found her love'.
10. *Daily Telegraph Mirror*, 13 January 1993.
11. *Daily Telegraph Mirror*, 14 January 1993, Fiona Wingett.
12. *Sydney Morning Herald*, 24 December 1994, Ian Verrender.
13. Byrnes's contract with Bond was seized by the AFP in September 1994. It was later filed in the Federal Court in Bond's bankruptcy, NB 1071 of 1992.
14. Byrnes to author, 1999.

13: Brain Damage

1. Affidavit of Dr William Barclay, 15 February 1994, filed in Federal Court NB 1071 of 1992.
2. Ramsay affidavit, 3 December 1992, filed in Federal Court NB1071 of 1992.
3. Since 1992, bankrupts have been automatically discharged

from bankruptcy after three years unless their trustee convinces a court that there are grounds for the bankruptcy to continue. After discharge, investigations by the trustee cease.

4. *Woman's Day*, 10 May 1993, p 2, 'Bondy bounces back'; and Lee Tate to author, 1999.

5. Quoted in affidavit of Karen Coleman, 3 February 1994, filed in Federal Court NB1071 of 1992.

6. *Sun Herald*, 12 December 1993, 'The Diary'.

7. Affidavit of Dr WM Carroll, filed in Federal Court NB1071 of 1992, citing report of 11 June 1993 and letter to Bond's lawyers, Galbally Fraser & Rolfe, 27 October 1993.

8. Affidavit of Tim Watson-Munro, 3 March 1994, filed in Federal Court NB1071 of 1992, citing report of 22 October 1993 and letter to Galbally Fraser & Rolfe 3 March 1994.

9. *ibid*.

10. Paul Barry, *The Rise and Fall of Alan Bond*, Transworld, Sydney, 1991 (paperback edition), pp 32–34.

11. *ibid*, p 38.

12. Letter from Alan Bond to Bob Ramsay, 24 July 1992, filed in Federal Court NB 1071 of 1992.

13. *Western Australian Police Gazette*, December 1952, cited in *Sun Herald*, 5 July 1998, 'Bond as you've never seen him', Jamie Fawcett. For conviction as an eighteen-year-old, see *The Rise and Fall of Alan Bond*, p 44.

14. Letter from John Saunders to Galbally Fraser & Rolfe, 29 October 1993, filed in Federal Court NB 1071 of 1992.

15. John Saunders gave evidence that Bond was suffering from minor brain damage and severe depression.

16. Ros Thomas to author, 1999.

17. Ros Thomas to author, 1999.
18. Affidavit of Dr William Barclay, 15 February 1994, filed in NB 1071 of 1992.
19. Affidavit of Michael Hunt, 3 February 1994, filed in NB 1071 of 1992.
20. Affidavit of Wally Knezevic, 3 February 1994, filed in NB 1071 of 1992.
21. *Sydney Morning Herald*, 10 February 1994, p 1, 'Alan Bond felled by Skase syndrome', Anne Lampe.
22. Affidavit of Dr Dennis Tannenbaum, 15 February 1994, filed in NB 1071 of 1992, citing reports to Galbally Fraser & Rolfe, 8 February 1994, 14 February 1994.
23. Barclay, *ibid*.
24. Barclay, *ibid*.
25. *Woman's Day*, 14 March 1994, 'Broken Bond on the mend', Ian Dougall.
26. *Australian Financial Review*, 12 April 1994. 'Bond IQ drops after heart surgery', Brook Turner.

14: Remember Me?

1. Supreme Court of Victoria, 9 May 1978. Brooking sentenced a witness in the trial of a Victorian police officer to six months jail for contempt of court. The witness claimed to have forgotten whether the officer had bribed him. (See text in this chapter, p 164 and 143 CLR 162–189, High Court of Australia, 1978–1979, *Keeley v Mr Justice Brooking*.)
2. *Sydney Morning Herald*, 4 May 1994, p 1, 'Memory fails a listless Bond', Peter Smark.
3. Bond section 81 bankruptcy examination in Federal Court, 3–5 May 1994, NB 1071 of 1992. Transcript, p 248.
4. Bond, *ibid*, p 14.

5. Bond, *ibid*, p 25.
6. Bond, *ibid*, p 29.
7. Bond, *ibid*, p 31.
8. Bond, *ibid*, p 31.
9. Bond, *ibid*, p 41.
10. Bond, *ibid*, p 40.
11. Bond, *ibid*, p 132.
12. Bond, *ibid*, p 51.
13. Bond, *ibid*, p 157.
14. Bond, *ibid*, p 146.
15. Bond, *ibid*, p 70.
16. Bond, *ibid*, p 85.
17. Bond, *ibid*, p 100.
18. Professor Lesley Cala, neuro-radiologist at Sir Charles Gairdner Hospital in Perth, swore an affidavit for Bond's lawyers on 28 February 1994 that Bond was indeed brain-damaged. Magistrate Ivan Brown reviewed her evidence during hearings about Bond's state of health in June 1994. He said that he did not accept her findings about the extent of the damage.
19. Bond, *ibid*, p 123.
20. *Four Corners*, ABC TV, 9 May 1994.
21. Bond *ibid*, p 252.
22. Supreme Court of Victoria, 9 May 1978. Justice Brooking's judgement was upheld by the High Court of Australia, which ruled: 'A court is justified in convicting a witness of contempt for refusing to answer questions if it is satisfied beyond reasonable doubt that the witness, by falsely asserting an inability to remember, has evinced an intention to leave the questions unanswered'. 143 CLR 162–189, High Court of Australia, 1978–1979, *Keeley v Mr Justice Brooking*.

Brooking had presided over the trial of a Victorian police officer accused of taking bribes from a certain Mr Keeley, who was the key witness for the prosecution. Keeley had given sworn evidence at the committal hearing that he had paid the bribe, but when it came to the trial he spent three days in the witness box swearing that he could neither recall his previous evidence nor the bribe itself. The policeman was acquitted, and Keeley was duly jailed for six months for contempt.

23. 1978–79 143 CLR, *ibid*, p 182.
24. Byrnes to author, 1999.
25. Cunningham to author, 1999.
26. Commonwealth Law Report, 1953, 90 CLR pp 573–582.
27. It wasn't just Alan Bond who lost his memory. His younger son, Craig, who was examined by the Dallhold liquidator on oath in May 1994, appeared to have the same problem. In late 1988 and early 1989, Dallhold had borrowed $103 million in the space of six months from the company that ran the Queensland Nickel Project, MEQ. Craig had been a director of both companies at the relevant time. So what could he remember about this $103 million? Well, nothing at all, basically. He sort of remembered the number but didn't know who had lent the money to Dallhold or where MEQ had got it from. Nor did he recall the important matter of the loan being interest-free. He might have known at the time, he said, but he had forgotten.

These details were important, because some of MEQ's $103 million really belonged to Standard Chartered Bank who had funded the nickel project, and Dallhold had been in such desperate straits that there was little prospect of it paying the money back. In fact, counsel for Dallhold,

Stephen Robb QC, suggested that Craig's conduct amounted to theft:

> Q: I suggest that Dallhold in fact stole all this money from MEQ Nickel.
>
> A: I wouldn't agree with that.
>
> Q: It had no means of repaying any of the money, and did not.
>
> A: I could not agree with that.
>
> Q: As a director of Dallhold in the period of December 1988 to the end of 1989 can you say what means were available to Dallhold to repay these loans?
>
> A: I don't recall.

28. Ramsay and his lawyers did try to persuade the Federal Court to resume Bond's examination, on the basis that he had not answered questions satisfactorily, but Bond's offer to settle with his creditors in December 1994 ended any such attempts.

15: Faking it

1. John Urch to author, 1999.
2. Lionel Berck to author, 1999.
3. John Urch to author, 1999.
4. The statement from Urch was taken by phone because he was in Sydney.
5. *Daily Telegraph Magazine*, London, January 1995, 'The name's Bond ... Alan Bond', Paul Spike.
6. *Sydney Morning Herald*, 19 July 1994, p 5, 'Bond on the ball in fraud hearing', Duncan Graham.
7. *Bulletin*, 13 June 1995, p 13, 'Expert witnesses. Their pivotal role in the famous (and not-so-famous) cases'.
8. Letter from John Saunders to Galbally Fraser & Rolfe,

29 October 1993, filed in Federal Court, NB 1071 of
1992.
9. *Bulletin, ibid.*

16: *Money, Money, Money*

1. Luke Atkins to author, August 1999. The loan of $10,000
    to Atkins by Byrnes is confirmed by a letter from Atkins
    to James W Byrnes and Associates of 14 March 1994,
    seized in raids by the Australian Federal Police in Septem-
    ber 1994 and obtained by Robert Ramsay via court orders
    in December 1994 and February 1995. In fact, much of
    what Atkins alleges in this chapter is backed by documents
    that the AFP seized.
2. Neil Cunningham to author, 1999.
3. Atkins to author, August 1999. Atkins and Asia Pacific
    advised Bond on deals like this for roughly nine months,
    from October 1993 to June 1994.
4. Australian Securities Commission records, February 1995.
    The fact that a company is struck off does not necessarily
    mean that it has gone bust. It has either ceased to do
    business or never started, but such a high proportion of
    failures is both rare and rarely blameless. One of Bryer's
    companies (but not Bryer) was also prosecuted (unsuc-
    cessfully) for insider trading and was the subject of
    complaints from investors.
5. Records in the Isle of Man do not disclose Tri Kal's true
    owners. Manx Corporate Services, which acts as the com-
    pany's registered office, told me in May 1999 that Tri Kal
    started life in 1986 as Keller Industries, at which time it
    owned the rights to a cement-lining process. Keller went
    bust in 1992 and was bought by 'Gerry Sklar and others',
    who changed its name to Tri Kal International. Sklar's

plan was apparently to use the company for property deals. But whether it found any was another matter. Tri Kal was struck off the Isle of Man companies register in December 1995 for failure to file annual returns.

Keller Industries had been listed on the NASDAQ, the US stock market that deals primarily with high-tech stocks. This listing was suggested by Manx Corporate Services as a reason why Sklar and his partners wanted to buy the company, but it either lapsed before or very soon after the company changed hands. NASDAQ told the author in July 1999 they had never heard of Tri Kal.

Apart from the deals mentioned in this chapter, Tri Kal was lined up to buy 25 per cent of St Bees Island and Craig Bond's restaurant Papparazzi in Perth for US$7.5 million. Tri Kal was also expressing interest in the Emu Brewery and Swan Brewery sites in Perth and a huge block of land on the corner of Park and George streets in Sydney, which were all properties that Alan had dabbled with in the past. It also had plans to purchase a casino called Aladdins in Las Vegas for US$75 million and there are documents to show that its bankers in Sydney had written to a firm in New York to say they believed Tri Kal had the financial capacity to complete the deal. Whether the letter was genuine is another matter. Atkins alleges that several such letters were forgeries.

Roger Bryer talked to the author about Tri Kal in January 2000. He said he had known Gerry Sklar for many years but couldn't remember how he met him. He also told me that he introduced Tri Kal and Sklar to Bond because the company was looking for deals to finance. Sklar had told him that the company had the capacity to raise money.

6. Atkins to author, August 1999. Bond maintained to Robert Ramsay that he was merely a consultant to Tri Kal, yet no consulting fees were ever paid. Bryer also denies that he was a shareholder but says that he was to be paid a commission if any of Tri Kal's deals came off, which he says they never did.

7. Atkins to author, August 1999.

8. Atkins to author, August 1999. Documents seized by the AFP support this. For example, Bond faxed Gerry Sklar in August 1994 to tell him what Tri Kal should say in a letter to a company in Scotland with whom they were negotiating an oil deal. Another fax in February 1994 from Bond to Jim Byrnes tells Byrnes how to arrange the paperwork for a transfer of Tri Kal shares.

9. Atkins to author, August 1999.

10. Atkins to author, August 1999.

11. Affidavit of Peter Menadue, 1 July 1994, filed in Federal Court, NB 1071 of 1992; and Vladimir D'Jamirze to author, 1999.

12. Australian Securities Commission media release, 6 February 1995. Nicolai and Alick were also banned for three years. The ASC said their lack of fitness was displayed in their management of Curly International Pty Ltd and Antonov Airlines (Cargo & Services) Pty Ltd.

13. In January 2000, osmium-187 was being offered for sale on the Internet at US$58,000 a gram, so Vladimir D'Jamirze's estimate of the sale price sounds too high. Documents seized by the Australian Federal Police in September 1994 do confirm that someone in Bond's circle obtained a sample of osmium-187 for testing.

14. Roger Bryer told me in January 2000 that he knew nothing about the osmium1-187 deal but did know about

the violin deal. He says he did not travel to Zurich with Vladimir but met him there. He also says his role was to introduce the D'Jamirzes to various Swiss banks who might finance their transactions. Bryer was at a loss to explain how he had such contacts.

15. Roger Bryer explained his involvement with the Bond family in a letter to Bond's lawyers, Galbally Fraser & Rolfe, dated 21 December 1994, the day before Ramsay obtained access to documents seized by the Australian Federal Police in their raids of September 1994. The letter, which was later filed in the Federal Court, included a history of dealings with the D'Jamirzes. He told me in January 2000 that he did not know what deals the companies were to be used for, but confirmed that the instructions came from Alan Bond.

Bryer said that, after discussions with Bond, he had set up three companies in the British Virgin Islands to deal with the D'Jamirze transactions. These companies, called Arabesque Investments Ltd, Exxel Data Ltd and Broken Hill Services Ltd, were each given a bank account at Banque Indosuez in Zurich, into which a sum of $10,000 was deposited to cover company fees, hotel bills and air-fares. Exxel Data Ltd had an additional account at Credit Suisse in Zurich. According to Bryer, the money came from one of Alan's friends, Geoffrey Ogden, who stood surety for Bond on the Bell fraud charges in January 1995. Bryer said that both he and Ogden were to receive 'a percentage of the profit' on the deals that these three British Virgin Islands companies were involved in.

Documents seized by the AFP showed that Arabesque entered a joint venture with Tri Kal and a Bond family company based in Australia called Hastings Finance, to buy Russian roubles. Hastings agreed to lend Arabesque US$1.65 million for thirty days.

Bryer says that when the deals fell through, he closed the companies' Swiss bank accounts and delivered all the documents, along with a record of expenses, to Alan's house at Cottesloe. Yet when Bond was challenged by Ramsay in December 1994 about his dealings with the D'Jamirzes he said he had no idea who owned Arabesque or the other two companies. This is hard to believe, not least because his family company, Hastings Finance, was lending Arabesque so much money.

16. Robert Ramsay report to Alan Bond's creditors, 24 January 1995, and attached schedule of documents seized by AFP, filed in Federal Court, NB 1071 of 1992.
17. Tony Weatherald interview with Jamie Fawcett, 1996.
18. Atkins to author, August 1999.
19. Weatherald to Fawcett, 1996.
20. Greg Barnes interview with Neil Cribb, representing Alan Bond's trustee in bankruptcy, Perth, 23 January 1995. Filed in Federal Court, NB 1071 of 1992. Kitarski is Bart Kitarski, who worked with or for Bond at this time.

The background to the SIDRO offer is as follows. Greg Barnes was a deal spotter in the mining industry with special knowledge of Eastern Europe, where he would make friends with academic geologists, research dusty archives, and unearth mineral deposits that could make millions of dollars for those who were smart enough to exploit them. For this reason, he regularly had Perth's mining promoters knocking on his door for deals, as Alan Bond did in February 1993.

Barnes had worked up a number of prospects at the time, of which the best was a deal that needed some

$600 million in finance. It was a huge East German coal company that owned three power stations and had a twenty-five-year exclusive contract to supply coal and power to three East German states. A similar company in the West would have been worth between $1,400 million and $1,600 million, or so Barnes reckoned, and this one looked like it could be cleaned up to be worth a similar amount.

Bond presented himself at the start as a consultant to a Swiss group that was interested in the deal, but he talked about it as though he planned to make a great deal more than a consultancy fee, telling Barnes, 'If this coal deal works, I'm out of my shit'.

Barnes was concerned about where the $600 million in finance would come from, and asked Bond whether he was sure he could find it. Bond assured him he could handle it, via his banking contacts in Switzerland, who would back him for the right deal. So who were these friends, Barnes was asked by Neil Cribb?

A: One was George Bollag ... and other contacts and friends in banks in Liechtenstein and Switzerland.

Q: So your understanding was that Bond would be contacting George Bollag to arrange the necessary finance?

A: Yeah.

Like so many of Bond's deals, the coal deal did not come off, because someone else snapped it up first. But Barnes met Bond to discuss a whole range of projects that included diamonds in Greenland and gold in Austria.

21. Robert Ramsay report to Alan Bond's creditors, 24 January 1995, and attached schedule of documents seized by AFP, filed in Federal Court, NB 1071 of 1992.

22. The Austrian gold-mining deal went the way of all the others that Bond was involved with at the time and the Perth investors lost their money. One of them, Steve Zielinski, who owned a businessmen's lunch club known as Slik Chix, which featured naked waitresses and girls with feather dusters up their vaginas that diners were invited to remove with their teeth, had been so impressed with Bond's enthusiasm that he had slung $100,000 into the project. And he was so angry that he had lost it that he told Bond he would go public by talking to Robert Ramsay's Perth representative, Neil Cribb, and the Australian Federal Police, which he did. He told Cribb that Bond accused him of being a dog (or informer) and threatened to dob him in to the taxman.

> Alan said 'Watch your back', sort of thing, and I said 'I'm not worried about my back, mate'. He didn't say it in those exact words ... but it was like a threat. So if you find me in the Swan River, you'll know where to look.

The Austrian gold-mining deal featured Broken Hill Services, one of the three British Virgin Islands companies set up by Bryer. This company also popped up after the deal fell through, when Bond tried to sell the same Austrian leases to a Perth mining company called Argosy Minerals. Peter Lloyd, the company's managing director, told me in 1995 that Bond came to his office asking for a payment of $1 million if Argosy went ahead with the purchase of the leases. The cash (which Lloyd understood to be a fee for Alan Bond) was to be paid to Broken Hill Services, which suggests that Bond owned it.

23. Affidavit of Peter Menadue, 1 July 1994, filed in Federal Court, NB 1071 of 1992.
24. Barnes to Cribb (Bob Ramsay's Perth representative), January 1995.
25. Atkins to author, August 1999. For example, the AFP seized a letter from the Suisse Volksbank in Berne to Atkins's Asia Pacific Group. This was a financial reference for another Liechtenstein company called Wira Establishment, which Weatherald identified as being a Bond/Bollag company. This said: 'Our valued client is considering entering into a contract with your group. We confirm that they have the financial capacity to enter into contracts up to $50 million US'.
26. Neil Cunningham to author, 1999.

17: The Enforcer

1. Luke Atkins to author, 1999.
2. The shelf company became Whitsunday Island Development Pty Ltd. In October 1995 it was put into liquidation, owing $4.7 million.
3. See, for example, Diana Bliss, section 77C examination, 24 June 1994, filed in Federal Court, NB 1071 of 1992.
4. This account of Diana Bliss's delivery of the hatbox containing $130,000 was given to the Australian Federal Police on 15 May 1995, and confirmed by Atkins to me in 1999. Banking documents confirm the deposit of the cash in St George Bank and the transfer to Singapore.
5. Atkins to author, 1999.
6. Tim Bristow to author, 1999.

7. Atkins to author, 1999.
8. Atkins to author, 1999.
9. The AFP's search warrants were filed as exhibits in the Federal Court, VG 427 of 1994, as attachments to the affidavit of Andrew Roderick Fraser, 30 September 1994.
10. Atkins to author, 1999.
11. Atkins to author, 1999.

18: Operation Oxide

1. Letter from Western Australia's Director of Public Prosecutions, John McKechnie, to Richard Moss, Inspector-General in Bankruptcy, Canberra, 20 October 1993.
2. Letter from Richard Moss to Allan Mills, Assistant Commissioner for Investigations, Australian Federal Police, Canberra, November 1993.
3. Australian letter of request to Swiss authorities for 'Mutual Assistance in a Criminal Matter', November 1991.
4. The Swiss police were always happy to deal with an official government-to-government request for assistance if a criminal matter was being investigated. They were not able to help Bob Ramsay in his civil investigations. But the 1991 request was unusual in that the Zuger Kantonal Bank seems to have surrendered the documents to Swiss police without triggering a legal challenge from Laurie Connell or Alan Bond. When the AFP used a similar request in 1994 to get documents from Switzerland, four years of legal challenges ensued.
5. The relevant law was the *Bankruptcy Act 1966*.
6. Request for Mutual Assistance in a Criminal Matter, made to Swiss authorities on 16 September 1994, p 17. Exhibit ARF2 in VG446 of 1997, Federal Court. The AFP also

obtained phone records for Bollag's London office, which showed that a large number of telephone calls were made from there to Western Australia.

7. Those who operate without one have no protection if a trustee runs off with their money. They can also find themselves in trouble if the trustee dies or goes insane, because they have no proof for the bank that their millions belong to them.

   Swiss fiduciaries like Bollag—who look after other people's money—are typically quite careful. They like to be insured against professional negligence claims, and they can't get insurance unless they tell the insurance company whose money they are looking after. For that reason, too, there is usually a contract in place.

   Bollag had certainly kept some papers relating to Bond's affairs. He had already admitted to John Lord, the Dallhold liquidator, that he had retained documents for Crasujo, the company that had received US$2.8 million from Dallhold in 1987 (recorded by Dallhold as a loan to Alan Bond) and for Lindsey Trading Properties, the company that owned Upp Hall.

8. Request for Mutual Assistance in a Criminal Matter, p 2, filed in Federal Court, VG 446 of 1997. A supplementary letter was sent on 4 November 1994.

9. These banking instructions from Touche Ross were obtained by court order from the Allied Irish Banks in Jersey in 1993. They were an exhibit in Bond's bankruptcy examination in May 1994, and filed in the Federal Court, NBV 1071 of 1992.

10. The request asked in general terms for all accounts that were conducted on Bond's behalf, so there is no doubt that the Xavier documents would in fact have turned up in the trawl.

The AFP also identified an account at the Ueberseebank in Zurich in the name of Andrew Benson, whose initials, coincidentally or otherwise, were AB, the same as Alan Bond's. This account had received £541,000 in 1989 from Balmoral Securities, the Touche Ross service company in the Channel Islands that had sent money to Connell in December 1987. The financial wizards who prepared the Financial Tracing Report for Western Australia's Royal Commission into WA Inc had traced a chunk of this money back to dividends paid to Alan Bond's private company, Dallhold. The Ueberseebank told Swiss police that they had neither documents nor accounts that related to Bond.

11. This is made clear in the affidavit of Andrew Fraser, Federal Court, VG 446 of 1997.

19: Getting Off

1. *Sydney Morning Herald*, 24 December 1994, 'The Bankrupt's friend is always on a Roll-er', Ian Verrender.
2. If the AFP discovered money belonging to Bond it would go to Australian taxpayers.
3. Ramsay letter to Alan Bond, 15 September 1994.
4. The Zug Cantonal Court order is referred to in the minutes of Bond's Committee of Inspection meeting, 27 February 1995, filed in the Federal Court, NB 1071 of 1992.
5. Dallhold report to creditors, December 1994. This eleven-page report filed in the Federal Court in the liquidation of Dallhold Investments, NG 3039 of 1991, sets out details of the claims against the Bond family and the prospects of their success.
6. John Lord and Stephen Robb believed they could show

Dallhold was insolvent by May 1989 at the latest. This would disallow (or void) any gifts made by Alan Bond to his family after that date.

On 1 May 1989, Bond Corporation Holdings was unable to pay its interim dividend on time because it didn't have the cash. (Dallhold relied on these dividends to stay afloat.) On the same day, Bond Corporation was downgraded by Australian Ratings to a CCC credit rating (from which no company had ever recovered). During this month its shares were valued by Baring Securities Australia at *minus* $1.80 per share.

7. Between October 1988 and June 1989 Dallhold received roughly $160 million from Bell Resources and JN Taylor, which were ex-Holmes à Court companies that Bond controlled. Bond was convicted of fraud for taking the Bell cash and was sued by the liquidator of JN Taylor for removing money from that company.

A further $100 million was channelled into Dallhold's coffers from MEQ Nickel, a Dallhold subsidiary that had pledged the money to Standard Chartered Bank under a loan agreement.

8. Dallhold report to creditors, December 1994, Federal Court, NG 3039 of 1991. This sets out the details of Bond's proposal to settle his $519 million worth of debts to the company.

9. *Bankrupt Estate of Alan Bond, Report to Creditors*, 8 December 1994, filed in Federal Court, NB 1071 of 1992.

10. *ibid.*

11. Dallhold report to creditors, December 1994.

12. *Bankrupt Estate of Alan Bond, Report to Creditors*, 8 December 1994.

13. Ramsay had won the legal battle over Bond's super fund, which had produced around $2.7 million for creditors, but his offshore investigations had produced no return. By the end of 1994, Bond's bankruptcy had cost $3.5 million, of which nearly $2 million had gone in legal costs. Most of this had been paid by Tricontinental, who had paid $2.16 million, and the Hongkong Bank, who had paid $841,000. The National Australia Bank and AGC had put up $75,000 between them. Affidavit of Robert Ramsay, 8 December 1994, Federal Court, NB 1071 of 1992.

14. *Sydney Morning Herald*, 20 December 1994, p 1, 'Bond clears the decks for a comeback', Colleen Ryan. Bond needed the backing of more than half of the creditors who voted and more than three-quarters of the $519 million debts by value.

15. *ibid*.

16. *Sydney Morning Herald*, 24 December 1994, 'The Bankrupt's friend is always on a Roll-er', Ian Verrender.

17. In mid-November, Ramsay had persuaded George Caddy, the Official Receiver for New South Wales, to serve the AFP with orders to hand over all the material they had obtained from Bond in the September raids. Within a week, the AFP had sent all the documents to Caddy's office in Sydney and Ramsay had arranged to inspect them. But before this examination could take place, Bond's lawyers had applied for an injunction.

    The orders were made under section 77C, which was introduced in 1991 to strengthen the power of bankruptcy trustees to get hold of documents. The law required the Official Receiver to issue the orders.

18. Comments by Sheppard J in making orders in Federal Court in Sydney, 22 December 1994, that Bond give

details of telephone calls made from the Sheraton Went-worth hotel between March and May 1994, and that he consent to the handover to Ramsay of documents seized from his house by the AFP in September 1994. Reported in *The Australian*, 23 December 1994, Sally Jackson.

20: Free

1. The creditor was Gerry Cavanagh, credit controller of Western International Travel, part of the West Australian Newspapers Group. This is verbatim from Cavanagh's file note of the meeting, made shortly after Bond's departure.
2. *West Australian*, 27 December 1994, p 1, Mark Drummond, 'Bond debunks Bollag "myth"'.
3. The quotes are from a letter written by Richard Moss, Australia's Inspector-General in Bankruptcy, to Allan Mills, Assistant Commissioner for Investigations, Australian Federal Police, Canberra, November 1993.
4. *West Australian*, 20 January 1995, p 1, 'DPP won't give up Bond secrets', Margot Lang and Mark Drummond.
5. *West Australian*, 23 January 1995, p 1, 'Bond investigator in papers backflip', Mark Drummond and Anne Lampe.
6. *Report to Creditors on the Bankrupt Estate of Alan Bond*, 24 January 1995, filed in Federal Court, NB 1071 of 1992.
7. Parker & Parker letter from Steven Paterniti to Bond's creditors, 27 January 1995. Paterniti's comments on Ramsay's report were carried in the *West Australian*, 26 January 1995, p 1, 'New blow to Bond bankruptcy plan', Mark Drummond.
8. This is verbatim from Cavanagh's file note of the meeting, made shortly after Bond's visit. The basis of Bond's argument that Western International Travel should vote 'Yes' was a letter from Bond to his old colleague, David

Aspinall, then a director of the company, dated 19 December 1991, and signed by both men. In this letter Bond recited the terms of an agreement between him and Western International Travel by which the company would accept a payment of $7,000 from Bond in settlement of a debt of $54,397.79 and vote for a Part X arrangement under the *Bankruptcy Act 1966*, if one was proposed.

However, the compromise that Bond was proposing in January 1995 was not a Part X arrangement, and Western International Travel's lawyers did not consider that the letter bound them to vote for it.

9. Out of the $3.25 million paid by the Bond family, $2.25 million was owed to the Hongkong Bank and Tricontinental, who had funded the trustee's investigations. This left roughly $1 million for distribution to creditors, who were owed $599 million in total.

10. The Australian Taxation Office had presumably read Ramsay's November 1994 report to creditors which pointed out that in the six years before his bankruptcy Bond had declared income of $2.5 million on his tax returns, yet had managed to give $32.5 million to his family and friends. After the annulment of Bond's bankruptcy, Treasurer Ralph Willis revealed that Bond was nearly given the chance to claim a further $20 million of tax losses on his debts. A tax official realised this just in time and the loophole was closed to prevent it happening.

11. Ramsay did not retire. In 1999 he was still working as a consultant to Bird Cameron.

12. *Sydney Morning Herald*, 28 February 1995, Colleen Ryan.

13. There is little reason to think that the claim against the Queensland Government would have succeeded. The

Dallhold liquidator, John Lord, did not even bother to pursue it. Even if it had succeeded, for Bond's sums to be right, the Greenvale Nickel Project would have needed to sell for around $800 million more than the $330 million it actually fetched.

14. The SULA banks (which sold the Greenvale Nickel Project for $330 million and pocketed all the money) lost heavily. They lent Bond US$335 million in 1990, and did not receive a cent in interest.

   The $5 billion figure for the Bond Group's total losses includes $519 million for Dallhold, $600 million for Bond's bankrupt estate and a final figure of $3.7 billion for Bond Corporation Holdings Ltd.

15. *Sydney Morning Herald*, 1 March 1995, Letters to the Editor.

16. *The Australian*, 1 March 1995, 'Bankrupt laws leave creditors in the lurch', Henry Bosch.

17. *Business Review Weekly*, 13 March 1995, 'How Bond beat bankruptcy', Philip Rennie.

21: Wedded Bliss

1. Australian Securities Commission statement announcing delivery of unpublished report from John Sulan QC.

2. A time limit of five years normally applies to bringing charges under the Companies Code. This time limit expired in February 1994. Leave was granted by acting Attorney General Duncan Kerr to bring charges outside this period.

3. Tim Phillipps to author, April 1999.

4. *West Australian*, 16 January 1995, p 1, 'Push to recall Bond men', Margot Lang.

5. An old Polish pre-communist extradition treaty existed, but

no one had attempted to use it with another Australian fugitive, Abe Goldberg, who went bankrupt in July 1990 owing $320 million and was wanted on a string of fraud charges. The Commonwealth Director of Public Prosecutions did attempt to use the treaty to get Oates back to face trial, and attempts to extradite him were still under way in early 2000.

Peter Mitchell returned to Australia of his own accord, pleaded guilty at trial, was sentenced to four years in jail and freed in late 1999.

Peter Beckwith, Bond Corporation's managing director, who also took a key role in the Bell Resources cash strip, died in 1990.

6. *Weekend Australian*, 4–5 March 1995, p 4, 'Bond for trial over picture purchase', Colleen Egan.

7. *ibid.*

8. *New Weekly*, 21 October 1993, p 24, 'I love him ... I always will', Suzanne Monks.

9. *Good Weekend*, 29 March 1997, p 16, 'The show must go on', Jane Cadzow.

10. *Sydney Morning Herald*, 17 April 1995, p 5, 'For richer, for poorer, Bond embarks on a life of wedded bliss', John Huxley.

11. *Hello!*, 29 April 1995, p 12, 'Australian entrepreneur Alan Bond marries theatre producer Diana Bliss', Interviewer, Prue MacSween.

12. *ibid.*

13. *Bond v Pacific Publications*, No 11213 of 1995, NSW Supreme Court. Amended Summons, 10 April 1995. See also Affidavit of Jim Byrnes, 12 April 1995.

14. *Daily Telegraph*, 30 March 1992, 'Page Thirteen', Fiona Wingett.

15. *New Idea*, 22 April 1995, p 6, 'Bond Case, Threats and

Intimidation', Fiona Wingett. Also Pam Lesmond to author, 1999.

16. *Daily Telegraph*, 7 April 1995, p 3, 'Bond stops intimate article on "sex life"', Naomi Toy.

17. *Bond v Pacific Publications*, No 11213 of 1995, NSW Supreme Court. Amended Summons, 10 April 1995.

18. *New Idea*, 22 April 1995, pp 6–7, 'Bondy and me. The story Alan Bond tried to ban'.

19. Cecelie Turner, signed statement to Australian Federal Police, June 1995.

22: Guilty

1. Court of Petty Sessions, Perth, WA, complaint nos: 349–355/9, between Timothy Graham Phillipps and Alan Bond, before Ronald J. Gething S.M. Reasons for decision of preliminary hearing, 17 January 1996.

2. Tim Phillipps to author, 1999.

3. *ibid*.

4. David Michael to author, 1999.

5. The purchase of the Manet was effected by buying the leasing company that owned it. By mid-1988, the residual on the lease was $1.6 million. Dallhold paid more than this because two lease payments were outstanding and because the owners of the leasing company, Macquarie Bank, demanded a premium for selling.

6. The ABC's *Four Corners* program brought these bogus profits to light in March 1989. In early 2000, Arthur Andersen & Co was still being sued for negligence by the liquidator of Bond Corporation Holdings Ltd, which by this time had been renamed Southern Equities Corporation Ltd.

7. The committee also examined several other problems thrown up by the audit.

8. WA District Court, charge 35568–35571 of 1993, *ASC v Alan Bond*, 20 August 1996, Justice Antoinette Kennedy, Sentencing Remarks for Alan Bond.
9. *ibid.*
10. ABC TV, *Australian Story*, 21 February 1997, 'The Parson's Daughter', produced by Wendy Page.
11. *Sunday Times*, 22 December 1996, pp 1–2, 'Jailbird Bond's barbecue set'.
12. *ibid.*
13. *ibid.*
14. WA Supreme Court, *ASC v Bond*, 5 February 1997, Murray J, Remarks on sentencing.
15. *Sun Herald*, 16 February 1997, p 23, 'Last straw for Bond', Candace Sutton.

23: Zuggered Again

1. In late 1999 the Swiss Federal Court finally ruled that the papers could be sent back to the NCA in Melbourne.
2. Parliamentary Joint Committee on National Crime Authority, April 1998.
3. Alan Bond, examination under section 81 of *Bankruptcy Act 1966*, Federal Court, 3 May 1994, p 48.
4. *West Australian*, 27 December 1994, p 1, Mark Drummond, 'Bond debunks Bollag "myth"'.
5. Federal Court of Australia, VG 446 of 1997, *Alan Bond and others v Andrew Tuohy and others*, Application for an order of review under the *Administrative Decisions (Judicial Review) Act 1977*.
6. Federal Court of Australia, VG 601 of 1995, *Alan Bond v Michael Rozenes and others*.
7. Federal Court of Australia, VG 446 of 1997, *Jurg Bollag and Alan Bond v The Attorney-General of the*

*Commonwealth of Australia, the Director of Public Pros-
ecutions for the Commonwealth of Australia, the Commissioner, Australian Federal Police; Reasons for
judgment,* Merkel J, 30 October 1997.

8. Hadgkiss, speech to ITSA National Bankruptcy Conference, Melbourne, November 1998.

9. In 1998 Benazir Bhutto and her husband Ali Zardari were
convicted of corruption by a Pakistani court, fined
US$5.3 million and sentenced to five years in jail. The
court found they had taken bribes from foreign companies
in exchange for granting contracts and had lied comprehensively about their income and assets to the Pakistani
tax authorities. Benazir Bhutto had declared an annual
income of only $42,000 in 1996 and paid just $5,000 in
tax.

  The Pakistani Government employed American
investigators Kroll Associates to investigate the case in
Switzerland. Kroll paid US$1 million for documents
apparently stolen from Jens Schlegelmilch's office. These
were important evidence and no doubt also helped persuade the lawyer to talk.

10. *Australian Financial Review,* 24–25 October 1998, p 3,
'AFP gives up Bond chase', Bill Pheasant.

24: *Cook's Tour*

1. Supreme Court of South Australia, 113 of 1996, *Southern
Equities Corporation Ltd and others v Alan Bond and
others, Amended Statement of Claim,* 19 October 1997,
para 132. Southern Equities Corporation Ltd (SECL) was
formerly Bond Corporation Holdings Ltd. The case is being
heard in South Australia because Richard England, the Bond
Corporation Holdings liquidator, is based in Adelaide.

2. *ibid*, para 223.1.1–223.1.2.
3. *ibid*, para 81.
4. Supreme Court of South Australia, 113 of 1996, *Southern Equities Corporation Ltd and others v Alan Bond and others, Further Amended Statement of Claim*, 19 October 1999, para 43. (Southern Equities Corporation Ltd—SECL—was formerly Bond Corporation Holdings Ltd.)

   In all, fourteen artworks were 'sold' to Way. It is not clear why Bond selected them. There were many more valuable pieces that he could have chosen from his collection, which was valued at $146 million, but the Captain Cook was a special favourite, and the others constituted the bulk of the pictures owned by Bond Corporation Holdings (as opposed to Dallhold). The majority were hanging in Dallhold's offices and gallery on the top three floors of the Bond tower, while one was at Alan's home in Dalkeith and another was on his yacht *Southern Cross II*.

5. Even though she wasn't quite sure what was happening, Diana de Bussy had severe misgivings about what she was being asked to do, but she was new on the scene at Bond Corp and was in no position to argue. Until ten months earlier, she had been running a small PR agency in the Scottish highlands, where she had imagined that being curator of Bond's art collection would be the job of a lifetime. Soon after this incident, however, she would decide she could stand it no more.

   It was not just the 'sale' to Way that was bothering her. A few weeks earlier she had arranged for two other prize pictures in the Bond collection to be taken down from the walls of Bond's offices and packed off to Jurg Bollag in Switzerland. These two paintings, *Portrait of Matthew Flinders* by the French artist Antoine Toussaint de Chazal and *Natives in the Eucalypt Forest* by the colonial artist John Glover, which were worth at least $1.5 million between them, had been bought for Alan in the early 1980s by his art dealer Angela Nevill and invoiced to his Jersey company Kirk Holdings. Yet Bollag had written to Bond in early December 1989 claiming they had been on loan.

6. Supreme Court of South Australia, 113 of 1996, *Southern Equities Corporation Ltd and others v Alan Bond and others, Further Amended Statement of Claim*, 19 October, para 88.2.

7. Examination of Angela Nevill, London, 19 August 1996, Supreme Court of South Australia, 2516 of 1993, *Southern Equities Corporation (in liquidation)*. Documents obtained by the author from the Isle of Man show that Firstmark was set up on 22 June 1989 in the Isle of Man by the same company agent that had established Metal Traders for Bollag in 1986. Its registered office was at Sovereign House, St Johns, a small village on the island. Its shares were held by Bollag's JF Consulting (formerly Crasujo) and it was administered by Bollag through Jersey. The company was struck off on 17 June 1997 for not filing annual returns to the Isle of Man authorities.

8. *ibid*, p 11.

9. Supreme Court of South Australia, 113 of 1996, *Southern Equities Corporation Ltd and others v Alan Bond and others, Further Amended Statement of Claim*, 19 October 1999, para 97.3.

10. *ibid*, para 122.

11. National Gallery of Australia archives: file note from August 1993.

12. National Gallery of Australia archives: submission for

acquisition of Captain Cook, 30 August 1993.

13. *Australian Financial Review*, 3 August 1993, '$1.5 million agreed for Cook portrait', Terry Ingram.

14. National Gallery of Australia archives: letter from Robert Bleakley, managing director, Sotheby's Australia, to Michael Lloyd, Assistant Director, Collections, National Gallery of Australia, 31 August 1993.

15. Examination of Robert Bleakley, Adelaide, 2 August 1996, pp 26–28, Supreme Court of South Australia, 2516 of 1993. Bleakley was shown newspaper articles about the sale of the Bond Corp paintings to George Way published in the *West Australian* on 21 and 25 May 1992. He admitted that he had read them and passed them on to Angela Nevill.

16. *ibid*, pp 77–78.

17. *Australian Financial Review*, 3 August 1993, '$1.5 million agreed for Cook portrait', Terry Ingram.

18. *Sydney Morning Herald*, 29 July 1993, p 1, 'Switzerland discovers our missing Captain Cook', Ava Hubble. Hubble reported: 'Mr Bleakley said he did not know the identity of the buyer, and he refused to name the agent he is negotiating with. But he said the agent is not the Switzerland-based businessman Mr Jurg Bollag'.

     Bollag's role in Bond's offshore finances and in 'lending' other valuable paintings to Bond had been exposed on ABC TV's *Four Corners*, 'Rich Man, Poor Man', 26 July 1993.

19. There have been repeated rumours about the weird and wonderful things hidden in the Freilager, some of which are possibly true. On one occasion, the Zurich District Attorney even rushed down with a warrant to search for $2 billion worth of looted Japanese gold, which was

enough to fill a couple of rail cars, and sealed off a large section of the facility, only to find nothing.

20. Lionel Bowen in conversation with author, 1999.

21. Peter Lundy in conversation with author, 1999, and advice given by Peter Lundy, now in National Gallery of Australia archives.

25: Gotcha

1. Examination of Craig Bond, 9 April 1997, Supreme Court of South Australia, 2516 of 1993, *Southern Equities Corporation Ltd (in liquidation)*. Bond was being asked about money transfers from a Jersey bank account to his companies in Perth. Craig prefaced most of his answers with the word 'Privilege' to ensure that they could not be used against him in any future prosecution.

2. Supreme Court of South Australia, 113 of 1996, *Southern Equities Corporation Ltd and others v Alan Bond and others*, Further Amended Statement of Claim, 19 October 1999, paras 152–158.

3. *ibid*, para 166.

4. *ibid*, para 151A.

5. Supreme Court of South Australia, 113 of 1996, *Southern Equities Corporation Ltd and others v Alan Bond and others*, para 151A1/2.

6. Supreme Court of South Australia, 113 of 1996, *Southern Equities Corporation Ltd and others v Alan Bond and others*, Further Amended Statement of Claim, 19 October 1999, paras 171, 175, 180.

7. Examination of Angela Nevill, 19 August 1996, p 62, Supreme Court of South Australia, 2516 of 1993, *Southern Equities Corporation Ltd (in liquidation)*. The same police raiding party descended on Upp Hall later on

19 March 1996. They were let in by the caretaker and gathered another twenty-two boxes of documents. Soon afterwards, Bollag's office in Chelsea was also turned over, as was his secretary's flat in Ealing. His London lawyers, Franks Charlesly, meanwhile, were trusted to hand over their files without coercion.

8. The Bond Corp liquidator filed the action via a protective writ on 2 January 1996, even though the evidence had not been fully gathered, to avoid being caught by the *Limitation of Actions Act*, which set a time limit for the filing of legal claims.

9. Supreme Court of South Australia, 113 of 1996, *Southern Equities Corporation Ltd and others v Alan Bond and others*, affidavit of Mark Hoffmann, 20 February 1997.

10. Examination of Craig Bond, Adelaide, 29 March 1996, Supreme Court of South Australia, 2516 of 1993, *Southern Equities Corporation Ltd (in liquidation)*. Craig Bond was told that he had to answer questions, even if he felt he might incriminate himself, but that his answers could not be used against him in later criminal proceedings if he prefaced them with the word 'Privilege'.

11. Examination of Craig Bond, 9 April 1997, p 382, Supreme Court of South Australia, 2516 of 1993, *Southern Equities Corporation Ltd (in liquidation)*.

12. *ibid.*

13. Examination of Nancy Lake, Nassau, Bahamas, 23 August 1996, Supreme Court of South Australia, 2516 of 1993, *Southern Equities Corporation Ltd (in liquidation)*.

14. The 'naval portrait' was the *Portrait of Matthew Flinders* by Antoine de Toussaint Chazal. This had been bought by Alan Bond's Jersey company Kirk Holdings in December 1987, so it had belonged (and probably still belonged) to

GOING FOR BROKE

Alan Bond himself. Its history and fate are dealt with in Chapter 26.

15. Examination of Craig Bond, 9 April 1997, Supreme Court of South Australia, 2516 of 1993, *Southern Equities Corporation Ltd (in liquidation)*. The evidence relating to money transfers from SHC is also set out in para 187 of the liquidator's statement of claim.

16. *ibid*.

17. *ibid*. The evidence is also recited in paras 187, 205 and 206 of the statement of claim.

18. *ibid*. The letter to Lake is quoted in para 162 of the statement of claim.

19. Craig's letter to Lake is quoted in para 168 of the statement of claim.

20. Examination of Craig Bond, 9 April 1997, 2516 of 1993.

21. Supreme Court of South Australia, 113 of 1996, *Southern Equities Corporation Ltd and others v Alan Bond and others*, Affidavit of Mark Hoffmann, 20 February 1997; Reasons of Justice Debelle, 21 February 1997. Affidavit of Richard Green, 19 February 1997; reasons of Judge Bowen Pain, 10 February 1997, Supreme Court of South Australia, 2516 of 1993, *Southern Equities Corporation Ltd (in liquidation)*.

22. Supreme Court of South Australia, *Bond v England*, Judgement of Justice Debelle, 1 August 1997. *Bond and Caboche v England*, Judgement of Justice Lander, 23 October 1997. Details of the hearing at Karnet Prison Farm and legal manoeuvrings are disclosed in these two judgements.

23. Examination of Alan Bond, Adelaide, 24 November 1997, Supreme Court of South Australia, 2516 of 1993, *Southern Equities Corporation Ltd (in liquidation)*.

24. *ibid*, p 52.

25. This evidence is recited in the statement of claim, paras 43, 127.

26. Examination of Alan Bond, Adelaide, 24 November 1997, Supreme Court of South Australia, 2516 of 1993, *Southern Equities Corporation Ltd (in liquidation)*.

27. Supreme Court of South Australia, 113 of 1996, *Southern Equities Corporation Ltd and others v Alan Bond and others*, Further Amended Statement of Claim, October 1999, para 122. Also Nevill examination, 19 August 1996, pp 17–18.

28. *ibid*, para 122. Also Nevill examination, 19 August 1996, pp 28–30.

29. *ibid*, para 122. Also Nevill examination, 19 August 1996, pp 39–43. Nevill stated on oath: 'I told Sir Evelyn 1.) that Mount Zero was formerly in the Alan Bond collection, 2.) Mount Zero was being sold by entities related to the Bond family'. She said she had told him the same things about the two paintings by Bull.

30. Examination of Angela Nevill, 19 August 1996, p 30, Supreme Court of South Australia, 2516 of 1993, *Southern Equities Corporation Ltd (in liquidation)*.

31. Examination of Robert Bleakley, Adelaide, 2 August 1996, pp 83–85, Supreme Court of South Australia, 2516 of 1993, *Southern Equities Corporation Ltd (in liquidation)*.

26: Free Again

1. *The Australian Women's Weekly*, April 2000, 'Alan Bond home free', Carol George, p 16.

2. *The Australian Women's Weekly* later published the list of charities that the money was donated to.

3. *Daily Telegraph*, 10 March 2000, pp 1, 6, 'Pure Bliss,

Alan Bond walks to freedom with wife Diana and $70 million', Mark Russell.

4. *Sydney Morning Herald*, 10 March 2000, p 1, 'One day in jail for every stolen million', Paul Barry.

5. *Australian Women's Weekly*, April 2000, 'Alan Bond home free', Carol George, p 16.

6. Various press reports in Australia and the UK had suggested that the Captain Cook had been seized by the Serious Fraud Office in March 1996 during its raid on Nevill Keating Pictures, but these had always been wide of the mark.

7. The Freycinet collection was bought by Angela Nevill in June 1985 for $1.55 million from a Sydney art dealer called Derek McConnell. It was invoiced to Alan's Jersey company Kirk Holdings, but Nevill made it absolutely clear in a letter to McConnell whom she was buying it for.

> I am writing to confirm the purchase of the Freycinet Collection from you as agents for the vendor, Mr David L. Bremer. We are purchasing it on behalf of Mr Alan Bond.

From the outset, it was a closely guarded secret that Bond had bought it, possibly because the works had once been stolen from a French museum. Angela Nevill referred to the collection in code when discussing the possibility of bringing it to Australia for exhibition, and Bond's art curator Diana de Bussy never set eyes on it, because it remained in the UK.

In December 1989, a memo from Dallhold's managing director Michael Cross recorded that the collection was held offshore. When Dallhold's liquidator John Lord inquired about it in 1991 he was told by Nevill that it belonged to Alan (and not the company). Yet Bond failed to declare it as a personal asset when he went bankrupt in April 1992 and Lord, amazingly, failed to tell Bond's bankruptcy trustee, Bob Ramsay, about its existence.

8. Examination of Angela Nevill, 19 August 1996, pp 6–7. *Natives in the Eucalypt Forest* is a magnificent example of John Glover's work, now worth around $1 million. After its disappearance in 1989 its whereabouts remained a mystery until Angela Nevill was examined on oath in August 1996 by the Bond Corp liquidator. Nevill revealed she had sent the painting back to Australia in 1992, shortly before Bond was declared bankrupt, to be sold for $400,000 to a Sydney psychotherapist, John Buttsworth. The deal was done through Robert Bleakley, then of Sotheby's, who shared the $40,000 commission with Nevill. According to Nevill, Bleakley was made aware that the painting was from the Alan Bond collection and that someone connected with Bond was selling it, but he almost certainly failed to pass this information on to the purchaser. Buttsworth, who was struck off in 1991 for having an affair with a patient, was unwilling to discuss the matter when contacted by the author.

The *Portrait of Matthew Flinders* was judged by the Supreme Court of South Australia in September 2000 to be an asset of Bond Corporation, to whom the court was told it had been transferred in 1989.

Some of the other 13 missing paintings have also been traced. Nicholas Chevalier's *Mount Zero* and Knud Bull's *View of Hobart Town* and *View of Boa Vista* were snapped up by Sir Evelyn de Rothschild for $350,000 roughly two years after Bond was made bankrupt. Angela Nevill, who was a family friend of Sir Evelyn, gave sworn evidence in August 1996 that she told him the paintings were from the Alan Bond Collection and someone close to Bond was selling them.

Sir Russell Drysdale's famous *George Ross of Mullengandra* was sold in 1992 for $210,000 to the Australian TV game show millionaire Reg Grundy and now hangs in his London home.

John Peter Russell's *Antibes, Alpes Maritimes* was bought by a Federal Court judge to hang on the walls of his Sydney chambers. Justice John Lockhart, now retired, paid $130,000 for it several months after Bond went bankrupt.

Justice Lockhart and Reg Grundy both bought their paintings via Robert Bleakley, then of Sotheby's Australia, without knowing their history or the identity of the vendor. According to Nevill's sworn evidence and Bleakley's own admission on oath, Bleakley knew that someone close to Bond was selling the artworks, but omitted to pass this crucial information on to the buyers. Sotheby's, meanwhile, entered into complicated back-to-back contracts that involved Nevill Keating Pictures buying the pictures from the vendor, then selling them to Sotheby's, who then sold them on to Grundy and Lockhart.

In August 1996, Robert Bleakley was examined on oath about the sale of these Bond Corp paintings and was asked in particular about the sale of *Antibes* to Justice Lockhart.

Q: Did you explain to your client about the George Way history?

A: No I didn't . . .

Q: What do you think your client would have
   done if you had told your client this ...
   'Look, Mr Lockhart, I need to disclose this to
   you: the price is very good at $130,000, it is
   a great price, but what you have to understand is that this was a Bond art collection
   painting and it was sold out of the Bond
   company to somebody called George Way, a
   horse trainer in Western Australia in highly
   suspicious circumstances ... Since then I have
   been told by Angela Nevill who has dealt with
   Bond, seen him in gaol, and knows him pretty
   well, that it has been through a number of
   companies in Europe. I don't know who they
   are and what it means, but I think you should
   know that before you pay $130,000.' Did you
   tell your client that?
A: No, I did not.
Q: What do you think he would have done if you
   had told him that.
A: As I was about to say earlier, I felt that any
   association with Bond tainted a work.
Q: What do you think he would have done?
A: I imagine that he would [have] probably
   either felt discouraged to pursue the purchase
   or he would have offered a much lower price.

As a judge in the Federal Court, Lockhart would have
been quite horrified to find that he was buying a painting
from a notorious bankrupt who was already being accused
of concealing assets from his creditors. He would have
been even more worried had he known where his money

may have ended up, for according to the liquidator's statement of claim, the $340,000 paid to Sotheby's by Lockhart and Reg Grundy found its way via Nevill Keating Pictures to Bond's secret money box at the Private Trust Bank in Liechtenstein, where it was paid into an account in the name of SIDRO Anstalt.

According to the liquidator's statement of claim, the $350,000 paid by de Rothschild to Angela Nevill for the three Bond Corp paintings he purchased was sent to the client account of Jurg Bollag's London lawyers. On all past performance, it seems more than likely that this money also ended up with Alan Bond. Naturally, no one mentioned this to the innocent purchasers.

9. *Sydney Morning Herald*, 22 March 2000, p 1, 'Bond's big kickstart'; 23 March 2000, p 13, 'On the Bond money-go-round', Paul Barry.

10. Supreme Court of South Australia, 113 of 1996, *Southern Equities Corporation and others v Alan Bond and others*, Affidavit of Jason Karas, 10 February 2000.

11. In September 1994 the AFP seized documents from Alan's house in Cottesloe which showed that SIDRO Anstalt had transferred $1.7 million from the Private Trust Bank in Liechtenstein to the Swiss Bank Corporation in Lausanne. The evidence suggests that the transfer was linked to one of the deals that Alan was trying to do with the D'Jamirze brothers.

12. Supreme Court of South Australia, 113 of 1996, *Southern Equities Corporation and others v Alan Bond and others*, Affidavit of Jason Karas, 1 September 1999; also Further Amended Statement of Claim, 19 October 1999, paras 188A-188L.

13. Examination of Craig Bond, 9 April 1997, Supreme Court

of South Australia, 2516 of 1993, *Southern Equities Corporation Ltd (in liquidation)*.

14. Supreme Court of South Australia, 113 of 1996, *Southern Equities Corporation Ltd and others v Alan Bond and others*, Affidavit of Jason Karas, 10 February 2000, para 18–18.9.
15. *ibid*, paras 26, 28–30.
16. *ibid*, paras 33, 34.
17. *ibid*, paras 12.2, 12.3, 47.2.1.
18. *ibid*, paras 3.5, 3.6.
19. *ibid*, para 3.7.
20. *Sydney Morning Herald*, 9 June 2000, p 4, 'Bond's lost Captain Cook stranded without a sale'; 27 September 2000, p 4, 'Flinders is homeward bound'; 8 August 2000, p 3, 'Captain Cook about to return to Australia', Paul Barry.
21. Supreme Court of South Australia, 113 of 1996, *Southern Equities Corporation and others v Alan Bond and others*, Judgement of the Honourable Justice Debelle, 14 September 2000, p 12.
22. Roughly $6 million had already been collected from the sale of the Cook and Flinders portraits, so the Bond Corp liquidator received around $18 million in total, to satisfy the original claim plus interest and costs.
23. *Australian Financial Review*, 28 March 2001, p 33, 'Paying the full Bond', Mark Drummond.
24. Supreme Court of South Australia, 113 of 1996, *Southern Equities Corporation and others v Alan Bond and others*, Application to Amend Statement of Claim, 16 March 2001, paras 64A8.3-64A8.7 and 64A10.1-64A10.8.
25. *Sydney Morning Herald*, 30 September 2000, 'The art of dealing', Paul Barry.
26. Kelvin Kenney to author, March 2000.

27: In Exile

1. *Sunday Telegraph*, London, 17 September 2000, Damian Reece and Mary Fagan.
2. *Sunday Herald Sun*, 1 April 2001, pp 1, 3, 'Trust me I'm Alan Bond', Helen McCabe and Christine Middap.
3. *Sunday Telegraph*, *ibid*.
4. *Payday Lending*, A report to the Minister for Fair Trading, Queensland Government, August 2000.

28: Facing the Music

1. Senator Murray, Senate, 19 November 1997, pp 8988–89.
2. There is no way of knowing from publicly available documents whether money changed hands between the Bonds and their former Swiss landlord when the handover of Upp Hall took place in 1995, but John Bond's testimony to the South Australian Supreme Court in late 1999 suggests it did not. He stated that a family company had 'acquired the leasehold interest from Dallhold in exchange for a payment of $1.5 million'. He went on to say that the same company 'acquired, at the same time, the freehold interest in Upp Hall Estate from Lindsey Trading Properties Inc as part of the overall transaction'.

   Note the words 'as part of the overall transaction' and the lack of mention of any money, least of all $11 million, changing hands between the Bonds and Bollag. But even if there had been such a payment, it would probably mean very little, given the way in which Bollag had looked after Bond's money since the mid-1980s.

   Supreme Court of South Australia, 113 of 1996, *Southern Equities Corporation Ltd and others v Alan Bond and others*, defence of John Bond, paras 151A.1, 151A.2.

3. *Business Review Weekly*, 13 March 1995, 'How Bond beat bankruptcy', Philip Rennie.

4. Until the 1960s, the bankruptcy laws in Australia employed the doctrine of 'reputed ownership', which ruled that if someone had the use of property and appeared to own it, then a court was entitled to conclude that the person did own it. This might have proved useful for attacking trusts, but it was repealed because it caused problems with goods acquired on hire-purchase agreements.

5. On 20 October 1994, the Federal Court in Perth upheld an appeal by Alan Bond against an earlier Federal Court decision (and a previous determination by the Administrative Appeals Tribunal) that gifts of more than $700,000 made to Bond by his family and friends should be classified as income. The law was redrafted in 1996 and now works as parliament intended.

6. The start of the bankruptcy is defined as the first act of bankruptcy. This might, for example, be the issue of a creditors' petition, and could be months before the actual bankruptcy date.

7. Conversation with author, May 1999.

8. *ibid*.

9. Conversation with author, May 1999.

10. These changes are recommended by David J Kerr, an insolvency practitioner with Lord & Brown in Sydney, in his excellent paper, 'Dealing with the well-advised bankrupt', in *New directions in bankruptcy*, December 1999, volume 9, no. 4, published by the Insolvency & Trustee Service Australia.

11. *Sydney Morning Herald* editorial, 1 March 1995, 'Bankruptcy and Fairness'.

12. Senator Murray, Senate, 19 November 1997, pp 8988–89.

13. Andrew Fraser was charged in September 1999 with trafficking, using and possessing cocaine. In November 1999 he was further charged with being knowingly concerned with the importation of 5.5 kilograms of cocaine. He admitted on radio that he had had a $100,000-a-year drug habit. Fraser was charged after twenty-two police raided his St Kilda home at 3.00am. His chambers and mobile phone had been bugged for more than a month. *Herald Sun*, 16 September 1999, p 3, 'Jeweller on drug charge', Sarah Pellegrini; *Herald Sun*, 10 November 1999, p 11, 'New charge for lawyer', Fay Burstin.

    On 14 December 1999, Tim Watson-Munro pleaded guilty in Melbourne Magistrates' Court to two charges of using and possessing cocaine. He was placed on a twelve-month good behaviour bond. He had given himself up after a listening device planted in a Melbourne office had recorded him buying the drug. *Herald Sun*, 15 December 1999, p 11, 'Drug sinks high-flyer', Fay Burstin.

14. *Bankrupt estate of the late Peter Beckwith*, 1276 of 1990 XI, circular to creditors, 18 February 1999.

Bond's Millions
at a Glance

1975–2001

1975: Alan Bond narrowly escapes financial ruin. He determines to protect his fortune. Two Alan Bond family trusts are set up in Australia. The Bonds' family house is the No 1 Trust's first asset.

1979: Bond's family lawyer, Harry Lodge at Parker & Parker, instructs Geoffrey Davies of Touche Ross in Jersey to set up Alan Bond's first offshore trust.

May 1982: Alan Bond instructs Touche Ross in Jersey 'to accept instructions from Robert Ashley Pearce concerning any matters associated with me'. Pearce is managing director of Bond's master private company, Dallhold Investments.

1983: Lodge and Pearce go to Jersey to set up a trust for Alan Bond. Icarus Trust owns 14 Selwood Place, Chelsea, where the Bond family live throughout the 1980s.

July 1984: Kirk Holdings is set up for Alan Bond in Jersey. It owns paintings, horses and houses for Bond. It also has millions of dollars in accounts at the Allied Irish Banks in St Helier, Jersey.

November 1986: Jurg Bollag takes over Bond's offshore finances. He sets up a company called Crasujo in Zug, which appears to be an acronym for Bond's children: Craig, Susanne and John, or Jody.

1987: In January, Crasujo's name is changed to JF Consulting. In February, Bond writes to Touche Ross in Jersey telling them to accept instructions 'in relation to my affairs' from Robert Pearce, John Bond, Harry Lodge and Jurg Bollag. Bollag sets up Juno Equities, a Panamanian company run from Jersey, to buy a Chelsea apartment for Bond's girlfriend, Diana Bliss.

Huge amounts of money wash through Kirk's Jersey bank accounts. Approximately $50 million pass through in the last two months of 1986 and first five months of 1987. Some of this money is sent to Switzerland.

April 1987: SIDRO Anstalt is set up by Bollag in Liechtenstein. It has an account at the Private Trust Bank in Vaduz, Liechtenstein. There is evidence that the company is a front for Bond.

June 1987: Bond grants Bollag an option to buy the debts of the Greenvale Nickel Project for $3 million. The option is described by Bond in a 1991 court action as being worth $700 million. It would allow huge amounts of cash to flow offshore, tax-free, to an Isle of Man company called Metal Traders Ltd, which Bollag runs from Zug, Switzerland.

October 1987: World stock markets crash. Bond Corporation Holdings is in trouble. It resorts to creating artificial profits to keep its shareholders happy.

1988: Bond's business empire is running desperately short of cash. In April, Bond Corporation Holdings buys 19.9 per cent of the Bell Group from Robert Holmes à Court in an attempt to grab almost $2 billion held by its subsidiary, Bell Resources. The Western Australian State Government Insurance Commission also buys 19.9 per cent, giving them and Bond effective control. The National Companies and Securities Commission launches an inquiry but agrees not to proceed if Bond bids for the rest of Bell Group's shares.

By August, Alan Bond has installed himself as chairman of Bell Group and Bell Resources, with Peter Beckwith, Tony Oates and Peter Mitchell as directors. They start stripping cash out of Bell Resources. By February 1989, $1,200 million will have been removed, in the biggest corporate fraud in Australian history.

May 1988: Susanne Bond and Armand Leone get divorced. A court in New Jersey, USA, hears allegations that Jurg Bollag manages Bond's offshore finances. Alan Bond says Bollag is just a good friend who buys horses and lets Susanne ride them. Armand Leone says Bollag sent them money whenever they asked for it, and alleges Bollag is just a front for Bond.

November 1988: Dallhold purchases Manet's *La Promenade* for $2.4 million, about one-sixth of its market price, from the finance company that has been leasing it to the Bond Group. All the lease payments since 1983 have been paid by Bond Corporation Holdings, but Alan's private company will reap the profit when the painting is sold. Bond Corp shareholders are cheated out of $15 million.

Dallhold defaults on a $30 million loan from National Australia Bank. Alan Bond meets the bank's chairman, Don Argus, and the loan is rescheduled. Lonrho, a UK company Bond is trying to take over, says that Bond's business empire is insolvent.

December 1988: Lonrho's analysis of Bond Corporation Holdings concludes that the group has assets of $8.7 billion and borrowings of $12 billion, which makes it worth *minus* $3.3 billion. It is also paying $1.2 billion in interest a year and pulling in less than half that in earnings.

Despite his empire being broke, Alan Bond gives $4.3 million worth of diamonds to his wife Eileen, including a $1.5 million ring. He also gives a $420,000 Bentley Turbo to Eileen, a $350,000 bracelet to Susanne and $300,000 in cash to someone whose identity he can't recall in 1992.

March 1989: ABC TV *Four Corners* report reveals that $154 million of Bond Group's $273 million profits in 1987–88 were not profits at all, but were manufactured in bogus deals to keep the shareholders and banks happy.

April 1989: $750,000 passes through Alan Bond's account at Arbuthnot Latham Bank in London on its way to Jurg Bollag at the Zuger Kantonal Bank in Zug, Switzerland. Bond's account at Arbuthnot Latham is labelled Alan Bond, c/o J Bollag.

May 1989: Bond Corporation Holdings can't pay its dividend to shareholders of $34 million because it has no money. Bell

Resources, which has now 'lent' some $1,200 million to Bond, can't pay its dividend either.

May 1989: Australian Ratings downgrades the Bond Group to a CCC rating, from which no Australian company has ever recovered. Baring Securities Australia concludes that the Bond Group has a negative net worth of $1.80 per share. Dallhold defaults on a US$10 million loan from Elders Finance and on two $25 million loans from Toronto Dominion Bank and R&I Bank.

June 1989: Lonrho's second report says that Bond Corporation Holdings's negative net worth is $5.31 a share and getting worse.

October 1989: Auditors raise questions over sale of Manet's *La Promenade*. They demand that bogus 'profits' of the previous year be reversed. Bond Group announces record loss of nearly $1 billion. Bond is seen in Perth's Mediterranean restaurant laughing and joking. Later, he is seen kicking up his heels with Tracey Tyler, whose friend says, 'Alan can't be bust—he's just bought Tracey a house and a new mink coat'.

November 1989: Bond Group accounts are published. Auditors express 'some doubt that the Bond Group will be able to continue as a going concern'. Van Gogh's *Irises* is repossessed.

December 1989: Two valuable Bond paintings, Glover's *Natives in the Eucalypt Forest* and Chazal's *Portrait of Matthew Flinders*, together worth around $1.5 million, are shipped to Jurg Bollag in Switzerland after he claims that his Isle of Man company, Firstmark, owns them. The paintings, which were bought by Alan's Jersey company Kirk Holdings in 1984 and 1987 respectively, are not declared to Bond's trustee in 1992 when he goes bankrupt.

Seven Bond Corp artworks, including Webber's *Portrait of Captain Cook*, are sold to George Way's gallery in Fremantle for $922,500, or one-sixth of their market value of $6 million. Way allegedly receives a $50,000 fee, while Bond Corp's managing director, Peter Beckwith, gets $250,000 to allow the transaction to proceed. The paintings are flown to London on 6 January 1990, where they will be sold by Bond's art dealer, Angela Nevill, on instructions of Jurg Bollag and Alan Bond.

Receivers are appointed to Bond Brewing Holdings, which owes $800 million to the National Australia Bank and others. The action threatens to bring down the Bond Group, since Bond Brewing Holdings provides almost all the cash. In March, the receivers are removed by the court, because the banks are judged to have acted too hastily.

January 1990: Standard Chartered Bank calls in receivers to Dallhold's nickel companies over a US$50 million debt. This also threatens to bring down Bond Group, but Hongkong Bank, Tricontinental and the Bank of New Zealand agree to assume the debt and lend more money under a new syndicated US$ loan agreement (SULA). A condition is that Bond signs a personal guarantee for US$194 million. This will bankrupt him two years later.

Alan Bond gives an interview to Teresa Poole of London's *Independent* newspaper. He looks fit, healthy, unruffled, and certainly not contrite. He says he won't go bankrupt.

March 1990: Federal government sets up committee under John Sulan QC to investigate the cash strip of $1,200 million from Bell Resources.

May 1990: The first interest payment of $7.9 million is due on the SULA loan. The banks agree to roll it over.

June 1990: Bond gives Tracey Tyler a $93,000 Mercedes Benz 190E Sportster.

August 1990: Second interest payment on SULA loan is rolled over; $16 million is now unpaid.

August 1990: Bond is forced out of the Bond Group. He receives a payout of $758,756 net of tax. Half a million dollars of that is his redundancy payment. The rest is accumulated long-service leave. He also gets $2.36 million paid into his super fund.

September 1990: Bond, Oates and Mitchell are forced to resign as directors of Bond Corporation Holdings. The group records a $2.2 billion loss, the biggest in Australian corporate history. Shortly afterwards, it is put into receivership. Expected deficiency is $3.7 billion for Bond Corporation Holdings. It is more like $6 billion if Dallhold, Bell and Alan Bond are included.

December 1990: Bond is charged with dishonestly inducing Brian Coppin to commit money to the rescue of Rothwells Bank in 1987.

March 1991: The SULA banks issue a notice of demand to Dallhold nickel companies for payment of US$335 million owing on their February 1990 loan. No interest has been paid and $35 million is now owing. Four days later, the banks call in Alan Bond's US$194 million personal guarantee.

June 1991: Richard England, liquidator of Holmes à Court's old company JN Taylor, sues Bond, Tony Oates and Peter Mitchell, as former directors, for $250 million damages. They have lent $288 million of JN Taylor's money to the Bond Group and Dallhold between December 1989 and March 1990, which will not be repaid.

John Sulan QC hands his report to the Australian Securities Commission (ASC), whose chairman, Tony Hartnell, concludes that offences have been committed.

July 1991: Alan Bond is removed as a beneficiary of the Bond family's Alpha and Beta trusts, which own at least $31 million worth of assets, including the Bonds' $7 million family house and $10 million worth of farmland at Dandaragan in Western Australia. The next day, the bailiffs move into Dallhold, Bond's master private company, and a liquidator is appointed.

September 1991: Judgement is given in the New South Wales Supreme Court against Bond on the US$194 million personal guarantee. The first attempt is made to serve him with a bankruptcy notice. A process server, Kevin Munns, chases Bond through the streets of Nedlands, Perth, and they clash outside a police station.

November 1991: Western Australian police, chasing millions of dollars that Laurie Connell has looted from Rothwells, ask Swiss authorities to obtain bank documents from Zug. These reveal an account at Zuger Kantonal Bank in the name of Jurg Bollag, held 'on behalf of Alan Bond'.

December 1991: The New South Wales Court of Appeal rejects Bond's appeal against the September judgement on the US$194 million personal guarantee. Bond is also denied leave to appeal to the High Court. A new bankruptcy notice is issued. Process server Basil Faulkner sits outside Bond's house for five days over Christmas. Later, solicitor Hamish Young from Mallesons serves notice on Bond at Sydney airport.

January 1992: Bond petitions Federal Court to set aside the latest bankruptcy notice on the grounds that the banks' lawyers have used the wrong exchange rate to convert the debt from US dollars into Australian dollars.

February 1992: The ASC delivers a 600-page report on Bond Group to the Commonwealth Director of Public Prosecutions. The ASC statement says police in South Australia and Western Australia have been investigating Bond since mid-1991, as a result of which, 'the ASC has identified major breaches of the law that may give rise to criminal prosecution of a number of individuals who formerly held office in the Bond group of companies'. Murray Allen, head of the ASC in Western Australia, says it will be only a matter of weeks before a decision is taken to prosecute.

Bond travels to Los Angeles, San Diego, Tulsa, New York and London with Di Bliss. He is seen shouting a meal for friends at a restaurant in New York.

March 1992: Justice Morling in the Federal Court rejects Bond's attempt to have bankruptcy notice set aside. Bond appeals to full court, which rules against him. Another bankruptcy notice is issued. Bond is in London, staying at 14 Selwood Place, Chelsea. His friend Jurg Bollag emerges and hits *Sydney Morning Herald* photographer Nigel Marple. Bond denies that anyone is trying to serve him with a bankruptcy notice. He also denies that he owns Selwood Place. Bankruptcy notice is served on Bond's lawyers in Australia instead.

April 1992: Bond returns to Perth to give evidence to Western Australian Royal Commission into WA Inc. In Sydney, the Federal Court makes him bankrupt. Robert Ramsay of accounting firm Bird Cameron in Melbourne is appointed trustee of Bond's estate. His personal debts of $622 million are a record. Ramsay asks Bond for statements relating to any bank accounts in the UK, the British Virgin Islands, Switzerland or anywhere else in the world. Bond replies by letter, 'I have no such bank accounts'.

May 1992: Ramsay writes to Credit Suisse in Davos and Zuger Kantonal Bank in Zug, Switzerland, asking them to give details of any accounts held by Bond or on his behalf, and telling them to freeze any funds. They refuse to help. Back in Australia, Bond is sentenced to two-and-a-half years in jail over the Rothwells rescue.

June 1992: Ramsay takes legal action to claim Bond's $2.7 million super fund. The trustees of the fund pass a resolution that none of the money will be paid to Bond's bankrupt estate.

August 1992: Bond is released from prison after ninety days. A retrial is ordered on the Rothwells charges. He is acquitted in November.

September 1992: Ramsay asks the Federal Court in Australia to send letters of request to courts in Jersey, Guernsey,

England, Switzerland and New York, asking them for assistance. He asks for the application to be kept secret because he is concerned that assets may be moved and files destroyed. The Federal Court agrees.

November 1992: Federal Court rules that Bond's $2.7 million super fund belongs to his creditors. Bond appeals.

February 1993: Bond is due to be examined on oath in the Federal Court by Ramsay's lawyers, who want to ask about foreign bank accounts and assets. The examination is postponed because Bond is sick—he has open-heart surgery at Royal Perth Hospital to replace a heart valve.

May 1993: Alan Bond's younger daughter, Jody, is married in Perth. Bond looks fit and healthy at the wedding.

June 1993: Bond is charged in Perth with fraud over Manet painting, *La Promenade*. Bond tells the author outside the court, 'you mention Bollag in your [*Four Corners*] program and I'll sue'.

July 1993: ABC TV's *Four Corners* reveals how Bollag runs a network of offshore companies holding millions of dollars of assets for Bond and his family—including high-priced horses, an Elizabethan manor called Upp Hall, a house in London, and various bank accounts in Jersey, London and Switzerland. Bond does not sue.

Webber's *Portrait of Captain Cook* surfaces in Switzerland. Robert Bleakley, then managing director of Sotheby's Australia, offers it to the National Gallery of Australia for $3 million, then reduces the price to $1.6 million. Bleakley says

the owner is unknown, and Bollag is not the agent he is negotiating with. He is in fact negotiating with Bond's art dealer,
Angela Nevill. The painting is in a high-security bonded warehouse in Zurich.

August 1993: Administrative Appeals Tribunal tells Bond he
must pay half his income to his creditors. It raises the amount
payable from $208,866 to $344,851, based on Ramsay's new
estimate that Bond has received $713,390 from friends like
Jurg Bollag and Graham Ferguson Lacey. Bond appeals.

September 1993: Ramsay asks Royal Court of Jersey for a
secret court order to examine two partners of Touche Ross in
St Helier about Bond's offshore finances. In Australia, the
Federal Court rejects Bond's appeal over his super fund. Bond
phones Ramsay to offer settlement to creditors.

October 1993: Psychologist Tim Watson-Munro tells Bond's
lawyers Bond is unfit to face examination by Ramsay because
he is anxious, depressed and has brain damage. Alan's friend
Dr John Saunders agrees. Bond flies to St Bees Island with Di
Bliss and negotiates to buy the island. The owners say he is 'as
sharp as a tack'.

November 1993: Ramsay flies to Jersey to examine the two
accountants at Touche Ross who have been running the Bond/
Bollag companies. They identify Kirk Holdings as being 'for the
benefit of Mr Bond'. They give evidence that the companies and
trusts were set up for Bond in the early 1980s and that Bollag
took over in late 1986. They produce a handwritten letter, signed
by Alan Bond in February 1987, telling Touche Ross to accept
instructions from Bollag in relation to Bond's affairs.

The Australian Federal Police (AFP) start chasing Bond. They name the case Operation Oxide. They have learned about Swiss documents showing Bond had a Swiss bank account containing millions of dollars in the late 1980s.

December 1993: Bond due to face court on Manet fraud charges. Lawyers argue that he should not have to face trial because he is depressed, suicidal and brain-damaged. Tim Watson-Munro testifies that Bond has severe memory loss and could not run a corner store. Trial is postponed for six months. Later that day, Bond gets angry with a Perth TV reporter, snatches her microphone and hurls it across a car park.

Bond is forced to direct Jurg Bollag to hand over all money and assets held by him to his trustee in bankruptcy. The letter has been drafted by Ramsay, and the Federal Court has ordered Bond to sign it. Bollag replies that it would be illegal for him to comply with the request unless ordered by a court to do so. Ramsay also gets short shrift from the Zuger Kantonal Bank.

January 1994: Bond is examined by a psychiatrist appointed by the Federal Court to determine whether he is fit enough to face his bankruptcy examination. Bond bursts into tears under questioning and stops the interview.

February 1994: Deadline expires to charge Bond over Bell cash strip. It is now five years from last transaction. Bond is taken to private hospital in Perth, suffering 'severe major depression'. He cheers himself up by making phone calls to Russia in the middle of the night.

April 1994: Federal Court is due to hear whether Bond is fit to face examination. Justice Sheppard refuses to suppress

Bond's psychiatric reports. Bond agrees to face examination after all.

May 1994: Bond is examined on oath in the Federal Court in Sydney. He is asked about the network of offshore companies and bank accounts. He can't recall a thing. Back at the hotel, his phone runs hot. Between 8 May and 14 May he makes sixty-five international calls, including a $66.50 call to a public phone box at Zurich railway station.

Bond's girlfriend, Diana Bliss, delivers $130,000 in a hatbox to Luke Atkins for one of Alan's attempted business deals.

May–June 1994: Bond is back in court in Western Australia on the Manet charges, arguing he's unfit to face trial. He collapses on his first day in court. The prosecution reveals he made calls to Moscow while in hospital for depression in February, and that he was then finalising negotiations to buy St Bees Island off the Queensland coast. The island's owners tell the court that Bond was mentally and physically fine and the toughest businessman they've ever dealt with. They say he was jogging and swimming just two days before his court collapse. Magistrate rules that Bond is capable of standing trial.

June 1994: Bond's creditors agree to take legal action in Switzerland to recover assets from Bollag.

September 1994: The AFP investigators chasing Bond for concealing assets from his creditors ask Swiss police to obtain records from Zuger Kantonal Bank, and carry out searches on Bollag's house and offices. They also ask for Bollag to be examined on oath about his relationship with Bond.

The AFP raid fourteen houses, offices and cars in Sydney

and Perth. Their search warrants allege that Alan and others have conspired to defeat the bankruptcy laws.

October 1994: Bond wins appeal in the Federal Court. He will not have to pay his creditors $345,079, which is half the $713,390 that he has received from Bollag and others. The law is apparently badly drafted.

November 1994: George Caddy, the Official Receiver for New South Wales, issues notices to the AFP to hand over documents seized from Bond's home in the September raids. Pending full court hearing, Bond gets an injunction to prevent the hand-over.

November 1994: Bond asks for his passport back so he can work offshore as a consultant for a mysterious Canadian company, Tri Kal International. The Federal Court turns him down.

December 1994: Swiss police raid Bollag's house and offices. Zuger Kantonal Bank agrees to hand over documents. Bond makes offer of $9.25 million to settle debts owed by Dallhold and his bankrupt estate. In exchange, Dallhold liquidator will have to drop legal claims against Bond family for $53.8 million.

Dallhold creditors accept Bond's proposal, which works out at 1.3 cents in the dollar. The deal is conditional on Bond's personal creditors also agreeing to settle. Their vote is postponed because Bond hasn't got the numbers.

Justice Sheppard in the Federal Court rules that Bond has to give details of the phone calls he made at the time of his bankruptcy examination in May 1994. He also has to tell the

AFP to hand over documents seized from his home in September 1994. Bond appeals.

The *West Australian* publishes a wide-ranging interview with Bond in which he blames the banks for his demise, and politicians for persecuting him since his collapse. Bond repeats his story that Bollag is just a good friend, and a business colleague. He also says he is much better. 'It just takes time . . . I was quite ill six months ago. I'm much better now, very much better.'

January 1995: Bond is at last charged with stripping money from Bell Resources. He is arraigned at East Perth Magistrates' Court on a Saturday morning. It has taken six years to complete the investigations, and the acting Attorney General, Duncan Kerr, has waived the normal five-year time limit on Companies Code offences. Bond has to put up $500,000 bail and report weekly to Fremantle police station. But, unlike most people in this position, he is allowed to do it by phone. Tony Oates and Peter Mitchell, fellow Bell Resources directors, are also charged, but Oates is in Poland, Mitchell in the USA.

Bond meets Ramsay in Sydney to answer questions about the documents seized from his home by the AFP. He has given an undertaking that he has no assets other than those already disclosed. But the AFP documents indicate the possibility of bank accounts in Liechtenstein and Switzerland.

Ramsay sends a letter to creditors advising them to vote against the settlement. The letter reveals details of almost two dozen schemes that Bond has been involved in. Ramsay tells creditors, 'there are very strong grounds for believing that monies held by or on behalf of Mr Bond or controlled by him, were transferred to Switzerland'. He points out that these amounts 'far exceed the amount which Mr Bond is currently offering to creditors'.

Ramsay applies to John McKechnie, the Director of Public Prosecutions in Western Australia, to hand over documents obtained by Rothwells Task Force investigator Joseph Lieberfreund between 1991 and 1993. The documents come from Jersey and Switzerland and show details of a Swiss bank account held for Bond. The problem is that they have been obtained in connection with a prosecution of Laurie Connell and can't be used in any other case without Swiss approval. The Swiss won't give it.

Bond's creditors meet again. The vote is postponed once more.

February 1995: The Federal Court in Melbourne decides that Ramsay can see *all* the papers seized by the AFP—including those from Bond's associates. Ramsay has only two days to read them and write a summary for creditors.

Bond's creditors meet again in Sydney. This time the vote takes place and Bond is discharged. Thirteen creditors representing 88 per cent of the debt vote to let him off. Only eight, including the Australian Taxation Office, are game to continue the chase.

Acting Attorney General Duncan Kerr tells parliament that 'the Australian Federal Police is conducting an investigation into allegations that Mr Bond committed offences under the Bankruptcy Act'. He warns Bond that if any assets are discovered, criminal charges will follow and the bankruptcy can be reactivated.

March 1995: John Bond meets Jurg Bollag in Singapore. Bollag's role in Bond's offshore financial affairs is allegedly being wound down.

$4.3 million is allegedly moved from SIDRO Anstalt in Liechtenstein via the British Virgin Islands and Texas to Bond companies in Australia. Bollag, Craig Bond and John Bond are allegedly involved.

Craig Bond sets up a new Bahamas company, SHC International, to own the *Portrait of Captain Cook*. He opens a bank account in Jersey for the company.

Ramsay tells Channel 9's *Business Sunday* that it is just a matter of time before the Swiss documents come into the public arena, possibly revealing undisclosed assets. He says he was only a month to six weeks away from getting them. He also says the documents handed over by the AFP show clear evidence of money transfers and bank accounts. The implication is that he will soon have Bond back in court.

Bond is committed for trial on four fraud and dishonesty charges over Manet's *La Promenade*. He looks fit and chirpy now that he's no longer trying to convince a court he's too sick to appear.

April 1995: Bond marries Diana Bliss on Easter Saturday in Sydney's Museum of Contemporary Art. His family stay away.

The *Portrait of Captain Cook* is moved to Christie's high-security warehouse in London, along with Chazal's missing *Portrait of Matthew Flinders*. Craig Bond pays the storage bill with a cheque drawn on his personal UK bank account.

June 1995: Bond's lawyers take action in Switzerland and Australia to keep the Zuger Kantonal Bank documents secret on the grounds that the bankruptcy has been annulled. They also try to stop the AFP's investigation.

September 1995: The first dividend is paid to Bond's creditors at the rate of .000415293 cents in the dollar, or 4 cents for every $10,000 owed.

November 1995: John Lord, liquidator of Dallhold, has virtually completed a 200-page report on the conduct of Dallhold's directors. It canvasses the possibility that Bond has committed a number of criminal offences, such as trading while insolvent, and breaching his fiduciary duty.

January 1996: Bond and Peter Mitchell are committed for trial on $1,200 million Bell fraud charges. Magistrate Ronald J Gething says a jury might conclude that their conduct was 'dishonest', 'deceitful', 'very imprudent and irresponsible' and that it demonstrated an 'extreme breach of duty'.

Bond Corporation Holdings liquidator, Richard England, starts secret action in Supreme Court of South Australia, alleging fraud by Alan and Craig Bond over thirteen missing Bond Corp artworks, valued at $6 million.

February 1996: Bond and Bollag lose action in Federal Court to stop Bollag being questioned in Switzerland.

March 1996: A lawyer acting for Craig Bond attempts to sell the Flinders portrait to the Art Gallery of South Australia for $600,000. In London, the Serious Fraud Office and the AFP raid the offices of Bond's art dealer, Nevill Keating Pictures, and find storage receipts for the missing *Portrait of Captain Cook*. Craig Bond is examined on oath about the missing paintings in the South Australian Supreme Court for the first time.

May 1996: Bond Corp liquidator obtains secret UK court order to secure the Captain Cook and the Flinders portraits. Both paintings remain at Christie's, but no one is allowed to disclose their whereabouts.

August 1996: Bond is jailed for three years over Manet's *La Promenade* after being found guilty on two counts of fraud and two of deception. He is sent to Casuarina maximum-security prison.

Craig fails to turn up for his second examination in the Supreme Court of South Australia over the missing Bond Corp paintings. Bond's art dealer, Angela Nevill, is examined in London. Robert Bleakley, then managing director of Sotheby's Australia, is examined in Adelaide. Nancy Lake, director of Craig's Bahamian company SHC, is examined in the Bahamas.

September 1996: Craig again fails to turn up for examination in the Supreme Court of South Australia.

October 1996: The AFP at last get their hands on documents obtained by Swiss authorities from Bollag and the Zuger Kantonal Bank. They seek a summons to examine Bollag.

US$600,000 is allegedly sent from the Private Trust Bank in Liechtenstein to Bond companies in Australia via Jersey and Texas. Bollag, Craig Bond and John Bond are allegedly involved.

December 1996: Bond goes quietly in Bell fraud trial. He pleads guilty to two counts of failing to act honestly as a company director, with intent to defraud. In exchange, the conspiracy to defraud charge is dropped, along with four Western Australian Companies Code charges. Mitchell, who has returned from the US, also pleads guilty. Tony Oates is still in Poland, trying to avoid extradition.

January 1997: Bollag is due to appear before Zug prosecutor Paul Kuhn. He fights summons in Swiss courts on the basis that they have no power to question him because no charges have yet been brought against Bond. He loses.

February 1997: Bond is jailed for four years over $1,200 million Bell cash strip.

Craig Bond fails for third time to turn up to the South Australian Supreme Court to be examined over the missing paintings. A summons for contempt of court is issued.

April 1997: Craig is finally examined. In Switzerland, Bollag appears before Zug prosecutor, Paul Kuhn, to answer questions put by the AFP. He stays silent, claiming privilege against self-incrimination. Bollag and Bond start legal action in an attempt to stop him having to take the stand again.

May 1997: Operation Oxide leader Andrew Tuohy resigns from the AFP. Statement of claim in the paintings case in the Supreme Court of South Australia reveals allegations of fraud by Alan and Craig Bond.

August 1997: Bond's sentence on the Bell cash strip is increased from four to seven years after the Commonwealth Director of Public Prosecutions appeals against the leniency of the sentence. The court rules that Justice Murray has given too much weight to Bond's pleas of mitigation, because the crime is the very worst of its kind.

November 1997: Bollag appears again before Zug prosecutor and says he will answer questions, then claims privilege again. Back in Australia, Bond is flown in protective custody to Adelaide to face examination over the *Portrait of Captain Cook*.

July 1998: Tony Oates wins his legal battle against extradition on Bell fraud charges. Bond is attacked in Casuarina prison in an argument over use of the telephone.

August 1998: Transcript of Bollag's interview with the Zug prosecutor in Switzerland is finally delivered to the AFP. They now discover how little he has said. More legal battles will be needed to force him to take the stand again. If he then defies the court, he will probably only be fined.

October 1998: The AFP abandon Operation Oxide. It has taken five years and $700,000 of taxpayers' money. Police reckon they have little chance of convicting Bond without Bollag's evidence, and little chance of making Bollag talk.

August 1999: Craig's friend Peter Philpott is examined on oath in Texas by lawyers for the Bond Corp liquidator. He tells them that the two alleged money-laundering transactions in 1995 sent $5.1 million from Liechtenstein to Bond companies in Australia, via US companies he set up for Craig Bond.

October 1999: New statement of claim filed by Bond Corp liquidator in South Australian Supreme Court action over the missing paintings. It raises the money-laundering allegations for the first time.

March 2000: Bond is released from jail after an appeal to the High Court frees him on a legal technicality. He has served 1,298 days for the Manet and Bell charges combined, or roughly one day for every $1 million. *Australian Women's Weekly* pays $50,000 for an exclusive interview.

Secrecy orders surrounding the *Portrait of Captain Cook* and the *Portrait of Matthew Flinders* are lifted. Both paintings are revealed to be in London. The press reveal money-laundering allegations for the first time. The AFP promise to look into them.

May 2000: The South Australian Supreme Court is asked to freeze assets of a Bond family company, Carindale Land Corporation, which has allegedly received the $5.1 million from Bollag in Liechtenstein.

June 2000: Justice Debelle in the Supreme Court of South Australia rules that the *Portrait of Captain Cook* belongs to Bond Corp.

August 2000: *Portrait of Captain Cook* returns to Australia. It has been purchased by the National Portrait Gallery in Canberra for $5.3 million, and is unveiled by Prime Minister John Howard.

Bond flies to UK, intending to make it his home.

September 2000: Justice Debelle freezes assets of a Bond family company, Carindale Land Corporation, on the basis that there is a prima facie case of art fraud. Debelle says the $4.3 million money transfer from Liechtenstein via the British Virgin Islands and Texas to Brisbane is 'a payment to Bond interests arranged by Bollag'.

Minister for Justice, Amanda Vanstone, promises that the AFP will examine the evidence on the money transfer and alleged art fraud, and decide whether to resume its investigations into Alan Bond.

October 2000: London's *Sunday Telegraph* reveals Bond is planning a business comeback. A Bond family trust has bought the UK rights to an Australian money-lending business.

March 2001: Art fraud trial begins in Adelaide. Angela Nevill, Nancy Lake and Peter Philpott are all set to give evidence. Bond settles after two days, paying the liquidator $12 million.

April 2001: *Sunday Herald Sun* investigation reveals Alan and Diana Bliss share a $3 million penthouse opposite Kensington Palace. The building, which was bought by a British Virgin Islands company, Bonaparte Investments, in early 2000 for $10 million, is up for sale for $12.7 million. Guess who's behind it. Alan Bond.

Photo and Text Acknowledgements

Picture Section 1

Page 1 News Ltd
Page 2 Nigel Marple
Page 3 Nigel Marple
Page 4 WA Newspapers
Page 5 WA Newspapers (top)
    The Age (bottom)
Page 6 The Age (top)
    ABC TV (bottom)
Page 7 ABC TV
Page 8 ABC TV

Picture Section 2

Page 1 ABC TV
Page 2 ABC TV
Page 3 Patrick Riviere/Sydney
    Freelance (top)
    Tony McDonough/Sydney
    Freelance
    (bottom)
Page 4 Channel 9 Perth
Page 5 Channel 9 Perth
Page 6 ABC TV
Page 7 ABC TV
Page 8 WA Newspapers

Picture Section 3

Page 1 Andrew Meares/Sydney Morning
    Herald (top)
    WA Newspapers (bottom)
Page 2 Andrew Meares/Sydney Morning
    Herald (top)
    Mark Drummond (bottom, left
    and right)
Page 3 Patrick Cummins/Fairfax
    Ben Rushton/Fairfax
Page 4 News Ltd
Page 5 News Ltd
Page 6 Photographer unknown (top)
    News Ltd (bottom left)
    The Fairfax Photo Library
    (bottom right)
Page 7 ABC TV (top left)
    Sydney Morning Herald/Fairfax
    (top right)
    West Australian/AAP Image
    (bottom)
Page 8 News Ltd

Cover Photo

WA Newspapers

Acknowledgements are due to the following authors, publishers and agents for permission to include extracts of newspaper and magazine articles, books and television transcripts.

Janise Beaumont, 'Now jitterbug Jackie's really found her love', *Sunday Telegraph*, 13 September 1992

Jane Cadzow, 'The show must go on', *Sydney Morning Herald*, 29 March 1997

Channel 7 Perth news report, 26 September 1994

Mark Drummond, *West Australian*, 27 December 1994, 20 January 1995, 23 January 1995, 26 January 1995

Four Corners, ABC TV, 'Rich Man, Poor Man', 26 July 1993, 'Bondy's benefactor', 9 May 1994

Peter Hartcher, 'What a hide: Bond's secret stash', *Australian Financial Review*, 12 March 1995

Terry Ingram, '$1.5 million agreed for Cook portrait', *Australian Financial Review*, 3 August 1993

Anne Lampe, Senior Business Journalist, 'Alan Bond felled by Skase syndrome', *Sydney Morning Herald*, 10 February 1994

Prue MacSween (interviewer), 'For richer, for poorer, Bond embarks on a life of wedded bliss', *Hello!*, 29 April 1995

Susan Mitchell, *Private Lives, Private Passions*, copyright permission is granted by the copyright owner c/- Curtis Brown (Aust)

Bill Pheasant, 'AFP gives up Bond chase', *Australian Financial Review*, 24 October 1998

Philip Rennie, 'How Bond beat bankruptcy', *BRW*, 13 March 1995

Sunday Times, 'Jailbird Bond's barbecue set', 22 December 1996

Candace Sutton, 'Last straw for Bond', *The Sun-Herald*, 16 February 1997

Thomson Legal & Regulatory Group, 'Coward v Stapleton' *Commonwealth Law Reports* (1953) No 90; 'Keeley v The Hon Mr Justice Brooking' *Commonwealth Law Reports* (1978–79) No 143; Dennis Rose, Lewis' 'Australian Bankruptcy Law' (1994), 10th edition

Brook Turner, 'Bond IQ drops after heart surgery', *Australian Financial Review*, 12 April 1994

Fiona Wingett, *New Idea*, 22 April 1995

Every effort has been made to identify copyright holders of extracts in this book. The publishers would be pleased to hear from any copyright holders who have not been acknowledged.

Index

INDEX

INDEX